# THE DUTCH MULTINATIONAL CORPORATIONS IN INDIA

# THE DUTCH MULTINATIONAL CORPORATIONS IN INDIA


G.K. LIETEN

*In Collaboration with*

USHA MENON
FONS VAN DER VELDEN
SRIDHAR KRISHNAN
AJAY KUMAR RATH
BASUTHKAR RAJENDER


*Foreword by*

GERRIT HUIZER


Sangam Books
1988

Sangam Books Limited
57 London Fruit Exchange
Brushfield Street
London E1 6EP

Published by
Sangam Books Limited 1988

By arrangement with
Manohar Publications
1 Ansari Road, Daryaganj
New Delhi-110 002, India



**ISBN 0-86132-196-0**

Printed in India by P.L. Printers, New Delhi

# *Foreword*

"Why is it that Dutch multinational corporations should be object of research?" was one of the questions first raised when the idea of doing such research was brought up in a meeting of Dutch social scientists. Of course the easiest answer would have been "Why not". This counter question was more to the point than expected. In fact it was rather evident that while indeed Dutch social research deals with almost any existing social phenomenon in our own or another society, big business enterprises had been conspicuously unresearched in the Netherlands. Apparently it hardly ever occurred to Dutch social scientists to deal with this topic, while about many other controversial and emotionally loaded topics such as the role of churches, religious practices, the family or political parties, libraries had been filled. The lack of research into what Dutch businessmen have been doing in the Third World is particularly conspicuous in view of the tremendous quantity of investigations of the economic activities and political behaviour of peasants, indigenous people, and other categories of fellow human beings, who can apparently be approached more bluntly for all kinds of information. Are the business people any less interesting? Or is there something else?

When thinking about the neglect to look at multinational corporations, there appeared some similarity with the subject of sexual behaviour. It was not until after the Second World War and the appearance of the famous Kinsey report *Sexual Behaviour in the Human Male* in the USA that this theme became empirically and seriously studied by social scientists. The Victorian Age and its—in this field—rather long aftermath had kept the topic under a certain taboo. Speaking publicly or even thinking about this topic was considered almost as indecent as doing certain things. Even ethical treatises only dealt with it in rather vague—but not misunderstood—terminology. Ethics in most cases seemed to restrict itself to this aspect of human behaviour, given minor importance to other fields of human (mis)behaviour or sins such as stealing or war-making.

The taboo of dealing in more empirical terms with sexual behaviour and sin was broken by neurologists, psychotherapists, and psychoanalysts because of the alarming problems and pathological disturbances that Victorian taboo morality produced in more and more people who most strictly tried to live up to it; not the common people but the upper and middle classes.

Now, reflecting upon our original question of why or why not to research the behaviour of multinational corporations, one wonders why this topic, at least in the Netherlands, has apparently been under a kind of taboo for so many decades. Does it also have anything to do with "ethics" or even with "sin"? Is it that the concentration of economic power, the entrepreneurial cannibalism (devouring or swallowing each other) and the kind of greed which seems to underly this trend has become so pathological that some of its protagonists start to get worried and confused? Or is it because of the obviously detrimental consequences of this behaviour for too many people, who no longer tolerate this in some areas of the world, that the taboo on this topic is now being broken?

I am convinced this latter is most obviously the case, and I learned this. not thanks to my good Calvinist upbringing in the Netherlands or my solid academic training in social psychology, but rather in spite of these. It was through working for over 20 years as a development worker among poor peasants in Third World areas, first as a simple volunteer and later as an "expert", that this fact became obvious to me.

In the Netherlands, the social implications of producing goods, selling them, doing business, making profits on a large or small scale were seriously and critically discussed only by a small group of people considered "communists" (and many of that small group openly stated they were), who therefore were—though not viewed as badly as common criminals—considered as a serious threat to the stability of our society and its morality.

As a student at the University of Amsterdam (known in those days as the only "red" university of the Netherlands, with some professors who were openly member of the Dutch Labour Party), I had become acquainted with the ideas of such "communists" (other students) which I found in my heart more akin to the strongly Christian ethics with which I had been indoctrinated as a member of the Reformed Church of the Netherlands than I expected. But I was at that time more drawn towards ideas of pacifism, world federalism and existentialist humanism and thus too much an individualist to see much good in any "totalitarian" system. Moreover I had had some traumatic experiences with "totalitarianism" during the former occupation of the Nertherlands in 1940-1945.

As a student I already was attracted to work in developing countries to help solve the tremendous problems that people there had to face, which appeared much more of a challenge than the reconstruction of Dutch society which seemed to be well on its way ten years after the end of the Second World War. So I came to work in 1955 thanks to a UNESCO scholarship in a small village as a kind of volunteer in the Eastern part of El Salvador in an earthquake-stricken area called Valle de la Esperanza, Valley of Hope.

By living in that village, trying—and initially failing—to motivate people there to participate in community projects, I soon learned that such a community under the surface was ridden by serious internal contradictions, particularly those between the powerful landowners and some of their allies—mainly public officials—on one side, and the rest of the village's poor and very poor peasants on the other side. The stability of that situation could only be maintained, I found after living there for some time, by a system which had many similarities to the highly oppressive totalitarian system that I had known during the Second World War, complete with razzias and other forms of terrorizing people by heavily booted and armed "policemen". It was clear that peaceful and constructive community development, as I had envisaged myself to get involved in, was rather impossible in an atmosphere of that kind. In fact such development for the poor was even considered "dangerous" by the higher placed pepole who as persons were on the whole nice men. When being occasionally amongst themselves they rather openly talked about their fear of people's "education" leading to rebellion, "communism" and they gave this as reason why they always carried pistols. Though people in the village never even seemed to dare to discuss such things, their behaviour indicated that they were well aware of them and strongly resented this situation. While nobody ever talked about "class struggle", it was there under the surface already in 1955, more than 20 years before it became overt in that area. Theoretical concepts such as "class" and "class struggle", which I had never cherished nor really understood, became a reality to me during that year in that village. At times I could not stop myself from feeling angry too about the humiliating way my neighbours and friends in the village were "kept in their place" by other friends, the elite and the officials, who came there from the town.

My first acquaintance with multinational corporations also occurred during that first year in a Third World environment when I found the walls of my neighbour's little house papered with calendar sheets (stronger than newspapers which most people used) of a Philips' advertisement calender that had found its way there. It showed attractive-looking girls very scarcely dressed in a way that could not possibly have been used in the Netherlands at that time for publicity purposes, but hardly aroused any comments in the village. That same year Philips had opened a branch in the capital San Salvador, though in my village, as in many others, there was no electricity.

I also found that the Netherlands' consul in San Salvador at that time was originally a Curacao-ean entrepreneur, now one of the richest men in El Salvador, called De Sola, owner of many coffee plantations and factories of coffee, oils and fats, soap and other products. He was a nice old man who praised me for my good work with the poor peasants but who saw industrialization as a way to solve poverty. He invited me to visit some of his family's enterprises which—without any doubt—had far better working conditions for men and women than I was accustomed to see in the Valle de la Esperanza. Years later I learned that the De Sola clan was one of the 13 richest families that ruled the country and that their firm was taken over by Unilever and rebaptized Unisol (sol means sun in Spanish).

Though suspicions about the influence of my businessmen compatriots had been raised I never heard in those years about them being involved in the kind of atrocities committed by American companies like United Fruit (which had practically taken over neighbouring Guatemala by violence and CIA-support a year earlier in 1954). The kind of "totalitarianism" with which El Salvador, and many other Third World countries in which I got involved in later years, were ruled seemed mostly determined by the landed oligarchies and their fear to lose their land and privileges, as had happened in the French, Russian, Chinese, and to some extent the Mexican, revolutions.

In the early sixties, many development specialists of the United Nations and its agencies, to which I had soon come to belong, had learned that, as most of the concentration of land property in the hands of few was not very efficiently utilized and moreover had come about through violence in the remote or recent past, a restoration of land to the tillers would be needed to make any serious rural development possible. Land redistribution, land reform was high on the agenda not only in countries which had passed through violent revolutions but also in many others as a reformist measure. As in Japan, Taiwan and South Korea where radical land reform had been carried out with strong support from American expertise, it was seen as a precondition for any other development, particularly for the creation of an internal market for mass industrial production of simple consumer goods. Several countries (e.g. Brazil) were seriously considering or had started to carry out such reforms and allowed the peasants to organize themselves for that purpose as had happened elsewhere (Mexico, Japan). Local industrialists were in favour of such reforms and in some cases were found to be supporting those peasant organizations.

The first indications that there were other kinds of business interests not in favour of such developments became obvious when the reformist government of Brazil was toppled by a military coup in 1964, directly supported by the CIA (as was much later admitted by US ambassador Lincoln Gordon). The tremendously growing influence of US and other multinational corporations in Brazil in the years after that coup, with some of the generals becoming top managers in their branches, gradually revealed that the worst obstacles for the poor peasants to get some land and a better life were not only the landlords, but the corporations which apparently could make more profits by producing their sophisticated products for an expanding middle class minority than to produce simple things for basic needs and mass consumption. The economic growth in Brazil was spectacular but only benefited the better-off minority and in fact impoverished the masses to such an extent that within ten years, in 1973, North-East Brazilian Catholic bishops felt compelled to publish a carefully but strongly worded Pastoral Letter in which they denounced the "class struggle" imposed upon the Brazilians by "international capitalist interests" as non-Christian and inhuman and as the main cause of "official terrorism" and violent oppression. I had come to know some of these men in the course of the years, and though originally found them, as any other churchmen rather on the conservative side, they were so upset by the growing poverty in their parishes and the rapidly growing potential for resistance of the poor that at least a number of them reacted with terminology which appeared derived from their arch-enemies, the "communists", and started supporting the people's movements. They were "converted" by the poor to a "theology of liberation".

Unfortunately a few years later, the tenor of their denouncements was confirmed by the military coup in Chile overthrowing the reformist Allende government with the direct intervention and support of CIA and US multinational corporations such as ITT but also of Unilever (through its local daughter company Indus Lever, a joint venture with the powerful Chilean Edwards clan). It was as a result of this involvement of multinational corporations in the overthrow of a democratically elected government that more and more people dared to question business practices and to break the taboos on investigating corporate behaviour. Church boards and groups of concerned citizens in the USA, in Britain and in the Netherlands started to call for, and in fact to fund modest efforts to find out what these powerful entities were actually doing.

As in the course of the years I had learned that to serve the cause of land reform and peasant organization, it was needed to carefully study and reveal its opponents, I had left the United Nations and had accepted an academic post in the Netherlands just before the Chile coup. While in the USA there were already at least a few critical and academic studies of corporate behaviour and the role of the "rich and the super-rich" or the "power elite", the Rockefellers, Mellons and other controversial names, in the Netherlands there was practically nothing in this field except for some material published years before by the Communist Party.

Even trade-union leaders recognized that they knew hardly anything about the practices of Dutch multinationals outside our borders, not to speak of their influence in the international and national political economy. One of those leaders created almost a row when observing once that in his view the Dutch economy was ruled by about 200 elite families. Such things were not said in our country, and hardly anybody knew their names anyway. In the one study that had ever been undertaken of Dutch business inter-linkages, precisely the 4 multinationals (Shell, Unilever, Philips, Akzo) had been left out because they were too difficult to come to grips with.

While, however, academics as well as politicians were groping in the dark, a proposal for a parliamentary investigation of Dutch corporations in the Third World by one of the small leftist parties did not get sufficient votes even to materialize. Was the Dutch international bourgeoisie's tradition of low key and inconspicuous operation since the 17th century, our "Golden Age", too well established a taboo to be challenged by "decent" scholars or parliamentarians?

Taboos generally concern mysterious or sinister forces or powers in men and nature, which can be beneficial but also terribly malevolent. The so-called primitive peoples are known to have many kinds of taboos. The so-called civilized people often consider themselves above such anxieties. This is perhaps due to their accumulation and production of many material goods and the ability to use these as a protection against the uncertainties of the natural environment. Material goods and wealth, however, have been or are being accumulated to such an extent and so far beyond what healthy human beings need, that they have become a sinister force themselves. Typical for a taboo, such accumulation is hardly ever seriously questioned by the majority of people.

Ironically enough, the business and development-managers of the multinational corporations and related institutions, including the World Bank and the International Monetary Fund have openly and clearly expressed their worries about the polarization between rich and poor for the world's security, but what have they done to correct the dangerous trends their own enterprises have enlashed? Why have they not looked more seriously at the few alternative and socialist experiments which—with trial and much error—are or were being carried out in some countries, but did everything in their power to destroy those? Lack of creative—or entrepreneurial?—spirit to help developing societies to find appropriate solutions? "Resistance to change" (an attitude for which these elites often blame poor peasants), in order to rigidly maintain what they have? An even more worrying question is : Have the mightiest multinationals limitlessly growing, swallowing others, doubling in size every 5-10 years, gone out of control even of their own managers, often well-meaning and honourable human beings? A Frankenstein monster? Expansion run out of hand?

Precisely in our small Dutch society, with a great dependency on these sinister forces, they remained for a long time taboo for academic researchers. Not rarely, while carrying out the research of which this book is a result, we were given the impression by some compatriots that *we* were doing something that had to be apologized for, something decent people shouldn't do, almost something "dirty". But the question is : Why should there be this unwillingness to face and discuss "inconvenient facts", which is the task of social sciences to deal with, even according to bourgeois sociologist Max Weber? Our Third World experiences (of my collegues and myself), however, helped us to see that precisely because of the controversy and embarrassment our study provoked, we were on the right track and were dealing with a real and sensitive issue. We were not surprised that one difficulty we had to face when collecting our material and exposing it, was to deal with it in a way that could even satisfy those who prefer to continue to cherish the taboos of our society. Honesty and objectivity—to which we tried to adhere as strictly as possible—oblige us to admit that we did not succeed in this. We regret this, but it was probably naive on our side that we expected and insistently tried to have a serious dialogue with the corporate power holders about the beneficial and the harmful effects of their corporations' activities for the common people in a country like India. We were happy that we found considerable understanding and support in India, where most of the research was carried out in close collaboration with Indian collegues, and where the final results are now being published. Each society struggles with its own areas of sin and taboo, but in India at least these issues of power and wealth and who controls what and at the cost of whom, can be openly and vehemently discussed by intellectuals as well as common people : a new democracy unhampered by the kind of taboos surrounding the impact and power of the wealthy that seem to prevail in old democracies, like the Netherlands. Why do businessmen and most scholars in the old democracies fear, and what? May be the better part of their own human selves. One of the important things I learned in that village in the Valley of Hope in El Salvador was that while aware of a great deal of the wealings and dealings of the local power elite, the poor are prepared to go a very long way to understand and to forgive their exploiters and give them another chance. Their patience is not eternal, however, as the present turmoil in that country and in others, such as South Africa clearly demontrates.

The facts and critical insights presented in this book will hopefully serve to feed the ongoing discussion in India and stimulate it in the Netherlands so that problems and contradictions arising from the functioning of multinational corporations can be solved in democratic and mutually agreed ways before they become too big and uncontrollable, and really become something to be feared.

It is—finally—a consolation that the breaking of taboos does not only or mainly depend on the role of scholars but that the victims of its effects, the poor, have time over again in past and present found ways to create conditions where harmful institutions, which yielded great and uncontrolled power, could gradually—or radically—be brought under democratic control by all or most people concerned.

Nijmegen, October 1986 GERRIT HUIZER

# *Acknowledgement*

One of the main objectives of the present study was to collect empirical data on the behaviour of multinational corporations in a Third World country which should be helpful in giving insights into the question of the extent to which that behaviour benefits the economic development of the country concerned or not. Most of the data were collected in the period 1981-1983 by a dozen of scholars attached to Jawaharlal Nehru University at New Delhi and the Third World Centre of the Catholic University at Nijmegen. Prabhat Patnaik and C.P. Chandrasekhar of the Centre for Economic Studies and Planning of JNU and Gerrit Huizer and Detlev Haude of the Third World Centre at Nijmegen have, on behalf of their respective centres, looked after the progress of the project and have never failed to give us advice and sort out administrative problems. I should however stress that they have neither interfered with the actual work of the project staff nor co-authored the manuscript. They should therefore be absolved for shortcomings, mistakes and interpretations in the present study. I hope that the trust which the Centre for Economic Studies and Planning, then under the chairmanship of respectively Krishna Baradwaj and Sheila Bhalla, has put in the project staff will be validated by the final product.

Many people in research institutes, government departments, trade unions and companies have been helpful in providing us with data and suggestions. I particularly appreciate the help extended by the managers of some of the smaller companies. It is regretted that the bigger companies in general refused to extend their cooperation. The project has tremendously benefited from the numerous scholars who participated in the workshop at JNU in May 1982, the symposium on MNCs at New Delhi in Augst 1982, the assessment proceedings organised by the South Asian Academic Council at The Hague in January 1983 and the round-table meeting in October 1983 at Nijmegen.

The project has been financed by the Indo-Dutch Programme on Alternatives in Development, a joint research programme of the Indian Council of Social Science Research (ICSSR) and the Dutch Institute for Social Science Research in Developing Countries (IMWOO). In the former organisation, my thanks go in the first place to Ajit Singh and especially to R. Barman Chandra. Despite their heavy work burden, they were always available for help and to lend us a sympathetic ear. The same is true for Pieter van Stuyvenberg and professor Enno Hommes, respectively the secretary and the then chairman of the Dutch chapter of IDPAD who have sorted out occasional problems and have given us numerous suggestions on how to proceed with the project work and the final reporting, among others in collaboration with professor Martin Doornbos and professor Ashwini Saith.

While checking the many files connected with the project one file stands out as significant. It contains the minutes of the fortnightly meetings of the project staff and reflects the democratic, enthusiatic and genuine spirit in which the associates and assistants, occasionally in the presence of the project advisers or project director, reported on their work and planned the tasks ahead. The reports which the staff have written have been taken as the basis for this study. Particular reference I want to make to :

1. Fons van der Velden et al., A General Survey of the Position of Dutch Companies in the Indian Economy, Chapters II and III;
2. Sridhar Krishna, in collaboration with Amitava Mitra and Jagan Mohan Reddy, Balance of Payments Implications and Financing policies of Dutch Companies in India, Chapter III;
3. Ajay Kumar Rath, Hindustan Lever Limited, a profile, and; A Case Study of Hindustan Lever and the Detergent Industry, chapter IV;
4. M.C. Paul, Lipton Tea Ltd., a profile of the company and its workers, Chapter IV;

5. Basuthkar Rajender, Peico Electronics and Electricals Limited, a profile, Chapter V;
6. Usha Menon, with assistance of K. Kumar, Survey of Research and Development by Dutch MNCs in India, and, Some Case Studies of Transfer of Technology, Chapters VI and VII.

I finally wish to express my thanks to the colleagues in the Department of South & South East Asia at the University of Amsterdam for providing my with the necessary research time.

December 1986 GEORGES KRISTOFFEL LIETEN

# Contents

# *List of Tables*

# *List of Abbreviations*

| | |
|---|---|
| CDRI | Central Drugs Research Institute |
| Cr | Crores (ten Million) |
| DGTD | Directorate General of Trade and Development |
| DST | Department of Science and Technology |
| ELMI | Electric Lamp Manufacturers (India) Ltd. |
| FERA | Foreign Exchange Regulation Act |
| GLS | General Lighting Service |
| HL | Hindustan Lever Limited |
| HMT | Hindustan Machine Tools |
| HPMV | High Pressure Mercury Vapour |
| HVM | Hindustan Vanaspati Manufacturers |
| ICOC | Indian Central Oilseeds Committee |
| IIC | Indian Investment Centre |
| ILS | Industrial Licensing System |
| INC | Indian National Congress |
| ISI | Indian Standards Institute |
| KVIC | Khadi and Village Industries Commission |
| MRTP | Monopolies and Restrictive Trade Practices |
| NOCIL | National Organic Chemical Industries Ltd. |
| NV | Naamloze Vennootschap (Limited) |
| OTAI | Oil Technologists' Association India |
| RBI | Reserve Bank of India |
| R&D | Research and Development |
| RRL | Regional Research Laboratory |
| Rs | Rupees |
| STC | State Trading Corporation |
| STPP | Sodium Tripoly Phospate |
| WB | World Bank |

# *Introduction*

## QUESTIONS FOR RESEARCH

The process of development in the Third World is confronted with a number of serious problems. In the field of industrialisation, the solution to the multi-faceted crisis involves at least four elements. In the first place, industrial development should break the foreign exchange constraint. In the second place, it must finance an expanding programme of government initiatives in the field of infrastructure and human resources. Thirdly, it must solve the urban food problem which will follow in more earnest in the wake of industrialisation. Finally, it must find avenues for keeping the vast numbers of people productively engaged.

Whereas the importance of a radical departure in these fields is beyond question if foreign companies wish to continue their operations in the Third World, the political and financial will to organise the programmes is often lacking. Stephen Hymer (1975, p. 59) has hence in a provocative manner asked the question whether "the age of multinational corporations is at its end rather than at its beginning". The question posed by Hymer concerns the ultimate self-defeating social, political and economic consequences of the growing abyss between the epicentre of the capitalist world and the Third World in general. This fact alone has given a dramatic importance to the debates among politicians, social scientists, journalists and business people on the role of private foreign investments.

The multinational corporations see themselves as the most appropriate, and in any case the most efficient instrument of international diffusion of resources, particularly of technology in its embodied and disembodied form. Also, the managerial expertise which accompanies private foreign investments is put forward as a positive characteristic. By its adaptability and flexibility, in combination with the command over vast resources in different parts of the world, MNCs are in a position, for the benefit of the country concerned, to save on production costs and to widen the scope of industrial activities. The activities are seen as a catalyst in increasing the technical as well as the commercial levels, and in stimultaing the involvement of local business. In the process, through the general stimulation of economic life, the problems of unemployment, poverty and backwardness, will be solved. The creation of emloyment, often merely by exploiting hitherto unused natural resources, will lead to higher income and consumption levels, which in turn will generate even more production and higher tax receipts by the government.

It should be added, however, that the claims of MNCs as agents of development, are not upheld with the same vigour as in earlier decades. The Anglo-Dutch Unilever company, in a publication on its role in developing countries, merely submits that in breaking the vicious circle of poverty or in activating the development process, it "can play" an important role : "It is, after more than half a century of international experience, our conviction that private initiative can provide an important stimulus in the further development of the countries concerned" (Unilever 1984, p. 3). Production on the basis of the free enterprise is advanced as the most important engine for economic growth and well-being, "and it is the task of the government to create a climate in which the enterprises can function efficiently" (Unilever 1984, p. 21).

The contribution of foreign firms to the realisation of national economic aims will be most outspoken in the countries which, accordingly, provide them with a reasonable degree of freedom in unfolding their activities. The World Bank nevertheless questions whether the equity forms of investment can expand : "equity investment is beneficial to developing countries and can be increased, but (it) is largely a complement to bank lending, not a substitute for it. Because it is narrowly concentrated in countries and sectors, its potential for expansion is limited" (World Bank Report 1985, p. 125). The maximisation of that limited potential would require liberal policies particularly in regard to foreign investments, as well as a stable economic and political environment.

Multinational Corporations are not so much attracted by their ethical desire to join efforts in breaking the chains of poverty and misery, but, as the World Bank puts it, "by a country's natural resources or its favourable economic environment; occasionally they are also attracted by the special inducements offered by the host countries" (World Bank Report 1985, p. 125).

Whatever the claims and intentions of the spokesman of the corporate groups, empirical evidence reveals a widening abyss between the wealthy home lands of the giant corporations and the immiserised vast stretches in the Third World. Many authors accordingly have come to the conclusion that a regulatory framework would be required in order to reduce the economic and political power of the internationally operating concerns. The works of broadly recognised authorities as Vernon, Dunning, Kindleberger, Streeten, Lall, Hymer, and others, have generally ended with the conclusion that the absolute free interplay of market forces would only aggravate an already lopsided economic situation.

Michael Vernon, in a book with the suggestive title *Sovereignty At Bay*, considers the MNCs as the best possible alternative for achieving an increase in the world aggregate productivity. He concedes, however, that in some industries, the existence of multinational corporations has been stifling to growth. In general, the distribution of profits over the lending countries and the receiving countries follows an asymmetrical pattern. As for the distribution of profits within the countries, Vernon does not see a trend towards a more egalitarian system. The growing economic polarisation has generated social and politicial tensions which are sharpened by the loss of national control over the foreign firms.

The rationale of the evolutionary scheme which ultimately would bring the promised advantages to the underdeveloped countries, is, according to Stephen Hymer (1975, p. 47ff.) confronted with two major problems. In the first place, the corporations seriously erode the power of the nation state. In effect, governmental policies diminish the more open the economy and the greater the extent of foreign investment. Since legal rights are defined in terms of property ownership, the subsidiaries are not really effective partners in a multinational development effort, but remain the property of the parent office. The parent company, though its economic and political instruments, tends to over-rule the sovereignty of the host country in all fields of life. Such an erosion of sovereignty could be tolerated if it did not generate unevenness. This, however, is the crux of the problem and constitutes a major issue which multinational corporations, according to Hymer, will have to solve.

The crux of the problem indeed follows from the conflict inherent in the territorial non-coincidence. The control over a large cluster of corporations in various countries has enabled the MNCs to enjoy the economics of scale in the production and distribution of knowledge. The geographical specialisation and integration allows them, according to V.N. Balasubramanyam (1980, p. 4.) "to share the costs and benefits" between the countries in which they operate. He, however, despite his sympathies for the MNCs as such, continues that the very strengths of the corporations, "have also proved to be their curse. The size and the control they exercise over operations are seen to pose a threat to the political sovereignty and economic independence of the new nation-states in the Third World. Their search for profitable opportunities and their emphasis on cost minimisation and efficiency are seen to be inimical to considerations of social justice and equity, however they are defined. Concern is expressed that their activities may thwart rather than promote national economic objectives such as the reduction of income disparities, increased employment opportunities and strengthened balance of payments".

The issue of foreign investments is related to the economic as well as to the social and political concerns. Even in conditions where the net economic contribution would be positive, the ex-patriate nature of the investments would reduce the jurisdiction of the national state and would increase the influence of a foreign power. It may be assumed that the negative political and social costs associated with foreign investments will be acceptable by the various layers in society as long as the direct and indirect benefits are noticeably bigger than the costs. Indirect economic, social and political costs and benefits (see Reuber 1973, pp. 15-25) in any case are complex quantities and qualities, and will not be assessed in the present study. Even if it could be concluded, on the basis of a comparison of direct costs and benefits involved, that indigenous firms have not performed better, in view of the expatriate nature of foreign firms, political questions could can be asked and have been asked.

The foregoing statement is relevant for an understanding of the direction of the study to be undertaken. In the host country where the research project was located, questions of sovereignty and indigenous development efforts have been a fundamental aspect of political, social as well as academic life. Negative features of foreign based companies thereby attract a more critical assessment than if the companies would have been national enterprises.

Precisely on the issue of disregard for national cultures and national governments, multinational corporations have received criticism from various, unexpected quarters. Reference could be made to the statement by the Assemblee of the World Council of Churches at Nairobi in 1975 : "Multinational Corporations form a typical example of the way in which capitalist forces join up at the international and national level in order to suppress the poor and to keep them in their power" (translated from TNO Werkgroep 1984, p. 9). Ten years later, the MNC committee of the Dutch chapter of the Council of Churches presented its report in a similar spirit of ethical indignation : "They consider their duty as limited to the stimulation of economic growth, and at the same time lack the knowledge, understanding and interest to assess the impact of their activities on the poorer sections of the population" (TNO Werkgroep 1984 p. 57). One of the conclusions of another Dutch report on MFCs and developing countries, like the previous report the end-result of many rounds of consultations between social scientists and representatives of the companies, is equally outspoken : "The powers wielded by states and multinational corporations cannot be separated. They are the result of an inextricable string of interests which more often than not lead to abuses of which the countries in the Third World are the victims" (Hommes 1985, p. 17).

It would be rather easy to supplement the ethical anxieties as quoted above with scores of similar comments. From those comments by institutions and scholars who generally are not opposed to the system of private capital, it can be deduced that the effect of multinational corporations on the Third World remains at the centre of attention. The question marks do not relate as much to the intrinsic capacity of the multinational corporations to bring about development, as to the most appropriate policy prescriptions : rather a more stringent supervision by the governments concerned so as to harness the powers of the MNCs in accordance with the aims of planned development and equity than a more liberal approach which would bring about development in the short run and equity in the long run through a trickle down effect.

The latter is clearly the the strategy proposed by the multinational corporations. The lack of development is located in the regulatory restrictions imposed by the governments in the developing countries. The liberalisation and privatisation of the economy is hence proposed as the only viable alternative for development. The research question, therefore, assuming that the multinational corporations are justified in claiming to be important agents for the process of development in the Third World, would be to locate the negative consequences which follow from the absence of government regulation.

Research efforts to establish the impact of multinational corporations have been undertaken quite frequently at an aggregate level. In-depth case studies on the effect of a limited number of companies in a particular country, instead of gross statistical aggregation, might throw more light on the sequences of development and the impact of foreign investments. We plan to carry out such an investigation in respect of India. India offers an excellent country-case because of its long standing policy, aimed at preventing the monopoly power of both national and foreign companies from blocking the development of small and medium scale industries. Despite the consecutive policy frameworks which have been worked out, and which we shall analyse in chapter two, monopoly power in industry has continued to grow. The regulatory policy which had already been eroded in practice, from the early 1980s onwards has definitely given way to a policy of economic liberalisation. The monitoring of the failure of that policy aimed at the prevention of the growth of monopoly power and the stimulation of the non-monopoly sector of the economy, as it has been defined in the Indian context, is an exercise which will do no more than to establish that islands of excellence have grown in a desert of stagnation and inefficiency. In addition, we shall, in the main body of the book, take up a number of case studies relating to the overall behaviour of the Dutch multinational corporations operating in India, particularly of the two major companies, Hindustan Lever and Peico.

In the light of various theoretical approaches which will be outlined in chapter one, particular attention will be paid to the following topics :

1. The modification in the behaviour of MNCs in relation to the government policy, and more concretely, the nature of its growth against the background of indigenisation;
2. The financing policy, including the effect on the balance of payments account, the generation of profits and its ploughback ratio.
3. The relation to the indigenous industry which will throw some light on forward as well as backward linkages and the degree of competition in some product branches;
4. The contribution to the national economy in terms of product-mix, spread effect, strain on the capital market and tax revenue;
5. The transfer of technology both at the level of import and assimilation of technology and at the level of generation of know-how by means of in-house Research and Development.

The information which forms the basis of the empirical chapters in the book, has been obtained from the following sources :

(a) published company reports, particularly the annual reports;
(b) unpublished company data collected by government agencies and departments in the legally prescribed form;
(c) published government material, particularly annual surveys and reports emanating from commissions which look after the implementation of government policy;
(d) interviews with representatives of management and

workforce of the companies concerned and occasionally with civil servants;

(e) interviews in and around ancillary units and in units belonging to direct competitors in a particular industrial field;

(f) reports and surveys published in newspapers.

Not all sources were equally accessible. The cooperation of government departments and trade unions was generally good, although in a number of cases information which had been promised was not forthcoming. This was, for example, the case with the government statistics on export prices and costs of production which would have enabled us to make an assessment of transfer pricing. The cooperation of the management of the smaller companies and of the competitors of the big multinational corporations was equally good.

The two biggest companies, in the sample were, however, rather hesitant to extend their cooperation, despite a number of efforts from the side of the project staff. One explanation for the unwillingness relates to the fact that in the final report the identity of the companies would not be concealed, and as a matter of fact, in view of the limited number of clearly distinct firms, could not be. Given the open nature of the end results, the companies preferred to take a cautious attitude. Another explanation which may have reinforced the uncooperative attitude relates to the fact that the intentions of some of the project staff may have stuck the management as being too critical. This at least was possibly the reason for the biggest company in the sample to break off its cooperation after an initial period prior to the visit of two of our researchers to the company premises. Our insistence to talk to the employees directly was, according to our understanding, the breaking point for Hindustan Lever. The other major company, Philips-Peico adopted a negative stance right from the beginning. The only net result of announced visits to the registered office in Calcutta and the head office in Bombay was an annual report of the company and a short meeting with the technical director. Both privileges were extended after insistency from our part. The technical director was quite outspoken in his explanation why cooperation would not be extended: apart from the general distrust of researchers from the Netherlands, the fact that the research project was located in a "left-dominated university with pre-conceived ideas" (i.e. the Jawaharlal Nehru University in New Delhi) was an added reason for not reciprocating our request. In later written communications, two official reasons were advanced. Since on the one hand the company had only a Dutch minority participation, it did not fall within the ambit of the study. On the other hand, labour unrest and the setback in production made any exercise involving workers with questionnaires untimely.

The official data, as contained in the annual reports, do not necessarily reveal the real state of affairs. The same restriction applies to the information which, in fulfilment of legal obligations or in support of requests for subsidies or programmes of expansions, supplied regularly to the Reserve Bank of India and to government departments. The only counter-check which could be made use of was the information which we solicited from employees in the concerns and from the concerned civil servants. Although we realise that on a number of issues the management may be better informed than the other two types of respondents, and that the empirical evidence has therefore a self-selective and incomplete character, the official data constitute the basis of analysis. In that sense we shall represent the reality as reported by the multinational corporations, but shall, for reasons of comparison and evaluation, make use of data and queries provided by third parties.

The present study is not intended as a sample study on behaviour and role of multinational corporations in India. The nature of the study, namely an investigation into the position of Dutch multinational corporations, including obviously the Anglo-Dutch companies, automatically identified the companies to be studied. No attempt will be made to determine how representative the companies studied are of all foreign investments in India. The implication is that no strong inferences can be drawn about all present and future MNCs in the country, especially since it appears that the sample companies are generally most active in the consumer sector and not in the capital goods sector. That caveat, however, does not diminish the relevance of the empirical data for the topics which will be the object of research.

# 1

# *Multinational Corporations in Development: An Overview*

While the specific analysis of any multinational corporation, or of any developing country for that matter, will come up with distinct features which are not applicable to all situations, generalisations about the role of private foreign investments in developing countries can be made, and actually should be made in order to present the specific analysis within the broader comparative framework. This first introductory chapter therefore concerns a topical overview of some of the major issues involved in the overseas investments by MNCs.

Among the relevant issues which will be dealt with in the empirical body of the book are the foreign resource constraints, the employment generation within an envisaged new international economic order, the extent of capital export in the decolonised world structure, and the complexity of the integration of foreign monopoly structures with a lopsided industrial formation. Prior to those aspects, we shall first present a selective view of the three main theoretical schools, namely the (bourgeois) mainstream economists, the neo-marxists and the marxists.

## 1.1. Modes of Analysis

The role of multinational corporations as a carrier of development has been the focus of interpretations and reinterpretations by the most varied types of economists. In general, mainstream economists have continued to appreciate their contribution to development by the introduction of advanced technology and management and the increase of overall industrial activity, but on the other hand have in a number of cases deplored the outflow of resources, the disarticulation with the indigenous sector and the manipulation of government institutions.

The export of capital to the countries in the Third World has, for long, been regarded as an essential prerequisite for the economic development of those countries (*e.g.* Rostow, Nurkse, Myrdal, Kindleberger, etc.). The development of the Third World was therefore necessarily tied up with the increases in private foreign investments. Since the less developed areas of the world, in view of the scarcity of capital, the abundance of raw material and labour, and the elasticity of the market, were moreover, seen as the natural direction for capital to flow, the bridging of the gap was considered to be a matter of time only.

As the decades drew on, the oil stain function of foreign capital in developing countries became less obvious as a natural phenomenon. The foreign resource gap did not exhibit a narrowing tendency, and the income differences between the developed countries and the underdeveloped countries went on increasing.

In the early seventies, Streeten still saw an amicable relationship emerging. The positive and negative results would find a mutually acceptable balance if both parties. *i.e.* the foreign firm and the local government, would decide to become partners in development. A number of arrangements for the remittance of profit and capital gains would attract foreign capital and know-how to the activities where they were most useful, but would release them, when the host government would buy out the firm, for new ventures elsewhere. Thus good use would be made of the finance and experience of foreign companies by keeping them in a revolving fund (Streeten 1972, p. 250).

During the second half of the 1970s the realisation of the oligopolistic power of the multinational giants definitely entered the picture, and led to a somewhat less naive analysis. Lall and Streeten in their study on *Foreign Investment, Transnationals and Developing Countries*, originally published in 1977, submitted that foreign capital would not be satisfied with such a pioneering role. Foreign capital would essentially flow to countries with a particular overall environment, namely one in which the host country "efficiently integrates with the international capitalist economy on terms favourable to private enterprise—mainly by offering stable economic, social and political conditions for growth of private investment and 'free' markets; sometimes by controlling the power of labour unions; by minimum interference with the activities of the firm; and generally by not tampering too much with the pattern of income distribution which evolves naturally with industrial development" (Lall and Streeten 1980, p. 194).

In order to make its investments competitive with the local entrepreneurs, it would be necessary for the investing firm to have some oligopolistic or monopolistic advantages not possessed by the potential local competitor. Such advantages relate to access to capital, modern management techniques, technology, marketing networks, economies of scale, etc. Although the control over these sources are the main consideration for governments in developing countries to invite the multinational corporation, they would continue to remain internal to the firm, and would not be allowed to come under the control of the government or the indigenous competitors. While accepting that state of affairs as an unalterable framework, the authors call for imaginative controls on the foreign exchange and monopoly regulation front. It is for the governments in underdeveloped countries to act skilfully in providing a right *ambience* for a constructive and beneficial use of the potentials of foreign firms: "Every measure offers a potential benefit to the host country but may also have a potential cost—if maladministered, it may inhibit desirable inflows, encourage distortions in the economy and negate the purpose for which it has been instituted". Since per definition it is accepted that the positive and negative effects can be separated, it follows that "it is neither necessary nor desirable to take either a completely laissez-faire or an extreme communist view. The skill in framing a policy and in negotiating a contract with transnational companies is to maximise the surplus of beneficial over detrimental effects that is still acceptable to the TNC. The key to policy then, is selectivity, not ideology" (Lall and Streeten 1980, p. 218).

The onus for the negative backwash of the multinational

domination over the economy has thus been transferred to the governments and people of the Third world. It is argued that unless there is a drastic change in the internal structures of the poor countries themselves, the undesirable effects will continue to be felt. What exactly the changes in the internal structure should consist of, is not made explicit except for the fact that it should not lead to communism or should not be obstructed by an overgrown bureaucracy fed on ideology and an over-regulating red-tape system. In his many recent contributions in *World Development*, *Journal of Development Studies* and other journals, Sanjaya Lall has made this approach ultimately into a plea for the liberalisation of the economy. Particularly with reference to India, the argument is that if the industrial economy of India is really to move forward, the basic rules of the games will have to be changed. The highly interventionist policy of the past has created serious distortions in the industrial structure, economic efficiency and international economic relations. The persistence with the policy of pervasive quantitative controls and self-reliance at all costs has vitiated the national advantages and has created widespread distortions and inefficiencies. For any dramatic change in the ossified system, governments will have to change the rules of the game in an outward looking policy in open confrontation with the MNCs.

From the mainstream economic literature, the view also emerges that conflicts are intrinsic in the relationship between multinational corporations and underdeveloped countries, and that the divergence of the goals of the opposite partners is most likely to be exacerbated where the bargaining power of the multinational corporation is at its greatest or where the perceptions of the desired course of economic development are different. The various shades of differences in the theoretical approaches, however, could be united around the eclectic view of Dunning (1984, p. 29; also Dunning, 1981) that "it is difficult to establish any generalised theory of international trade or production", and that therefore it would be just as difficult to draw up any generalised code of conduct or policy recommendation. The major exception to this view is represented by Hymer who has highlighted the anti-competitive aspect of the growth of multinational corporations and the resulting reinforcement of a pattern of uneven development not so much based on interdependence as on dependence. The position of Hymer followed logically from his reading of the monopolistic elements in the capitalist economy. Monopoly formation is not perceived as a deviation from the ideal type of free competition in a market economy, but as the quintessence of the economic and political power structure which is dominated by the multinational corporations. Within the non-marxist tradition, Hymer went far beyond the accepted political conclusions. His defense of strict control and even of a ban on international sourcing by multinational corporations as well as his plea for national planning processes and nationalisation of companies (Hymer 1970, p. 448) came quite close to the orthodox Marxist understanding.

The orthodox marxist theory on foreign investments, which in the developed capitalist countries, attracted an important following around 1970, in the recent decade has lost ground to the appeal of "neo-marxist" theorising and to the contributions within the world system and unequal exchange models. Although these theories do not usually deal with the role of private foreign investments but rather with the asymmetrical relationship between such descriptive entities as the North and the South or the Centre and the Periphery, they do deal with the problems caused by the domination of the international finance, trade and production monopolies. André Gunder Frank's approach to the question may be considered typical for many of his dependencia colleagues. In his 1980 book on *Crisis in the World Economy*, only three cursory references are made to the position of multinational corporations. The oversight is not accidental. In the analysis of Frank, underdevelopment is not to be explained by the inherent operation of the multinational concerns, but by "a whole hierarchy of exploitation—a chain of metropolis—satellite relationships moving from the world metropolis, which is no one's satellite, via nations, capitals, cities, regional and local centres, large landowners and merchants, small peasants and tenants, right down to the landless labourer at the bottom"(Frank 1967, p. 95).

The usefulness as well as the theoretical coherence of the dependency theories have been the subject of germane critique, in Lall (1975), Nabudere (1978), Limqueco and McFarlane (1984), Szentes (1985) and Patnaik (1986). The relevant point for our purpose is that some of the theorists of dependency and unequal exchange, particularly Emmanuel and Bill Warren, have elaborated on the theory of imperialism, and have come to the conclusion that MNCs play a potentially useful role in the development of as yet underdeveloped countries.

In the view of Bill Warren (1973; 1980), the phenomenon of dependency has suffered "an irreversible" decline after the formal political independence of the countries in the Third World. The increase in institutional control over their domestic economies in combination with an increase in trade and foreign investment rivalries has created a situation in which the imperialist firms and states have to compete increasingly for the favours of the Third World governments. The intensive battle for markets has led to an increased leverage of power within the southern hemisphere. The prospect for a successful capitalist development of the major underdeveloped countries is accordingly quite good. In so far as there are obstacles to this development, "they originate not in current imperialist-Third World relationships, but almost entirely from the internal contradictions of the Third World itself; the imperialist countries' policies and their overall impact on the Third World actually favour its industrialisation" (Warren 1973, p. 2).

According to the "neo-Marxist" view of Warren, the multinational corporations ultimately will offer to the developing countries all the advantages which non-marxist economists tend to predict, such as improved technology control over resources, export oriented growth, generation of employment and even independence in partnership. In respect of the latter assertion, he expressed more confidence in the self-regulatory power of the free interplay of market forces than for example Vernon and Hymer:

> Indeed . . . it is not easy to imagine large geographical centres of industrial and economic power indefinitely controlled from elsewhere. For manufacturing alone, technical economic factors are bound, over time, to bind it by a thousand ties to the local environment and thus bring

> it under the control of that environment. As industrial power spreads, political power follows.

In fact, "private investment in the Third World is increasingly creating the conditions for the disappearance of imperialism as a system of economic inequality between nations of the capitalist world system, and . . . there are no limits, in principle, to this system" (Warren 1973, p. 40).

Arghiri Emmanuel, another major "neo-marxist" author, also expects foreign capital to initiate the development of the Third World, although in his view, this could be undertaken on the basis of mechanisation in agriculture and should not necessarily imply industrialisation. It is not so much agricultural specialisation which has prevented development, but the depression of wages. By unilaterally increasing the wage level, developing countries would, so runs the argument, gain on two counts, namely by buying cheaper foreign products and by selling more expensively on the world market. Higher wages would, as a consequence, allow for the import of machine goods and would expand the market of consumer goods. This, in the view of Emmanuel, is the crux of the solution. Foreign capital at the moment is not in a position to expand its investments in developing countries outside the enclaves because of the lack of a consumer market. Although the investors would prefer to extend their activities and bring about development, as they have done in such previously agricultural countries as Canada and Australia, as long as the developing countries keep their wages at the existing low levels, there is no scope for a substantial contribution by foreign capital. At the same time, the present investments do have a positive impact : "Although it is lopsided and asymmetrical, the 'extraverted' development, precisely on account of the fact that it is restricted to enclaves and is not rooted in the internal economic structure, does not block anything. If it had not been there, nothing would have taken its place. The underdeveloped countries would in that case even have lost the revenue which, however meagre, accrue to them on account of salaries, taxes and the sales of local products to the enclaves" (Emmanuel 1970, p. 91; see also 1978 and 1982).

Samir Amin, on the other hand, although an advocate of a

modified form of Emmanuel's unequal exchange theory, has an outspoken pessimistic view of multinational corporations in developing countries. External dependence is considered to be at once the origin and the result of the situation of under-development. The essence of development is not to be found so much in the absence or presence of growth, as in the integrated mobilisation of resources : "The disarticulation of the economy prevents the development of any one sector from having a mobilising effect upon the rest" (Amin 1974, p. 17). Any effect which might emerge is usually transferred abroad. The onslaught from without originally by means of trade, carried out by the "central capitalist mode of production" upon the pre-capitalist formations, caused certain crucial retrogressions, and led to a decline of the crafts without their being replaced by local industrial production : "The subsequent investment of foreign capital does not have the effect of correcting these retrogressive changes, because of the extraverted orientation of the industries that this capital establishes in the periphery" (Amin 1974, p. 391). The extraversion of the central capitalism as it operates, i.e. the distortion towards export activities, forms the decisive element in the explanatory model of underdevelopment and international unequal specialisation. According to Amin, foreign capital first serves to open up the peripheral countries but afterwards automatically engenders a flow a profit transfers in the opposite direction. The transition of the phase of "opening-up" to foreign capital to the phase of "exploitation at cruising speed" marks the beginning of a negative balance of payments situation which can only be brought back to equilibrium by a very rapid growth of exports. Exports should necessarily grow faster than the gross national products and would result in the development of underdevelopment.

In the Marxist approach, both in its Leninist and in its Luxemburgean variation, the monopolistic control by a decreasing number of financial and industrial empires has been earmarked as the specific feature of developed capitalism. Instead of arguing on the best possible name for the concerns (multinationals, transnationals, corporate-enterprises, etc.), orthodox marxism in fact uses the concept of International Monopoly Capital. Arising out of the tendency of the rate of profit to fall with the increasing organic composition of capital, capitalists must look for ever new opportunities to increase productivity. This continuous process can be realised by either a vertical intensification through cost-cutting innovations and the establishment of monopolistic positions, or by a horizontal expansion over the regional borders.

The production of capital aimed at the production of ever more capital, which is considered to be the essence of the capitalist mode of production, in the second half of the nineteenth century led to the twin process of concentration and centralisation and to the internationalisation of capital, i.e. the change-over from the export of commodities to the export of productive capital. The new developments which started emerging one century ago were conceptualised by Lenin as the final stage in the development of capitalism, namely the imperialist stage. Apart from the export of capital on a large scale, imperialism was characterised as a monopoly formation in which the so-called finance capital ("controlled by banks and employed by industrialists") and the state organs were closely interlinked. The latter aspect of the concept of imperialism is often missed by present day "neo-marxist" critiques of Lenin, although it constitutes its essential part.

The failure of capitalism to develop industrialisation gradually throughout the whole world has been the subject of theoretical as well as polemic attention by marxists over the last half a century. When Marx wrote in the middle of the nineteenth century about the role of the East India Company in India, he predicted it to fulfil a double mission, namely the destruction of the archaic stagnating economy and the building up of a modern industry. Also Lenin, in his writings on imperialism, expected an expansion of capital throughout the world and an acceleration of the development of capitalism in the then territorially subdued nations.

While in previous epochs capital moved in function of trade, with the emergence of imperialism, trade was integrated as a function of capital. In the view of Lenin, the expansion would necessarily lead to the reproduction of the conditions of capitalist production on an extended level. The hunt for larger monopoly profits would necessarily induce a movement of finance capital in that direction. It was, however, not stated explicitly that the direction would automatically be towards the backward countries, or that the integration in the world capitalist system would necessarily lead to the introduction of the capitalist mode of production, as many "neo-marxists" tend to believe. The notion that imperialism in fact could have a dampening effect was introduced during the debates within the Communist International in the 1920s. Imperialism, so sounded the official theory, originally had given rise to native capitalism, but now tended to impede its development. By destroying agriculture, imperialist finance capital with the support of the indigenous pre-capitalist vested interests, narrowed down the base for further development of industry. (Lieten 1984, pp. 101-106). In contemporary Soviet writings, this position has been elaborated by Pavlov and Ulyanovsky (1973), Gromyko (1985) and particularly by Simoniya (1985) in his penetrating analysis of *The Destiny of Capitalism in the Orient*. Credit for the outstanding and most comprehensive contribution in the orthodox marxist field goes to Tamas Szentes (1983 and 1985). Szentes, extending the analysis made by his Hungarian compatriot Göncöl in the 1960s, argues that while in the pre-imperialist stage of the capitalist international economy, the debtor-creditor relationship was basically the consequence and function of the international exchange of goods, in the present imperialist stage on the contrary, the international exchange of goods has become more and more the function of the debtor-creditor relationship. With the debtor-creditor relationship becoming the determinant of the international exchange of goods, the capital of the developed industrialised countries has obtained a determining role in forming and changing the production structures of the backward countries, subordinating them to its own needs and including them in its own circulation process.

Szentes concludes that the "monopoly-capitalist character (which restricts) the sphere and efficiency of competition" contradicts the conditions which are necessary for the harmonious equalisation between the flows of money and commodities at the international level. He theoretically establishes that the flow of capital exports "necessarily leads, under the given circumstances, to the cumulative process of over-borrowing and over-lending" (Szentes 1983, p. 160). This aspect shall be taken up in the next section.

## 1.2. The Foreign Exchange Gap

In the optimistic view, the MNCs, because of their power to command capital and technology on a global scale, are expected to spread production more evenly over the world's surface, and to act as a force for diffusing industrialisation to less developed countries. The trickle-down system would coincide with a reinforcement of the centralised decision making. By and large, mainstream economists belonging to the various theoretical persuasions agree that advantages remain unevenly distributed between the corporation and the host country. Unlike the marxist and dependencia theorists, many would, however, be in agreement with the view that a bilateral monopoly situation exists in which the host country can effectively bargain with the foreign corporations.

In such a situation, according to Charles Kindleberger (1973, p. 261), the impact of direct investment on the balance of payments of the receiving country is adverse in the short run, but helpful in the long: "Typically the advantage in a bilateral monopoly situation starts out all on the side of the investing company and gradually shifts to the host country".

The particular contribution of private foreign investment is not generally attributed so much to the addition to total available foreign exchange, which in fact may be negative, as to the particular productive form of the resources transferred. Its merits lie not so much in contributing to filling the foreign exchange gap or even the savings gap, but, as Streeten (1972, p. 444) submits, "in helping lay the foundations for further growth in the economy and in strengthening the base from which domestic savings and foreign exchange are generated". Listed as some of the positive effects are the contribution to the tax revenue and budgetary balance, the transfer of technology, management and marketing skills, the growth of local entrepreneurship by local subcontracting, the penetration into foreign markets, the competitive spirit, etc.

However, a number of obstacles need a solution before a new balance can be found. The obstacles may be located in respect of practically every field for which the contributions of the multinational corporations are considered beneficial in the underdeveloped regions of the world. A brief treatment of the foreign exchange, employment and linkages effect will show that expected positive results are not as straightforward as the earlier generation of economists and the multinationals themselves have predicted.

Private overseas investments have not yet achieved, and Streeten (1972, p. 438) agrees, "with all its merits, can probably not achieve a large and sustained transfer of foreign exchange resources to developing countries". Such a conclusion that foreign companies plough more profit out of the country than they introduce fresh capital, is the logical result of a number of operations. In the first place, there is the profit mechanism itself. In general, foreign capital grows faster than domestic capital. This follows logically from the fact that the return on capital in foreign dominated firms exceeds the growth of national income. Between 1973 and 1980 the GDP growth rates of all developing countries together as well as the middle income oil-importers separately, was of the order of 6.3 per cent. Some regions, like India and Africa, were below the 4 per cent mark (World Bank 1984, p. 11). On the other hand, the profitability rates attained by the multinational corporations have been substantially larger, and moreover have left profit rates in the home countries far behind. This has been the case not only in the extraction sector, but also in the production sector proper (Dunning 1981, p. 186; Astapovich 1983, p. 17).

The higher profits, if transformed into capital, would have led to an ever increasing capital stock in the developing countries and to a diminishing importance of the OECD countries in the operations of multinational corporations. The opposite course of events indicates that only a part of the profits has been ploughed back into the local economy, and that Third World countries throughout the years have been used and continue to be used as a source of surplus generation. The logical construct can be strengthened by direct evidence. During the two years 1979-80, developing countries made almost half of the recorded outgoing payments on foreign investments, but received less than a quarter of the reported foreign investments. Whereas during both the years, on an average 12.8 billion US dollars were registered as outflows on account of profits, only 5.8 billion dollars (net of 2.1 billion dollars re-invested earnings) of new productive capital were added to the capital stock (United Nations 1983, p. 19).

The deficit position, it should be added, is influenced by the special position of oil-exporting countries, who accounted for two-thirds of all payments by developing countries on foreign direct investments (United Nations 1983, Table II.13; Friedländer 1981, Table 13).

It may be argued, as Eberhard Czaya (1975, p. 110) does, that the return flow of profits does account for only one part of the drainage of surplus. Some of the outlays of daughter companies, such as the payments of interest on loans to the parent company, royalty payments and fees for management services, in fact contribute to the profitabillity of the parent company and to the foreign exchange outlay of the daughter company in the underdeveloped country. As such, the rapid growth of international trade in patents, licenses and know-how has provided the major companies with a new form of profit generation. A distinct feature of international economics is the development of intra-firm trade in technology. The trade in both embodied and disembodied forms of technology indeed has increased considerably. It is estimated that the receipts of OECD countries from developing countries in the form of royalties, fees and remuneration for technical services during the 1970s grew at an annual rate of 15.6 per cent from US $ 610 million in 1970 to US $ 2620 million in 1980. The income from technology and services accounted for nearly forty per-cent of total receipts from developing countries by the MNCs in Japan, nearly thirty per cent in the case of the U.K. and around twenty per cent in the USA (United Nations 1983, p. 162-166; Rana Singh 1982, p. 43).

The transfer of capital and technology is usually accompanied by the export of machinery, equipment, supplies and raw materials, and thereby automatically ties the developing countries to a long-term import commitment. The import-oriented production process may generate a more reverse impact on the balance of payments situation than the straight import of a selected range of commodities would have. According to Lall and Streeten, the greater the extent of reliance on imports for production, the less is the linkage of the industry to the local economy, the greater is the direct foreign exchange cost, and the fewer, as a consequence, are the growth and spread effects of the investment. In their study of six developing countries, they found the extent of import dependence to be very high, with the exception of India (only 14.5 per cent of sales of the companies concerned). They argue that a low extent of import dependence could be advocated on the basis of considerations of political economy, namely an economic strategy based on "less integration into the world economy and a different pattern of distribution, consumption and social organisation domestically" (Lall and Streeten 1980, p. 143). On the consideration of "conventional theory", however, a low optimum level of import dependence is not necessarily on the cards.

The most immediate effect of the import dependence, however, remains, namely a giant foreign exchange crisis which affects all Third World countries in general (see Table 1.1) and the so-called newly industrialised countries in particular. The countries with the highest ratio of foreign direct investments (Argentina, Brazil, Mexico, South Korea and Indonesia) also suflered the most severe imbalances on the balance of payment accounts, and have landed themselves in a seemingly intractable debt crisis.

**Table 1.1 : Debt Indicators for Developing Countries 1970-1984**

| Indicators | 1970 | 1974 | 1978 | 1982 | 1984 |
|---|---|---|---|---|---|
| Ratio of Debt to GNP | 14.1 | 15.4 | 21.0 | 26.3 | 33.8 |
| Ratio of Debt to Exports | 108.9 | 80.0 | 113.1 | 115.0 | 135.4 |
| Ratio of Dept Service to Exports | 14.7 | 11.8 | 18.4 | 20.5 | 19.7 |
| Ratio of Interest Service to GNP | 0.5 | 0.8 | 1.1 | 2.3 | 2.8 |
| Total Debt Outstanding (billions) US dollars | 68 | 141 | 313 | 546 | 686 |

*Source* : World Bank, *World Development Report*, 1985, p. 24.

The current account deficit of the developing countries in any case illustrate the growing imbalances. The deficit as a percentage of the GNP increased from 1.8 per cent in the five year period 1970-1974 to 2.3 per cent during 1980-1984. In the case of the African countries, the ratio went up from 5.7 per cent to 10.3 per cent. In the latter period, despite the harsh measures which the debt servicing countries were required to introduce, cutting down their imports and pushing their exports, the balance of payments deficit has risen to 3.5 per cent of the GNP (World Bank 1985, p. 17). In addition to the current account deficit of $ 36 billion in 1984, the interest payments of all developing countries totalled $ 58 billion, thereby illustrating what Fidel Castro in his 1982 address to the conference of the Non-Aligned Movement has called the bankification of the international economy: "The sharp worsening of the Third World's international economic relations while an appreciable volume of surplus capital was available in the developed capitalist world created the conditions for turning flows of financing into a generator of even greater indebtedness, dependence and domination for the poorest countries" (Castro 1984, p. 85). As a consequence of the growth of borrowing, debt service payments have increased from $ 9.3 billion in 1970 to $ 100 billion in 1984.

The growth of borrowing was, a.o., linked to the relative decrease in non-debt creating financial flows. Official development assistance as a share of total external finance dropped from 43.3 per cent in 1970-72 to 35.6 per cent in 1980-82. During the same period the flow of direct investments also decreased from 17.6 per cent to 12.9 per cent. Private flows for direct investments as a matter of fact even in nominal terms declined from 17.2 billion dollars in 1981 to 7.8 billion in 1983 (World Bank 1975, p. 21; Kannapin 1985, p. 39).

Amortisation and interest payments will have to be financed by the generation of new resources. Commercial credits will be insufficient for the purpose. The data contained in the World Bank annual report over 1985 reveal that for the third consecutive year, interest payments alone ($ 58 billion) have been higher than the newly granted loans ($ 36 billion). Ultimately the repayment potential will depend to a considerable extent on the stimulation of economic activities in the Third World. The governments of the OECD could participate in this process by taking subsidising and investment insurance measures in order to stimulate foreign investments in the debt countries. More investments would enable them to improve their export performance and meet their payment obligations. This at any rate was the message which the then IMF director De Larosière gave to the annual management symposium in Sankt Gallen in 1984. The launching of a new sister organisation of the IMF, the MIGA (Multilateral Investment Guarantee Association) in October 1985, was taken in hand with that purpose. The MIGA should insure foreign private investors against political risks such as nationalisations, and contribute to a growing preparedness to invest.

Third World countries may ultimately be obliged to accept the services of the multinational corporations on an export-oriented platform. MNCs in some Latin American countries as a matter of fact have started baling out the indebted governments. In this procedure the company pays part of the debt to the international banks and in return gets from the government concerned an approximately equivalent amount of local resources and the license to invest. The procedure, if extended on a major scale may undermine all the well-intended foreign investment regulations which most of the developing countries have enacted.

Even without changes in the regulatory mechanism itself, the change-over from the import-substitution strategy to an export-oriented strategy, given their control over the international trading and services network, implies a stronger reliance on multinational corporations.

The so-called footloose or runaway industries, which seemed to be spreading fast during the 1970s, illustrate this point. G.K. Helleiner (1973, p. 31) submitted that processing, assembly and component manufacture for export within vertically integrated structures was the inevitable trend: "Manufacturing for exports is the 'new frontier' for international business in the less-developed world, and process and component specialisation is likely to become the chief, or at any rate the easiest avenue for less developed countries seeking to expand their manufacturing exports". Helleiner, however, also introduced a number of caveats and warned that in a number of cases the developing country is better off without the footloose type of manufacturing industry (Helleiner 1973, p. 46; see also Deepak Nayar 1978).

A number of caveats were further explicated by Gyorgy Adam (1975, p. 102): "Summing it up: instability, dependence, 'over-kill' of incentives, the lack of linkages, etc. make world-wide sourcing a doubtful tool in the longer term for solving the problems of the Third World, despite some job creating and export earnings. Stressing the creation of too much labour intensive industry conjures up the danger of an over-supply of these goods—banana republics becoming pyjama republics".

In the whole debate, the comparative export behaviour of the multinational corporations in the developed and developing capitalist countries, has escaped notice. A detailed comparison, for example on the basis of the US Survey of Current Business, establishes that the export propensity is the highest in the case of the MNCs operating in the developed countries and that, therefore, investments in developing countries take place mainly for the local market. Whereas in the mid-seventies, the US manufacturing companies operating in the Third World exported only 8.5 per cent of their output, in the developed capitalist countries as much as 27 per cent of the output was exported (Ludeman 1982, Table 16; also Magdoff 1969, p. 58). The Free Trade Zones may not tip the scales in favour of increasing investments for exports, unless some specific locational advantages prevail.

In general, the existence of a local mass market for the mass production which is typical of the multinational plant, is an added reason for the companies to invest in most developing countries. Philips N.V., when it justified its expansion in South East Asia in the early seventies, advocated as one of the reasons, apart from the availability of cheap labour for the specific labour processes, the possibility "to participate in the growth of the market" (Philips, *Annual Report* 1973, p. 12). As long as the global trading network remains unaffected by restrictions based on a policy of import substitution, the corporation may, however, prefer to continue exporting from its politically secure home base to those areas in the Third World which are not politically safe or which do not have a sufficiently developed market. Let us have a look at the case of Philips. In

1981 it had a sales figure of around fifteen billion dollars. As much as 23 per cent of the production originated in the Netherlands where, however, only 7 per cent of the overall production was sold at an average profit on sales of 0.6 per cent. Europe and North America accounted for 62 per cent of output and 71 per cent of sales at an average profit rate of between 2.6 and 4.7 per cent. The countries in the Third World finally produced only 11.5 per cent of the world-wide output of Philips, but provided 18 per cent of the sales, at an average profit of between 11.3 per cent in the case of Asia and 16.9 per cent in the case of Africa (Philips N.V., *Annual Report* 1981). The exports, around forty per cent of sales, found their way to a large extent to the highly profitable *markets in the developing countries*, where the local production units may serve as a channel for organizing the imports and the transfer pricing benefits. The theories on export-orientation and a new international division of labour on the basis of the world-wide operations of any company appear to be questionable (see Chandrasekar 1983, for a well argued critique of the so-called Starnberg group, Frobel et al. 1980).

One reason, in addition to the aforementioned ones why MNCs are not likely to emerge as the solution to the export trauma, may be highlighted. Intra-firm trade in commodities is an activity which, as the seminal work by Vaitsos (1974) has suggested, allows for a substantial transfer of profits to the parent company. The vertical trade transactions, like the intra-firm technology transactions, are hardly liable to accounting. This captive trade system seems to become even more important in the field of the exports of manufactures and semi-manufactures as the tide of vertical integration sweeps forward. According to an ECLA study (quoted in Castro 1983, p. 68), whereas only 23.7 per cent of primary commodities exports from Latin America to the USA originated from US subsidiaries, this was the case with 51 per cent of manufacturing exports (see also Lall, 1979, p. 61 and United Nations 1983, pp. 160-162). The absence of wide-ranging empirical studies does preclude a foolproof assessment of the exact magnitude but not of the phenomenon itself: "Since the arm's length prices do not exist for many of the products forming the subject of intra-firm trade, the prices at which these products are transferred are set in the light of considerations internal to the company concerned" (United Nations 1983, p. 6).

## 1.3. Modifications in the Export of Capital

The negative foreign exchange impact, particularly during the 1970s, was not considered a necessarily longlasting side effect of foreign direct investments. Indeed, the then current theory of a new international division of labour predicted a reshuffling of industrial activities over the globe and an increasingly equal role for the newly industrialising countries. A small number of countries do seem to have benefited from the close integration with the western world. It should be stressed that the number of countries is very small indeed, and that the countries themselves are very small as well. In the second half of the 1970s, around sixty per cent of the finished and semi-finished products imported by the developed capitalist countries from the Third World, originated in the Far East (Heininger 1978, p. 46; Sanjaya Lall 1980a). The Four Tigers in the Far East (Hamilton 1983) did not excell so much in low wages, as in low labour costs per unit of added value. Gallex and Troupin (1981) have done some interesting calculations on the differences in value added per worker in the industrialised countries, in underdeveloped countries and in the Far East. In the latter region the share of salaries in the added-value was roughly one-third below the figures in the OECD countries. This is one reason, in addition to the land reforms, why the runaway industries have bypassed the poorest countries like India, where the lower wages were outstripped by a relatively much lower labour productivity. Another reason was the availability in some of the newly industrialised countries of the right type of labour, both in the technical and the psycho-political sense.

In recent years the cost effect of the excessive dependence on the shifting requirements in the global strategy of the multinational corporations has come to the forefront.

Partly due to the continuation of the global recession and partly due to the improved productivity, unutilised capacity has been building up and has led to a severe pressure on profitability. In order to restore the overall profitability of the corporate group, the industrial structure had to be re-adjusted. The management of Philips N.V. has put the direction of that change rather bluntly as follows: ". . . the characteristic development of Philips in the past, involving the establishment of industries in the national economies of the many countries in which our Company's operations had involved, means that our production is widely scattered, and this has been accentuated by the regionalisation of industrial activities within a particular country when the situation on the labour market called for it. *Gradually, the technological and economic conditions have changed so much that this has ceased to be the most effective structure*" (Philips N.V., Annual Report 1980, p. 5; stress added).

The new strategy would imply that the new international division of labour which during the 1970s has touched only a very limited number of people and products, seems to be restricted in time as well. In any case, the employment generation effected appears to be weakening. Despite a fairly widespread notion to the contrary, multinational corporations have not really made a substantial contribution to solving the unemployment problem in the Third World. It is estimated that the total direct employment provided by multinational corporations ranges from 13 to 30 million, and that, even of the most liberal estimates are accepted, the proportion of the total global industrial employment accounted for is only 4.8%. In the Third World, the MNCs are credited with the creation of between two to four million jobs representing 0.3% of total employment and 2% of the aggregate industrial employment (Ballance et al. 1982, p. 234).

There are vast differences between different countries and industrial sectors. In general, although no hard figures are available, it may be assumed that comparative advantage of MNCs in any country, where labour wages for all competitors are an equal denominator, consists in a more capital-intensive production and less generation of employment. In particular industries, depending on the extent of backward linkages, the corporations may generate significant indirect employment. The indirect employment effects are, for two reasons, likely to be of less significance than those of the domestic manufacturers. Apart from the fact that foreign firms are generally larger net importers of intermediate goods, their output-mix is generally attuned to the more demanding luxury market of the high income groups. Because luxury goods are relatively capital-intensive and are patterned on specifications in the industrialised countries, their production tends to generate relatively less direct or indirect employment (Ballance et al. 1982, p. 234). Since, moreover, the MNCs, who decide to invest and start subsidiaries abroad, are transferring fairly complex technologies, very few domestic linkages will be created: "the rapidly changing technology, the demanding specifications and requirements of cost minimisation reduce the scope for domestic linkages to practically nothing" (Lall 1978, p.247).

The evidence available for Dutch multinational corporations suggests that the growth in employment generation has been halted. After the initial significant growth in the early seventies, the increase during the last couple of years has been negligible, if not negative. Unilever's total employment went up gradually from just over 300,000 in the mid-sixties till it reached 383,600 in 1978, and then started declining. Employment in 1984 without the newly added Brooke Bond employees, stood at 301,000, thus below the figure reached two decades earlier. Once the decline set in, the effect was felt most immediately in the countries of the European Common Market. The shrink in employment in the developing countries was delayed by three years, but also there the employment level started falling from the top level of 167,000 reached in 1978 to 132,000 in 1984.

The trend as a matter of fact is typical of the Dutch Big Four (Shell, Unilever, Philips and Akzo), as can be seen in Table 1.2. North America stands out as the only area where employment figures have not fallen sharply, reflecting the increasing flow of capital to the United States.

The declining generation of employment suggests that the extension of economic opportunities in the Third World does not necessarily follow in the wake of foreign investments. This is not only due to the high productivity of the investments, but also to the limited investment flow in itself. For long, the less developed areas of the world, in view of the scarcity of capital, the abundance of raw material and labour and the potential of the market, were seen as the natural direction for capital to flow.

**Table 1.2 : Global Geographical Employment Position of the Dutch Big Four, 1955-1984 (x 1000)**

| Region | 1975 | 1976 | 1977 | 1978 | 1979 | 1980 | 1981 | 1982 | 1983 | 1984 |
|---|---|---|---|---|---|---|---|---|---|---|
| Western Europe | 644 | 627 | 611 | 600 | 586 | 568 | 535 | 517 | 495 | 482 |
| North America | 113 | 115 | 119 | 129 | 130 | 132 | 135 | 129 | 131 | 128 |
| Rest o/t World | 221 | 236 | 271 | 283 | 277 | 270 | 265 | 255 | 247 | 246 |
| Total | 978 | 973 | 1001 | 1012 | 994 | 971 | 933 | 901 | 873 | 860 |

*Source :* Annual Reports of Shell, Unilever, Philips and Akzo-Enka.

*Note :* The regional classification by the Dutch Big Four do not coincide, but the absolute employment in the areas which are not always included under the same geographical area (e.g. Japan, New Zealand and Australia) is of such a marginal nature, that the overall region-wise trend is not basically affected.

In the decades following the first world war, the world has undergone many profound changes. Against the background of the tempestuous growth of the national liberation movement, the downfall of the system of colonialism and the danger of the emergence of communist-inspired revolutions, the free deployment of private overseas investments was rendered less practicable. Accordingly, the role and impact of multinational corporations in many Third World countries has been modified. The penetration of the capitalist mode of production has not induced a horizontal expansion in the various countries which otherwise onpure economic or rather econometric calculations could be expected. If only considerations of factor endowments and locational advantages were at play, the spread of private investments over the globe would have had a more significant impact on the industrialisation process and generation of employment that it has turned out to have.

Investments, particularly in sovereign states which are not directly integrated with the power structure of the home country of the multinational corporations, represent a political and hence economic liability. This may turn out to be a major reason why MNCs have not really engaged in a process of a world-wide re-allocation of resources. International re-allocation has taken place, as is suggested at the aggregate level. The growing internationalisation of US capital for example has led to a situation in which the ratio of production abroad by US firms to exports from the USA has risen from 266 in 1960 to 431 in 1975 (Friedländer 1981, p. 42).

Economic reasons for overseas expansion are readily at hand. Where the continued expansion in its home market is likely to cut prices and profits, a company may opt to go abroad and expand in a non-competing area. According to Kindleberger (1972, p. 393), "a firm need not earn more abroad than its local competitors, so long as it earns more than the long-term government bond rate at home and is able to avoid depressing home profits".

The export of capital to the countries in the Third World, in the perception of mainstream economists, is an essential prerequisite for the economic development of those countries Since the less developed areas of the World, in view of the scarcity of capital, the abundance of raw material and labour, and the elasticity of the market, are moreover, seen as the natural direction for capital to flow, the bridging of the gap is only a matter of time.

Particularly the second premise appears to be based on partial evidence. The understanding that the multinational corporations have been engaged in a process of world-wide re-allocation of investments, which at the aggregate level appears from the trends in internationalisation of capital, needs some substantial modification. The enormous rise in foreign investments, the accumulated stock of which has been calculated by John Dunning (1983) to have risen from 14 billion US $ in 1914 to 63 billion in 1960 and 373 billion in 1978, has not followed a straight course. In Table 1.3 we have arranged the major developments which have taken place. In the respect of the origin of capital, the growing importance of the United States and the concomitant decline of the countries of Western Europe appears as the most significant development between the two world wars. The relative decline of Europe was mainly on account of the liquidation of German and Italian foreign investments as a consequence of the two world wars, and of the blow to UK investments following the decolonisation process. During the last two decades a new spurt of activities by MNCs from the UK,

Germany, the Netherlands and Switzerland has re-established Western Europe as an important source of direct foreign investments, mainly directed at other countries in Western Europe, but also at the United States of America. The total foreign investments stock in the USA increased from 7.6 billion $ in 1960 to 42.4 billion $ in 1979. The inward flow to the USA, as a percentage of inward flows in the thirteen richest capitalist countries, went up dramatically from an average of 3% in 1961-67 to an average of 27% in 1974-78 (OECD 1981). The flows indicates that the US in the last decade has risen to become the largest recipient of foreign direct investments, and continues to be the largest source of investments as well.

**Table 1.3: Global Distribution of Inward and Outward Investment Stock, 1914-1978**

| Area | 1914 | | 1960 | | 1978 | |
|---|---|---|---|---|---|---|
| | Out-ward | Inward | Out-ward | Inward | Out-ward | Inward |
| USA and Canada | 19.5 | 16.0 | 56.0 | 37.6 | 47.0 | 23.6 |
| Western Europe | 76.9 | 7.8 | 39.7 | 22,9 | 41.0 | 37.7 |
| Japan | 0.1 | 0.2 | 0.8 | 0.2 | 6.9 | 1.7 |
| Developing Countries | — | 62.8 | 1.1 | 32.3 | 3.2 | 27.8 |
| Others | 3.5 | 13.2 | 2.4 | 7.0 | 1.9 | 9.2 |

*Source* : Calculated from Dunning, 1983 and Magdoff, 1969, p. 56,

Before the second world war, only 35 per cent of all private capital exports went to the economically developed capitalist countries. During the last quarter of a century, the picture has changed quite dramatically. By 1980, the share in capital inflows had gone up to more than three quarters. By contrast less than one quarter (21.8 per cent in 1980) went into the direction of developing countries (United Nations 1983 , annex

Table II.2).* The decreasing relative importance of private investments in developing countries is accentuated by the fact that foreign firms operating in those countries tend to repatriate a share of the profits to the parent company which is much higher than the normal practice with the affiliates in the developed countries itself. For example, US firms over the period 1960-1980 undertook a net transfer of around 85 billions dollars out of 115 billion dollars net profit. The return flow of profits thus amounted to 74.8 per cent of net profits, to 195 per cent of the capital stock and to 573 per cent of the new capital flows. The return flow was even twice as high as the total expansion in capital stock (re-investments plus new inflows). On the other hand, out of the 199 billion dollars net profits in developed capitalist countries, only 114 billion dollars (53.3 per cent) were repatriated. The return of flow of profits amounted to 215 per cent of the fresh capital flows and to only 84 per cent of the total expansion in capital stock (Luedemann 1982, p. 69; see also United Nations 1983, pp. 283-287).

We may note that there are ample locational advantages in the developing countries, resulting in a higher rate of profit, and that nevertheless the flow of private foreign investments has largely been transformed into an internal affair of the OECD countries, with the United States gaining paramount importance. The political factor, i.e. the labile political situation and the competitive control over the state power by the indigenous bourgeoisie in the developing countries may turn out to be the most decisive factor influencing the decision not to

---

*The inequality among nations in terms of GNP, which has grown at a rapid speed over the last decades, is not as outspoken as the inequality in terms of new investments. The richest underdeveloped countries comprising 7 per cent of the Third World population in the mid-seventies accounted for 29 per cent of the GNP of the Third World and 42 per cent of the new investments. On the other hand, the poorest countries of the Third World. i.e. countries with then an income per head of less than $ 200 per year (58 per cent of the Third World population) still accounted for 20 per cent of the GNP, but for only 7 per cent of the new investments in Africa, Asia and Latin America (Nukhovich 1981, p. 57).

invest,* and to concentrate on the most powerful bulwark of private capital, the United States of America.

## 1.4. Integration with Local Capital

The unsettled situation and the potentially decisive influence of the local bourgeoisie in the Third World has induced a peculiar merger of foreign capital with local capital. In a number of countries the merger, in the sense of a share in the equity of foreign firms, has been legislated by the state. Among others this has been the case in India where in the early seventies the Foreign Exchange Regulation Act was introduced with the explicit purpose not so much to regulate the foreign exchange impact of the foreign firms as to compel them to sell a majority of shares to local shareholders. The use of local capital by multinational corporations has actually become a normal policy even in countries which do not impose legal restrictions.

The tendency to go in for a partnership with the local bourgeoisie can be attributed to a number of causes. Apart from the scope of an extended financial basis, the policy of risk reduction is certainly of major importance.** National capital in a number of countries has grown reasonably strong and is in a position to use the state power for the consolidation of national independence and for the imposition of

*The increasing OECD centered flow of capital for private investments has been induced by other considerations as well: the technological revolution (requiring less labour input), the economic and political integration of the European Common Market and the North Atlantic Treaty Organisation, and the increasing role of the state in providing guaranteed outlets, e.g. in armaments production and in loans for financing the budget deficits.

**It is symptomatic for the policy of risk sharing that before the beginning of the 1970s, direct investments made up half of all private capital exports from the leading Western powers to developing countries. Towards the end of the 1970s the percentage dropped to 28 per cent. The share of export credits increased to 20 per cent and portfolio investments (capital investments connected with the acquisition of equity without establishing control over the company) shot up from 7 per cent in 1970 to 45 per cent in 1979 (OECD figures in Friedländer, 1981, p. 15).

restrictions on foreign capital. MNCs originating from less powerful developed countries may not always be able, on their own, to generate enough countervailing power to scotch this process and would, at first sight, have to find a mutually acceptable agreement. The more powerful the home state, the less inclination the MNC would have to share its equity basis with local capital in developing countries. The second survey on multinational corporations by the United Nations (1978, p. 229) indeed establishes that: (a) US firms tend to have a much higher rate of consolidated companies than European firms and show in fact a behaviour which is the mirror image of companies in Japan and underdeveloped countries who had a minority participation in three-fourths of their overseas investments; (b) the percentage of fully owned and majority-owned affiliates has witnessed a sharp decline since 1951. Whereas in the case of West European MNCs the percentage of majority-owned affiliates came down from 54.5 per cent in 1951 to 35.4 per cent in 1971, the share of minority-owned affiliates went up from roughly 10 per cent to 42 per ccnt. US MNCs around 1970 still had at least half the equity in 75.2 per cent of the affiliates in developing countries.

Smaller companies in general and smaller or newly emerging companies from less powerful nations in particular may be assumed to be more sensitive to potential political and economic risks than the bigger companies (see also United Nations 1983, p. 354, and for indigenisation of management, ILO, 1976).

The risk reduction advantages for the foreign companies are matched by advantages accruing to the local entrepreneurs. While, in general, as a class, they in many countries may continue to regard the international monopolies as dangerous competitors, as individual entrepreneurs, they may urge their governments to create a favourable climate for foreign investments in exchange for tangible awards in the form of access to technology, increases in profits, new management techniques and access to foreign markets.

In course of time, the indigenous bourgeoisie, having significantly less bargaining power in the face of the foreign control over technology, may be reduced to junior partners and may ultimately be compelled to sell out their company to the foreign partner. Celso Furtado considers the long-term negative effect of this development as crucially important, namely the weakening of the independent local entrepreneurial class by the multinational corporations : "Their financial power made it possible for the international concerns to gradually extend their power over the dynamic sectors of the industry. All those who would have been in a position to stimulate local industry, found themselves absorbed into the new ruling class tied-up with the concerns" (quoted in Moslowski, 1978, p. 116).

The ongoing process of integration and ultimate subordination of local capital by the multinational corporations, which has taken on new forms in the period after de-colonisation, represents the fundamental problem of development. The inherent necessity for all capitalist enterprises in developing countries to depress the production costs and to reach higher rate of profit, would logically lead to a partnership of individual already better situated companies, with the foreign monopoly firms. The latter indeed can offer all advantages the local entrepreneur is in need of in order to either keep up with or do away with his competitors. Ultimately, however, it will lead to the skipping of the stage of free competition which was typical of the process of industrialisation in the western world. It will lead to the formation of monopoly, or for that matter oligopoly power, in the most dynamic sectors of industry at a moment that the capitalist mode of production is still in the process of formation.

Paul Baran was probably the first western scholar in the post-colonial period, to isolate this monopoly formation as an essential feature of the morphology of backwardness. The monopolistic industry, in his view, extends the merchant phase of capitalism by obstructing the transition of capital and men from the sphere of circulation to the sphere of industrial production. Thus in most underdeveloped countries, capitalism had a particularly twisted career : "Having lived through all the pains and frustrations of childhood, it never experienced the vigor and exuberance of youth, and began displaying at an early age all the grievous features of senility and decadence. To the deadweight of stagnation characteristic of pre-industrial society was added the entire restrictive impact of monopoly capitalism" (Baran 1962, p. 210).

Baran's seminal contribution in fact pointed at the impossibility for Third World countries to break out of a state of economic dependency and questioned the historically progressive role of capitalism under the changed circumstances. The problem with the statement that in its monopoly phase capitalism has lost its potential of a revolutionary transformation of the socio-economic structures in developing countries, is that a direct positive proof of the prevalence of multinational corporations as the only or major causal factor cannot be provided easily. Although at the macro-level, there is abundant evidence that apart from some island of rapid though dependent industrialisation, the Third World has witnessed a relative if not an absolute stagnation and immiserisation, other causal factors may be singled out to account for the state affairs. Both of the trend-setting work by Gunnar Myrdal on the *Asian Drama, An Inquiry in the Poverty of Nations* (New York, 1971) and its East European rejoinder *The Asian Dilemma* by Pavlov and Ulyanovsky (Moscow, 1973), agree on some other fundamental causal factors, such as the pre-emption of markets and foreign sources of capital accumulation, the existing economic and social backwardness in confrontation with the technologically developed and efficient production in the developed countries, etc. These categories of obstacles are a result of historical development and are irrevocably unavoidable. Some other causal factors, however, are in principle subject to redress and should receive paramount attention : the international terms of trade, the drain of surplus and the either deliberate or inherent policy of foreign companies to establish a monopoly position and to hamper the emergence of a indigenous industrial class.

Before leaving the general introductory field, and moving over to the interaction between policy and economic reality in India specifically, a short recapitulation of the argument thus far can be undertaken. The thrust of the argument was to establish that the functioning of multinational corporations in developing countries is influenced by the specific position of the Third World countries. The question whether MNCs contribute to the development or underdevelopment cannot be answered in isolation from the international as well as national inhibiting structures of which the corporations are an integral part. In this context we have, among others, referred to the developmental conflict between the oligopolistic, capital-intensive character of MNC's and the need for a broad-based and competitive development of indigenous capitalism. We have occasionally also referred to the possible role of government action. The latter aspect we shall look at in more detail in the next chapter.

# 2

# *Foreign Investments and Policy Framework*

The respective governments of the Republic of India, from the date of independence in 1947, have defended an industrial policy aimed at blocking the distorting influence of both the foreign and the indigenous monopoly sector. The dramatic economic developments during the colonial period had driven home to many leading politicians in the independence movement as well as to many of its economic spokesmen that the active intervention by the state apparatus had become necessary in order to save the country from a further downward spiral of immiserisation, polarisation, and exploitation.*

On the eve of independence, India was still embedded in a basically feudal agriculture and an archaic social structure. On the industrial side, there had been some progress, but the development was stark lopsided in terms of technology, ownership control, product orientation and pricing structure. Amiya Kumar Bagchi (1975, p. 442) concluded his study on private investments during the colonial period with an important addendum:

> Moreover, there was already a shadow of the shape of things to come in the penetration of Indian industry by large foreign capitalists. . . Thus even before Indian capitalists had wrested control over the economy from the pre-capitalist

*See e.g. Dadabhai Naoroji, *Poverty and Unbritish Rule in India,* 1901; R.C. Dutt, *The Economic History of India*, 1906; D.R. Gadgil, *The Industrial Revolution in India in Recent Times*, 1924 and 1942; R.P. Dutt, *India Today*, 1926 and 1947.

elements and from the old European-controlled Indian firms, they had to witness the invasion of new fields of industry by international cartels.

An important aspect of the industrial scene in India which, however, should not be overlooked, and which put the country apart from many colonial countries was the presence of a relatively strong internal bourgeoisie. Some of the indigenous industrial houses had a definite nationalist orientation and were looking forward to the establishment of an independent state for the defense of their interests (Rajat Ray 1981; Chandra 1979; Lieten 1984; Levkovsky 1966; Sumit Sarkar 1983; a.o.)

Even before political independence in 1947, the indigenous business community as well as the Indian National Congress (INC) under the chairmanship of Jawaharlal Nehru, who became the first Prime Minister after 1947, developed plans and policies for the containment of foreign capital. As early as 1931, in its famous Karachi resolution, the INC committed itself to state ownership of key industries and services. A national planning committee of the Congress Party in which different social groups and interests were represented, was constituted in 1938. The majority of the committee was of the opinion that the defense and other key industries should be state-owned and that all business should be licensed and regulated by a public authority. The indigenous Indian business community partially shared Nehru's hostility towards British and other foreign capital. There was some degree of commonality between Indian business and the political leaders regarding the proposed treatment of foreign capital after Independence (Watkins 1980, p. 17). It was a declared policy that after independence foreign capital would be removed from key industries and would be carefully controlled in those sectors where it remained. This line of thinking culminated in the so-called 'Bombay plan', a blueprint for the industrialisation of India after the second World War, which was formulated during the closing year of the war. A number of prominent Indian industrialists, headed by Tata and Birla, who conceived the 'Bombay plan', accepted certain essentials of state-planning, including the need for a central directing authority, rigorous measures of state control and state ownership of some industries.

The planning framework which came into being after independence was continuously the object of pulls and pressures from the different economic pressure groups and political movements. For purposes of a rough survey of the ensuing changes in the industrial policy, the four decades after independence can be divided into four main periods: the period 1947-1956 which evolved from hostility towards private enterprises in general and foreign enterprises in particular to one of cautious acceptance of both; the second period 1957-1965 which emerged with the severe foreign exchange crisis in 1957-58, and which provided a new lease of life to foreign capital; the third period 1965-1980 which was a period of renewed skepticism and restrictive policy towards new investments; finally the present period of renewed liberalisation which had already set in during the Emergency period (1975-77), but which took a clear shape with the re-election of Mrs. Gandhi and the formation of a new Congress-I government at the beginning of 1980.

## 2.1. Policy Fluctuations

With the many problems facing the government immediately after independence, the question of foreign investments was seen as just one of a multitude of pressing issues relating to the industrial policy that needed a solution. The Indian government, in accordance with the pre-independence thinking, adopted a planned and integrated approach to industrial policy. It announced in April 1948 an Industrial Policy Resolution (IPR), which embodied the directive principles for industrialisation of India. The 1948 IPR somewhat retreated from some earlier radical positions regarding private industry and foreign investments. The resolution stated that

> Government was decided to let existing undertakings . . . develop for a period of ten years during which they will be allowed all facilities for efficient working and reasonable expansion (cited in Watkins 1980, p. 20).

It was stated that for the time being the government would merely expand its present activities by concentrating on new units of production rather than on acquiring and running existing units. The resolution in fact stated that "private enterprise, properly directed and regulated, has a valuable role to play", but that, "while it should be recognised that participation of foreign capital and enterprise, particularly as regards industrial technique and knowledge, will be of value to the rapid industrialisation of the country, it is necessary that the conditions under which they may participate should be carefully regulated in the national interest. Suitable legislation will be introduced for this purpose" (cited in Watkins 1980, p. 20). It was proposed that each individual case of foreign participation was to be scrutinised and approved by the Central Government. As a rule, it would ensure that the major interest in ownership and effective control should be vested in Indian hands. The resolution mentioned that in case the rule of Indian control was waived, the Government would insist on the training of Indians for the purpose of eventually replacing foreign personnel.

Subsequently in 1949 the Industries (Development Regulation) Bill was introduced as a first step towards implementation of the various policy statements. The bill was adopted in 1951 as the Industries (Development and Regulation) Act 1951 (IDRA). This act provided the state with powers to control and regulate private industries. Under its provisions, all industries above a certain size are required to obtain a licence from the Licensing Committee before they can start operations. The act also authorizes the Government to examine the working of an industrial undertaking and to issue instructions. It is noteworthy, however, that the IDRA did not provide guidelines for its implementation. These were to emerge largely from the industrial Policy Resolutions (Amendments) and from the Five Year Plans.

The second Five Year Plan (1956-61) was finalized in mid-1956, under the direction of Mahalanobis. It differed from the mere indicative first plan by putting more emphasis on industrialisation, especially on heavy industry in the public sector. Although, in accordance with the 1956 IPR, the second Plan did not modify the guidelines for foreign investment, the severe foreign exchange crisis of 1957-58 would lead to a reversal in policy.

The foreign exchange crisis forced the Indian Government to cut imports of capital goods, to temporarily suspend all import licenses and to cut public expenditure by about 20 per cent. The relative decrease in public expenditure led to investments by private capital in spheres reserved for the public sector. Thus the foreign exchange crisis not only set limits to the functioning of the public sector, but provided a basis for a change in the Government policy toward direct foreign investments. The Government response to the crisis indeed was to improve the strained relations with Western countries as well as foreign capital. The then Minister for Commerce and Industry, Mr. T.T. Krishnamachari, in 1957 went on a loan-raising trip to the West. The Government also demonstrated in a concrete manner its changing attitude towards foreign capital. A series of tax concessions favouring foreign companies were announced: foreign capital was invited to take up projects in the state-reserved industries; an agreement was signed with the USA Government providing for the repatriation of profits in dollars; and a permanent World Bank Mission was allowed in New Delhi (Kidron 1965, pp. 158-9).

In the Third Five Year Plan (1961-66), references to the private sector were far more positive than in either of the earlier plans. The Plan did not discuss the official policy toward foreign investment, but made it implicitly clear that more foreign collaborations and investments were needed if the planned industrial targets in the private sector were to be realized (Watkins 1980, p. 34). But, despite the positive statements concerning foreign investment in the Third Plan, during the latter part of its implementation, the relatively liberal policy began to tighten. This tightening was due to the success of earlier investments and, more importantly, to a renewed skepticism as to the net benefits to the Indian economy. There was a growing concern over the heavy burden of India's future balance of payment burden caused by foreign investments.

The Fourth Five Year Plan (1969-74) was presented to Parliament in early 1970. The first major objective of the Plan was the recovery from the preceding economic recession.

The second major objective was attaining 'national self-reliance'. Halving of the net inflow of foreign aid by 1974 and its complete elimination by 1981 was aimed at. The Plan document discussed two other items at length: the problems of economic concentration in the economy and the need for less direct foreign control of the economy. Regarding the first point (economic concentration), two points of action were undertaken: the nationalization of the fourteen largest Indian commercial banks in 1969 and the enactment of the Monopolies and Restrictive Practices Act (MRTP Act) which came into effect in June 1970. The stated aims of the new act were the prevention of monopoly power. For this purpose all applications for expansion, new production lines, mergers or takeovers attracted the provisions of the law in the case of all companies with assets of over Rs. 200 million and of those companies with assets of at least Rs. 10 million which controlled one-third of the production or trade of a particular commodity. By the 1980s, the number of companies registered under the act had increased to around 1500.

The Fifth Five Year Plan covering the period 1974-79 announced as 'strategic goals' the removal of poverty and the attainment of self-reliance. The attainment of complete independence from foreign aid was projected to be achieved by 1985-86. This was to be done through an increase in exports and a renewal of import substitution efforts. Concurrent with the beginning of the Fifth Plan was the coming in force of FERA, the Foreign Exchange Regulation Act 1973. The objectives of FERA, as spelt out in the Act, are to conserve the country's foreign exchange, to guide foreign investment into high priority areas in the core sector, the export sector and those area of production which employ sophisticated technology. Section 29 of FERA requires all foreign companies to dilute their non-resident share-holding to 40 per cent. However, in accordance with earlier policy decisions, manufacturing companies in high technology areas and export-oriented companies were allowed to retain up to 74 per cent of foreign ownership. The guidelines of FERA were amended in 1976. The requirements for companies wanting to retain more than half of foreign equity were slightly relaxed. A new mid-resting point of 51 per cent was introduced short after the foreign dominated associated chambers Assocham made a representation in favour of a flexible approach in defining technology on a graduated scale: medium technology should qualify for a 51 per cent equity (Verma 1983, pp. 149-150).

After the period of Emergency (1975-77) and the first signs of a new liberalisation, the Janata government of Morarji Desai took some initiatives in enforcing the FERA as a consequence of which some companies, notably IBM and Coca Cola, left the country. A new Industrial Policy Resolution was announced by Minister of Industry, George Fernandes. The focus of his statement was on the small-scale sector. Regarding foreign investments, he stated that the dilution under FERA would go on and reiterated that ownership and control of companies should be in Indian hands. (Exceptions were again made for highly export-oriented and/or sophisticated technology areas.) In general the Janata policy did not imply any fundamental change in India's foreign investment policy (Lieten 1980).

The Janata coalition under the leadership of Desai, remained in power for less than three years. Internal disagreements led to the split of the party and the fall of the Government. Elections were held in January 1980. Mrs. Gandhi's Congress-I party obtained a two-third majority and formed the new government. Six months later, on July 22, the then Minister of State for Industry, Dr. Charanjit Chanana, announced the Industrial Policy Resolution of the new Congress government. The main points included the recognition of the excess capacity built up in violation of the Industries (Development and Regulation) Act 1951, and the decision to liberalise the existing investment restrictions on both Indian and foreign monopoly companies with an eye on increasing exports.

This more liberal policy formed the basis for the Sixth Five Year Plan. Industrial progress was henceforth seen to depend on technological excellence, and therefore on a 'judicious blend' of imported and indigenous technology. The import of technology should not only be liberalised, but should also be reoriented towards an active instead of a passive acquisition policy. Underlying the new policy initiatives was the statement that "the framework or rules and regulations relevant to the nascent stage of development are not necessarily appropriate to the complex industrial structure (in which) much greater attention will have to be paid to securing greater efficiency and competitiveness" (Sixth Plan 1980, p. 261).

The Sixth Plan suggested "a greater emphasis in the direction of competitive ability, reduced cost and greater mobility and flexibility in the development of investible resources", but added that the growth of monopolies will have to remain regulated in the larger public interest (Sixth Plan 1980, p. 86).

The post-1980 developments, *e.g.* the cancellation of the exclusive small-scale sector schedule by an "illustrative list" of twenty-two industries where no foreign collaborations "is considered necessary", and the upward revision of licensed capacity bringing it in line with the actual production, indicate an important shift in government policy. R.K. Hazari, who in the mid-sixties had conducted an indepth study on concentration, ownership and control in the corporate private sector, concluded that although there was a concentration in economic power, there was no immediate need or economic necessity to break that power: "Till such time as the medium and small groups can achieve their 'take-off', only the State can countervail the economic power of the large groups. In the meanwhile, there need be little fear that the large groups will eat up the smaller fry for the opportunities for expansion are almost unlimited. (Subject, of course, to the availability of foreign exchange, local resources and various kinds of licenses, etc., the distribution of which is admittedly biased in favour of the larger groups) . . . . The task of public policy is, therefore, to see that, in future, the large groups do not take away a disproportionate part of the available opportunities" (Hazari 1967, p. 360).

With the emergence of Rajiv Gandhi in the turbulent last months of 1984, all seemed set for the dismantling of that countervailing public power structure. Official thinking moved even more rapidly than during Mrs. Gandhi's days in the direction of the liberalisation and privatisation of the economy, and of the free expansion of the monopoly sector, in particular the foreign companies. The terms of conditions linked to the massive 1981 IMF loan as well as the composition of the immediate power circle around Rajiv Gandhi, the computer boys with their instant desire to launch India technologically into the 21st century, worked for major changes in the industrial policy framework. Quite a few changes were indeed introduced, both in respect of the import-export policy and in respect of the industrial licencing policy. With regard to the former, many more products have been put on the Open General License. To the exporting companies many incentives were granted which were earlier available only to the companies operating in the half a dozen export processing zones, such as tax holidays on investments, export rebates, priority allotments of scarce material, exemption from import excise, etc. With an eye on the acquisition of new technology, firms were stimulated to go looking abroad for technical collaboration agreements.

The imported technology, equipment and spares have given a strong impetus to what could be called the screwdriver economy and in a number of cases have caused a crisis in the traditional Indian production firms. The drastic lowering of import duties on capital goods for example has brought many domestic capital equipment producers into disarray and has induced the government in August 1986 to abrogate the earlier concessions. Such incidental policy measures may not make a dent on the burgeoning foreign trade deficit which was a whopping Rs 87 billion in 1985-86 as compared to around Rs 55 billion in each of the preceding years.

In general, the new policy effort is not to provide protection to the domestic industry against imports, but to go in headlong for a stimulation of exports, one example of which was the decision in September 1986 to increase the subsidy on vegetables and fruit exports from the earlier 14 per cent to 22 per cent and to charter special planes to facilitate their quick transportation (*Economic Times*, 10.09.1986). A new series of initiatives has brought the export policy of India quite close to the principles of a market-led policy, as A.S. Ganguly, the chairman of the Anglo-Dutch Hindustan Lever, advised the government in a confidential report: agricultural exports should be freed from "local demand pulls" so that India can establish itself abroad as a reliable supplier (*Business India*, August 1986, p. 47). The exports may, as in the past, mainly be on account of traditional exports such as plantation products, raw materials and handicraft items. The engineering companies, on which some hope rested for an expansion in the export value, as a matter of fact have shown a rather negative performance. A study of the top hundred engineering companies has calculated that whereas they spent Rs 20.4 billion on imports, their export earnings were not more than Rs 5.4 billion, leaving a trade deficit of Rs 15 billion (*Economic Times*, 10.9.1986)

Although the FERA regulations remain on the statute book, it was decided in July 1986 to provide amnesty to the companies who had flouted the act in the past. The intention to deal more strictly with the new offenders after the amnesty period may not carry much weight in view of the simultaneous decision to conduct a clause by clause review aimed at amending the Act. One such amendment allows an unlimited production expansion to companies, albeit on condition that the extra production is exported. Given the sequence of the operation—first expansion of capacity, then increased production and then the vagaries of exports—the condition attached to the expansion may not be upheld for long, either in practice or in legislation.

The MRTP and FERA regulations which continue to be operational may not have much regulatory power left. There is at least one indication that the companies do not feel constrained by the MRTP act. The ceiling of assets for undertakings coming under the purview of this act was raised from Rs 200 million to Rs 1000 million in May 1985. More than one year later only 550 of the expected 1900 undertakings had taken the trouble of applying for deregistration (*Economic Times*, 19.07.1986).

The dismantling of the public sector, which for many Indians had already lost much of its intended functions, did, however, not figure in the seventh Five Year Plan (1985-1990). The plan document actually stated that "the public sector will continue to play an important role in the core sector of the economy. It will also be a pace-setter and encourage emerging new high technology industries. . . . A major employer of the country's engineering manpower, the public sector will play a leading role in stimulating development of efficient ancillary manufacturing; and will strengthen the sinews of industry" (Seventh Plan 1985, p. 17).

Government companies continue, in terms of paid-up capital, to be by four times more important than private companies. In 1985, the capital of companies operating in the manufacturing sector totalled Rs 133 billion and 42 billion respectively. As compared to 1980, the public sector companies had increased the paid-up capital by 87 per cent as compared to 23 per cent for the private sector (Annual Report Companies Act 1985, parim). It may be added here that, unlike its private counterpart, the public sector manufacturing companies have made a relatively important contribution to employment generation, an increase with 77 per cent during the ten-year period 1974-1984 as compared to less than 7 per cent in the private manufacturing units. During 1984-85, employment in the private sector even decreased by 0.3 per cent (*Economic Survey* 1985-86, pp. 142-43; *Times of India*, 29.05.1986). It may also be added that the state-owned enterprises, contrary to a widespread understanding, are actually not causing a strain on the exchequer. Gross profit before tax, net of depreciation, of the 150 manufacturing enterprises during 1984-85 was actually 7.9 per cent of capital employed. Total profits of the enterprises amounted to Rs 46 billion, which signalled a definite increase over the Rs 14 billion recorded in 1980-81. The contribution by the public sector enterprises to the exchequer in the form of direct taxes increased from 2.2 billion to 11.9 billion (*Economic Times*, 08-08,1986; *Annual Survey* 1985-86, pp. 71-75).

The pivotal role which the public sector is supposed to have played in modernising the Indian economy and in reducing the concentration of economic power may, however, be losing momentum, as the Seventh Five Year Plan figures indicate. During the new plan period gross public sector investments in industry will be lower than the private sector investments. Private capital is expected to take over the generative function from the public sector.

The reasons for an increasing role of the private sector are two-fold. On the one hand, in view of the resources constraint, more stress is being laid on efficiency and productivity. From this premise, it follows that public sector units which have not shown high rates of return will have to forego new investments. They are mainly to be found in three basic infrastructural sectors, namely steel, chemicals and fertilisers. On the other hand, the tight foreign exchange position may lead the country into a debt burden that cannot be sustained:

> . . . it has to be recognised that the scope for managing our international payments through large scale import substitution is considerably reduced. Thus in addition to sustained emphasis on efficient import substitution, pursuit of self-reliance demands a much more vigorous export promotion effort than has been forthcoming in the past. A rapid growth of exports will require changes not merely in trade policy but also in fiscal, monetary and industrial policies" (Seventh Plan 1985, p. 6)

Given the fact that the public sector enterprises are specifically directed at the internal requirements, changes in the industrial policy with an eye on increasing exports would necessarily make more facilities available to the private sector.

In the meantime, the expansion of the private corporate sector has gone ahead on its own steam. It has led to a situation in which, despite all the pious hopes expressed in the consecutive Five Year Plan documents, neither self-reliance nor equitable distribution have come any nearer of their goal. On the contrary, whereas on the one hand, the Indian market gets flooded with sophisticated products with a high import content for consumption by the affluent section, the vast majority of the people are still faced with the short supply and high prices of basic consumer goods. With the relaxation of government restrictions and guidelines, the government has progressively given out of hand a number of regulatory mechanisms. The typical Indian solution, a mid-way station between the free play of national and international corporate enterprises and the drastic curtailment of all forms of monopoly capitalism under a socialist system, has lost its momentum.

Did the change in the attitude and policies towards monopolies and concentration come about independently, or was it due to the influence exercised by the private organised sector in general and the top industrial houses in particular? Some internal government reports on the techniques used by top industrialists on leading politicians and top bureaucrats suggest a strong lobby to be operative quite successfully in getting their case settled. The secrecy of the reports suggests the general suspicion and hearsay evidence to be true. "After all, if one needs evidence of state patronage, it is only the government records that can prove the point, either way. So long as the curtain of secrecy is not lifted, no objective discussion can take place. . ." (Goyal 1979, p. 107). Without having to turn to instances of corrupt practices,* it would be sufficient to assess the changes in government policies in the light of representations by the industrial houses and their apex bodies, the FICCI and the ASSOCHAM, as Verma (1983) has done. In the direct association of company directors with government committees and financial institutions, in addition to the post-retirement employment of government officials, he sees an important explanation for the lukewarm application and the gradual relaxation of the official government policy:

> The importance of this phenomenon can not be understated. The boards of subsidiaries of MNCs are deliberately formed so as to include senior government officials and influential state people who are utilized to further the interests of the multinationals. A number of government functionaries and persons playing an important part in the political life of the country, often in the course of work come in contact with representatives of the foreign controlled companies and have to make decisions affecting the latter. Even when there is no direct contact there is usually an indirect influence through the activities of peers. The possibility of a prestigous directorship after retirement often would tend to make serving government officials more sympathetic to the MNC affiliates. Moreover, a number of relatives of government officials and political personages are employed by the companies (Verma 1983, p. 221).

The case of Hindustan Lever, the topmost foreign company, may serve as an instructive example. Some of its directors have earlier served as high-ranking directors with the Ministry of

*The political donations to the ruling Congress party, which has been revealed in the past (Sachar Committee 1978, pp. 99-140) and which may be assumed to continue, are probably only one of the various ways in which payments are being made.

Food or as a member of the Planning Commission (particularly J.S. Raj, H.C. Bijawat and V.G. Rajadhyaskshya). Others after leaving the company, went to occupy important government jobs.* The first Indian chairman, R.L. Tandon, after retirement went to the Punjab National Bank and then became the president of the National Council of Applied Economic Research and the chairman of the Government Task Force on Free Trade Zones. Hindustan Lever's Dr. S. Varadarajan first moved to the Indian Petro Chemicals Ltd., then in 1981 became the secretary of the department of Science and Technology and later the Director-General of the Council of Scientific and Industrial Research. Even acting managers of MNCs function on important government advisory and funding councils. In November 1985, a new premier advisory council, the Scientific Advisory Council to the Prime Minister, was set up. The seven member council contains two managers of private companies, one of which is A.S. Ganguly, the chairman of Hindustan Lever. In August 1986, a new fund was created under an agreement with the USAID, the Indo-US Programme for Advancement of Commercial Technology. The binational board of PACT comprises eight members, among whom, on the Indian side, are A.S. Ganguly and M.S. Patwardhan, the managing director of the Indo-Dutch Nocil company.

Although there may not always be a direct pay-off effect to the private company concerned, the presence of ex-managers and present managers in important official positions, establishes an additional channel of interest which the other companies, particularly the medium and small enterprises, do not possess. Such an explanation has been put forward by Pramit Chaudhuri (1978, p. 243): "Because the licensing procedure is both highly centralized and specialized, it gives a large firm certain built-in advantages in playing the system. It can afford the time and the resources needed to file applications and undertake the necessary 'lobbying' to get them through". The residential managers which

*Whereas the top level management in the private corporate sector has been calculated to earn a total of Rs. 223,00 per annum (1978) on an average, the topmost executives in the public sector and with the Central Government earned Rs. 84,000 and Rs. 67,500 respectlvely (Sachar Committee 1978, p. 306).

most large companies maintain near the centre of power in New Delhi have specialised in finding their way in the corridor network in the ministerial department and, even without having to take recourse to unsavoury practices, have an edge over their less resourceful competitors.

In the next subsection we shall have a look at the changing position of foreign capital in India.

## 2.2 Profile of Foreign Capital in India

In line with its colonial past, India at the time of its independence had most of its foreign trading and investment links with the United Kingdom (see a.o. A.K. Bagchi 1973; Levkovsky 1966; Rungta 1970). Till the mid-fifties, the foreign investment flow was minimal. It was only after the foreign exchange crisis of 1957-58, that capital flows increased considerably, mainly on account of UK and US direct investments. To a great extent this was due to the institutional assistance by the World Bank and the IMF and the constitution of the Aid India Consortium. The gross inflow of capital for productive investments increased sharply to Rs. 1066 million in 1965, but then again declined to between Rs. 100 million and Rs. 500 million in the 1970s. At the same time, however, total investments, including reinvestments of profits by subsidiaries, increased four and a half times between 1955 and 1973 (RBI Bulletin, July 1975, p. 442 and March 1978). The corporations increasingly succeeded in mobilising domestic and internal sources to finance their growth. S. Chaudhuri (1979, pp. 1431-1435) has calculated that for the fifty largest subsidiaries of foreign companies during 1956 and 1975, only approximately five per cent of the finances originated from foreign sources. Four-fifth of the financing consisted of non-cash inflows, mainly in the form of plant machinery and technical know-how, the price of which is often a matter of arbitrariness (RBI Bulletin 1975, July, p. 442). The Reserve Bank of India data indicate that the picture has not changed in the ensuing years. The data relate to all companies who take recourse to the capital market and do not distinguish foreign companies from Indian companies. They nevertheless establish that the import of equity capital by multinational companies is extremely small. In the period 1976-1980, it amounted to hardly 32 million Rs. or 0.26 per cent of the financial sources. In the same period, government subsidies and loans from government financial institutions totalled Rs. 84 million and Rs. 5649 million respectively, which clearly establishes the major role which state finances play in the process of industrialisation (RBI, 1980-81, volume 2, pp. 92-93).

The overall consequences of foreign investments and foreign collaboration agreement are difficult to assess. The outflow on account on the import of capital goods, designs tools, materials and chemicals, may presently be well over Rs. 10 billion a year. If we look at the foreign exchange flow on account of profit remittances, royalties and know-how (Table 2.1), the outflow which till 1978 had grown at a rate which exceeded the rate of inflation by four per cent (M.S. Patwardhan, *Economic Times*, 26.05. 1982), during the last years has increased dramatically, mainly on account for know-how payments. Payments for royalties and know-how in 1981-82 totalled Rs. 2867 million and were more than four times higher than the outflow on account of profits and dividends.

The trend which emerges from the Table is definitely going to continue. The foreign collaboration agreements, which for a number of years have remained at the stable position of around 400 per year around 1980 (see later Table 6.9), after 1983 suddenly lept to as many as 1039 in 1985. In regard to the cases in which foreign investment is involved, Japan (with a total investment of Rs. 160 million in 1983-84) appears to have taken the lead, closely followed by the USA and the UK and, trailing far behind, the FRG and the Netherlands (Department of Industrial Development 1983-84, p. 19).

As per the aims of the import substitution policy which was in operation till roughly the mid-seventies, foreign controlled firms were expected to generate savings in foreign exchange through a positive saldo on their current account transactions. The overall results for both subsidiaries and foreign-controlled minority companies, however, turned out to be negative, even with the exclusion of the oil-importing companies (RBI, 1974, pp. 148-156). The period following the enactment of the FERA, with its export provisions for subsidiary companies, has been

**Table 2.1: Remittances to Foreign Companies 1969-1982 (Rs. billion)**

| Year | Profit | Dividends | Royal-ties | Technical know-how | Interest | Total |
|---|---|---|---|---|---|---|
| 1965-66 | 135 | 194 | | 29 | 70 | 428 |
| 1966-67 | 145 | 287 | | 51 | 104 | 587 |
| 1967-68 | 159 | 327 | | 43 | 147 | 676 |
| 1968-69 | 129 | 302 | | 49 | 180 | 660 |
| 1969-70 | 127 | 314 | 58 | 130 | 93 | 723 |
| 1970-71 | 131 | 435 | 52 | 206 | 128 | 952 |
| 1971-72 | 99 | 389 | 59 | 139 | 121 | 807 |
| 1972-73 | 155 | 391 | 73 | 113 | 157 | 889 |
| 1973-74 | 219 | 376 | 62 | 141 | 163 | 961 |
| 1974-75 | 72 | 185 | 85 | 126 | 367 | 835 |
| 1975-76 | 204 | 248 | 105 | 257 | 246 | 1060 |
| 1976-77 | 194 | 485 | 159 | 378 | 251 | 1467 |
| 1977-78 | 101 | 680 | 195 | 281 | 228 | 1485 |
| 1978-79 | 102 | 543 | 126 | 555 | 314 | 1640 |
| 1979-80 | 144 | 509 | 95 | 440 | 252 | 1440 |
| 1980-81 | 121 | 559 | 89 | 1049 | 223 | 2041 |
| 1981-82 | 122 | 589 | 160 | 2707 | 411 | 3989 |

*Source*: K.V. Swaminathan and S. Varadarajan. In: M. Satyapal, *Technology Imports, Economy aud Trade*, November 1984, p. 37; Nagesh Kumar, *EPW*, M-104, August 1985.

credited with producing a positive account. D.K. Ghosh (1980) has calculated the net inflow of foreign exchange (exports net of imports) to be quite substantial, e.g. Rs. one billion in 1976-77. S.K. Goyal, on the other hand has calculated the balance to have been negative by approximately Rs. 200 million, excluding oil imports, in the preceding years (S.K. Goyal 1979, p. LVI). The differing results appear to be due to the sharp rise in the export price of tea during 1976-78*. This

* In 1975-76, there were 46 net earning subsidiaries. More than half of the net contribution by these companies was accounted for by the Brooke Bond Tea exports. The sudden drop in the value of tea exports in 1978 (from 604 million US dollars in the preceding year to 162 million dollars) caused a one-fourth decline in exports of subsidiary companies.

single fact would indicate that even subsidiaries, which, it should be added, after the FERA guidelines of 1974, were allowed to remain as subsidiaries on the conditionality of an excellent export performance, in normal conditions do not produce a positive trade balance.

Among the explanations which have been put forward for the export behaviour of foreign companies are the concentration on import substitution, the non-competitiveness of Indian products on the world market and the protected and hence lucrative local market. In an "inward looking economy", it is argued, "all manufacturing firms, local and foreign, would tend to export relatively little", but in those industrial sectors where the multinational corporations have monopolistic advantages, foreign-controlled firms turn out to have "higher export propensities than local firms, and this propensity rises with the extent of foreign shareholding" (Sanjaya Lall in Indu Emencee, 1982, p. 12). The "inward-looking" character of the Indian economy, if it had ever existed as an innate force, had definitely come to an end by the mid-seventies. Increase in production and export promotion were then elevated as the two panacea for India's stagnating production of basic commodities and balance of payment problems. In addition to the monetary and fiscal incentives and the liberalisation of imports, to which the Import Policy Statement in April 1976 had given the green signal, in the early eighties, the cheap labour supply was included in the advantages India could offer. Addressing the Davos Symposium of European industrialists, bankers and policy makers, Narayan Dutt Tiwari, the Minister for Industries, welcomed the companies to take advantage of the "economically dependable and low cost Indian production basis to increase the competitiveness of the European industry in world markets" (*Economic Times*, 30 January 1982).

In the meantime, two outstanding studies had established that such an export boom was not on the cards. The study of Subramaniam and Pillai (1979, p. 82) concluded with the warning note that "the performance of foreign-controlled firms was found poorer than indigenous counterparts, indicating a limited motivation or "willingness' of multinational corporations to the export development of the host developing country". Sumitra Chisthi, who investigated the strategy of the multinational corporations, submitted that even if exports occur temporarily at a higher level, the companies tend to use it as a leverage for access to the domestic market (IIFT, 1981). Present developments indicate that, either despite or because of the operations of multinational corporations and the corresponding international linkages, the gap between exports and imports is ever widening, as Table 2.2 brings out in full clarity. A positive balance could be maintained in the trading with the socialist countries and with the ESCAP countries, although in the latter case the positive balance has recently turned into a negative one, mainly on account of imports from the newly industrialising countries in the Far East. It is interesting to note that whereas for example in 1983-84, 51.4 per cent of Indian imports originated from the OECD countries, only 44.2 per cent of the exports went in that direction. From 1982-83 onwards, India had managed to stabilise the trade deficit gap up to 1985-86, when a dramatic deterioration emerged. The stabilisation of the deficit was caused by the massive export of crude oil (approximately 18 billion in 1984-85). A sizeable amount of this new export item may have found its way to the European market and would somewhat alter the above-mentioned negative trade pattern with the OECD which appears from the official statistics.

The onus for the gloomy trading deficit cannot be attributed solely to the high oil prices. The half-open door policy for the import of manufactured goods and (semi) knocked down production kits appears to bear a substantial part of the responsibility. Although some would argue that it is still too early for the positive impact of the new "outward looking" policy aimed at the export of compatible manufactured products to have made a headway, the nightmarish foreign exchange crisis which the major proponents of the open door policy (Mexico, Brazil, South Korea, Argentina) have run into, may serve as a good pointer for things to come if the present policy is continued.

For long, India has been presented as the example of a developing country which has effectively prevented the multinational corporations from getting an effective foot-hold in the economy. Statistical information which tends to support such a view even indicates that the monopoly sector

**Table 2.2: India's Regional Foreign Trade Balance, 1970-1984 (Rs Billion)**

| Region | 1970-71 | 1975-76 | 1977-78 | 1978-79 | 1979-80 | 1980-81 | 1981-82 | 1982-83 | 1983-84(P) | 1984-85(P) | 1985-86(P) |
|---|---|---|---|---|---|---|---|---|---|---|---|
| USA & Canada | —3.3 | —9.5 | —2.1 | —1.8 | —2.7 | —10.5 | —7.4 | —6.7 | —6.5 | —3.0 | —4.4 |
| EEC | —0.4 | —2.4 | —1.2 | —5.2 | —4.3 | —11.3 | —16.5 | —19.0 | —21.0 | —22.1 | —32.2 |
| OPEC | —0.2 | —5.3 | —6.5 | —6.5 | —16.9 | —27.7 | —28.3 | —30.8 | —23.7 | —32.4 | —25.0 |
| Eastern Europe | +1.3 | +1.1 | +2.8 | —0.1 | —2.6 | +1.9 | +4.7 | +3.1 | —3.5 | +0.9 | +1.8 |
| World Total | —1.0 | —12.3 | —6.1 | —10.9 | —26.8 | —58.0 | —58.0 | —54 9 | —58.9 | —55.3 | —87.4 |

(P)—Provisional.
*Source*: Government of India, *Economic Survey*.

as a whole has not advanced extraordinarily. N.K. Chandra (1981) on the basis of official estimates has concluded that the share of the monopoly houses in the total assets of the private corporate sector has shown a zero trend since the mid-fifties. The same conclusion could be reached for the share of the organised private sector in the total net national product which would indicate that the importance of the monopoly sector has remained virtually static though with noticeable fluctuations. The fluctuations could be associated with the periods of booms and crises in the economy leading respectively to a reinforcement and a decline in the monopoly share. In any case, the zero trend would indicate that the process of increasing concentration and centralisation of capital, which has been the hallmark of economic developments in the North Atlantic area, has not become operational in India. N.K. Chandra (1981, pp. 375-6) rather than regarding this as a negation of the Marxist theory on increasing concentration and centralisation, puts forth a set of explanations for the different trend in India. In the past as well as in the present, foreign domination, feudal relations in agriculture, lucrative opportunities outside industry in moneylending and mercantile activities as well as the emergence of monopoly sectors, have constituted effective barriers to the emergence of all-round capitalism . Moreover, an overall transition from relatively low paid to relatively high paid and highly productive occupations did not take place, and hence did not increase the purchasing power of the mass of the people. The infiltration and ultimate monopolisation of the vast Indian market by modern industries did not come about in a significant way:

> With an eye on quick profits and control over the labour process, monopoly capital, which was already well entrenched found contemporary western technology much too attractive, even if in the process industrial employment and the size of the home market got narrower, and the country became financially and technologically more dependent on the major foreign powers (Chandra 1981, p. 376).

If the skipping over of the competitive stage in capitalist development can be construed as one of the reasons for the continuing stage of underdevelopment (cfr. also Czaya 1975, pp. 131-136), then the kernel for the strategic importance of multinational corporation and Indian monopoly capital should be sought in the first instance not in their growing size but in their established monopoly power. Malyarov (1977, p. 178 ff) has produced sufficient evidence to conclude that Indian planners and scholars in the 1950s and 1960s were sufficiently aware of the danger of the emergence of the twin phenomena of monopoly formation and stagnation. The Report of the Monopolies Inquiry Commission in 1965, after summing up the advantage to be derived from the concentration of economic power (growth in capital formation, supply of managerial talent, attracting foreign technology, etc.), pointed at certain evil effects on the economy (high prices, corruptive power, restrictive trade practices, and the deterrent effect on the entry of small units). The concentration of economic power increases independence from government regulations. The misdirection of investment ultimately increases the disproportions in the economy and slows down its growth (M.I.C., 1965, pp. 135-138 and R.C. Dutt's Note of Dissent, pp. 193-197). Malyarov (1977, p. 174) infers that the concentration of economic power by the mere fact that it hampers the growth of small enterprises, and, one would like to add, the full-fledged development of capitalism, itself could weaken this tendency towards concentration.

A mere statistical survey of the share of multinational corporation in the Indian industrial sector would, in light of the just mentioned considerations, give information on only one aspect of the totality of factors. The mathematical share in total assets or sales does only give a clue to the extent of economic power, but is not identical with it, as Goyal (1979b) has forcefully argued.

Nirmal Chandra in an earlier contribution had argued that paid-up capital and total assets are not the most useful indication of foreign control over the organised sector. In an era of inflation, assets may be misleading since the age-composition on fixed asset can vary considerably. Sales data and gross profits are free from this deficiency and therefore give a better approximation:

Besides, it is generally recognised that the market power of a company is better gauged by its sales volume than the size of its assets, a good part of which may be used inefficiently as is probably the case with many public-sector companies. The other variable which is obviously crucial is pre-tax profits which will show the share of foreigners in the surplus generated by the corporate sector (N.K. Chandra 1977, p. 7).

On the basis of the Reserve Bank of India statistics for the period 1957-1972, Chandra has calculated the share of foreign controlled companies in the Indian corporate sector to have grown considerably as table 2.3. indicates.

**Table 2.3: Share of Foreign Companies in the Indian Private Corporate Sector**

| | Assets | Sales | Gross Profits | |
|---|---|---|---|---|
| | | | I | II |
| 1957-58 | 20.77 | 26.1 | 35.7 | 26.00 |
| 1959-60 | 20.40 | 26.4 | 30.7 | 22.32 |
| 1961-62 | 22.88 | 26.8 | 31.3 | 25.28 |
| 1963-64 | 25.91 | 26.5 | 29.5 | 29.90 |
| 1965-66 | 26.66 | 25.8 | 31.6 | 40.10 |
| 1967-68 | 27.69 | 25.5 | 38.9 | 37.27 |
| 1969-70 | 28.58 | 26.7 | 29.7 | 40.31 |
| 1971-72 | 25.61 | 30.8 | 50.0 | 39.15 |
| 1972-73 | 26.17 | 29.8 | 50.0 | 38.98 |

*Source*: Sau (1981, pp. 101-103) for assets and gross profits (estimate 2); and Nirmal Chandra (1977, p. 11) for sales and gross profits (estimate 1)

R.K. Sau (1981) on the basis of the same data has done a similar exercise with a somewhat different result but indicating the same trend. It appears from the aggregate data that in the period before the promulgation of FERA in 1973 the foreign sector had been edging its way up, and accounted for around thirty per cent of the sales and fifty per cent of the profits in the prive corporate sector.

After 1973, the first impression one gets from the rough data, is a marked decline in the number of branches and subsidiaries of multinational corporations.* Between 1973 and

*Whereas brandches are companies established outside India, subsidiaries are firms which not only operate in the country, but also have a registered office.

1979, the number of branches declined from 540 to 315, and of subsidiaries from 188 to 118. At the same time, the assets continued to increase. The value of assets of 434 branches in 1973-74 amounted to Rs 18 billion and increased to Rs 24 billion in 1978-79 (for 288 branches). The assets of 242 subsidiaries in 1969-70 amounted to Rs 11 billion. They increased to Rs 17 billion in 1978-79 (for 125 subsidiaries). During the period the paid-up capital increased by 22 per cent to Rs. 357 crores of which Rs 215 crores was held by the foreign companies (Sangal 1981, pp. XLII—LIII; Goyal 1979, p. 12.)

The aggregate growth figures do not appear to be excessive. Such a conclusion, however, would be erroneous. The decline in numbers indeed does not mean that the companies have left the country. It in most cases simply means that the foreign subsidiaries have diluted the percentage of foreign-held equity to a level that lifts them out of the category of subsidiary companies. The dilution of foreign equity to forty per cent or less has turned the local companies of major multinational corporations such as Cadbury, Colgate, British American Tobacco (ITC), Nestlé (Food Specialities), Philips (Peico), Imperial Chemicals, Swedish Match (Wimco), Brooke Bond Liebig (Brooke Bond—Unilever) and British Oxygen (Indian Oxygen) into Indian companies (Goyal 1983, pp. 131; also Goyal 1979).

The new category of foreign controlled Indian companies seriously distorts the official figures on the foreign involvement in the Indian corporate sector. The ministerial information which is regularly supplied to parliament tends to exclude the data relating to the ex-FERA companies. Statistical exercises, e.g. by D.K. Ghosh (1980), have therefore only a limited value. Apart from controls which can be exercised through the sale of technology and inputs, legally speaking even a block share of only one-tenth of the equity would provide certain safeguards. It would allow the foreign company to attract the intervention of the court for any change in management which could unfairly prejudice the shareholder (Aggarwal 1982, p. 119). The question as to when a subsidiary ceases to be so in legal terms, moreover, is not a mere arithmetic exercise of assessing the foreign equity share. A subsidiary, in terms of the Companies Act of 1956, is any company of which a parent company controls the composition of the Board of Directors or in which it "exercises or controls" more than half of the total voting power (Sangal 1981, p. XLI). It would not be difficult to establish that the above-mentioned companies, although they hold less than fifty per cent of the paid-up capital in the Indianised company, nevertheless control more than half of the voting power and the composition of the Board of Management. The Company Law contains a large number of provisions for the protection of minority shareholders. The important provisions, however, are null and void for a large number of them. Most multinational corporations operating in India have tens of thousands of small shareholders. As a rule the rights, for example the right to introduce resolutions, are given to members representing not less than one-twentieth of the total voting power or to a block of at least one hundred thousand rupees (Aggarwal, 1982, p. 118). The provisions in fact demonstrate that most of the shares held by the public do not constitute a balance impeding the controlling power of the multinational corporation concerned.*

The spread-out ownership of shares in multinational corporations, on the contrary rules out the possibility of the emergence of a major contending bloc of shareholders. It has rather created "a situation in which a very large number of shareholders can be mobilised to create public opinion against government if any policies were expected to be adopted for stricter regulations, which in turn, could reduce profitability of the shares" (Goyal, 1979, p. 19). The insurance

*For the trade unions in the major companies, it would not be impossible to bring together hundred shareholding union members. Assuming that they could be brought on one line against specific instances, to get a motion discussed at the annual conference (which in no way amounts to its adoption), the combined value of shares held by them would not be sufficient to meet the minimum requirement. This at least is the conclusion to be derived from a sample of 550 workers in Dutch multinationals in India, the results of which are still to be published.

against a possible gevernment crackdown on foreign capital may also be one of the considerations for establishing joint ventures with major Indian industrial houses. Such an association has the added advantage of taking over an established marketing system.

In the current debates, the protagonists and antagonists of the role of monopoly house, including the multinational corporations, put forward their arguments in a vehement style. The former tend to concentrate on the modernisation of the economy and the overall effect this may produce in the future when the government will finally decide to follow a correct policy. In the debates, it is easily forgotten that the present and the future have a past as well. The warnings of the past as a matter of fact turn out to be as relevant today as they have ever been.

Before moving over to the detailed analysis of the Dutch MNCs in India, we should, therefore, in the conclusion of this chapter, prefer to refer to a long quotation from the Report of the Monopolies Inquiry Committee (MIC 1965, p. 136):

> One social consequence of the concentration of wealth and income in a very small percentage of the population which is the inevitable effect of concentration of economic power in the control of industries deserves special mention. Part of this wealth aud income, has, it is true, been put back into industry; but the remainder has gone to the creation of a new caste in this already caste-ridden country—the very rich. Many of them flaunt their superiority in riches in palatial buildings, limousines, and a retinue of servants, and make no secret of the fact that they think themselves to be a class apart, well above the rest of their fellow countrymen. . . .
> Inevitably, the position and glamour of these very rich persons has also seriously undermined social values in the country. Culture and education, scientific pursuits and research are for many young men, at a discount, compared to a career that is likely to help to climb the dizzy tops of business success"

# 3

# *Survey of Dutch Private Investments in India*

We have seen in the first chapter that India till recently has followed a restrictive policy vis-a-vis the multinational corporations. In this chapter, we shall seek to draw a picture of the operations within that framework of the MNCs belonging to one specific country. Although the choice for the particular firms has been dictated by fortuitous circumstances, the sample as such does represent a significant number of important companies.

The Dutch multinational corporations are by no means small. In terms of turnover, the Royal (Dutch) Shell presently occupies the second rank among all corporate groups at the world level with a turnover of 82 billion dollars and a net profit of around 4 billion dollars in 1985. In the same year, the gross national product of India was valued at roughly US $ 110 billion. Whereas Unilever, after Toyota Motors the biggest non-American private company in the non-oil sector, generated sales to the tune of 22 billion dollars, and by large margins outstretched the performance of its immediate competitors, Philips (US $ 18 billion sales in 1985) was in stiff competition with the other major MNC in the field of electricals and electronics, Siemens, with which it shared the top positions in terms of employment, namely around 350,000 (*Fortune*, 04. 08. 1986).

Apart from the enormous turnover, which explains their oligopoly position in many fields, the corporate groups operate in numerous countries, in addition to the selling agencies which they maintain in practically all non-socialist countries of the world.*

The major Dutch MNCs are truly multinational (and not only transnational) in the sense that their ownership is spread over more than one country. The cases of the Shell and Unilever are most obvious in this respect. Both have headquarters in the Netherlands and in England, from where two identical boards of management supervise the production and transactions of the consolidated and non-consolidated companies who are formally grouped under either the Dutch Naamloze Vennootschap or the English Private Company Limited.

Even Philips, which historically has been and continues to be the property of the Philips family at the provincial town of Eindhoven, has gone 'multinational' in the sense that it is constituted of two interrelated corporate structures, namely N.V. Bezit (Ownership Ltd.) and the U.S. Philips Trust. The two holdings own respectively around hundred per cent and around sixty per cent of the Philips Gloeilampenfabrieken on the one hand and the North America Philips Corporation, the operating company restricted to North America, on the other hand. The Board of Governors of the N.V. Bezit is appointed by the general meeting of shareholders from a list of nominees drawn up by the priority shareholder, the family foundation Dr. A.F. Philips Stichting, which is incorporated in the Netherlands Antilles.**

*For a more detailed treatment of Dutch multinational corporations see Baruch (1962), Wilson (1970), Paerl (1971), Teulings (1975), Schellekens (1980), Crone and Overbeek (1981), IPSO (1982) and Lieten (1982).

**The multinational aspect of the Dutch companies is also reflected in the international composition of its boards and management. Particularly the Royal Dutch Shell excels in this respect. Its Supervisory Board of eleven men in 1981 included the Frenchman R. Marjolin, formerly vice-president of the EEC Commission, H. Merkle, the Chairman of the German Bosch concern, the Dutch E. Wellenstein, formerly secretary-general of the European Coal and Stell Community, O.B. Wormser, formerly governor of the Banque de France, H. Witteveen, former Dutch minister of finance and managing director of the International Monetary Fund, J. Zijlstra, former prime minister of the Netherlands and president of the Dutch National Bank, and R. McNamara, former U.S. Secretary of Defence and President of the Word Bank.

In this chapter, we shall bring together some descriptive material which illustrates on the general plane the activities of the Dutch companies in India and shall follow it up with a more detailed treatment of their balance of payment effect. Prior to that, we shall deal with the other economic relations between India and the Netherlands, namely in the field of trade and development aid.

Since the early sixties, India has been one of the main recipients of Dutch development aid. It was actually the first developing country to receive financial assistance from the Netherlands. In the early sixties, India experienced a severe shortage of foreign exchange. At that time, it was difficult to import from countries which did not provide development assistance in the form of loans and grants. A number of Dutch exporters faced difficultes in their trade with India and they, together with the Indian Government, approached the Dutch Government to provide credits. This led to a conditional sanction of Fl. 100 million financial assistance to India for the years 1961-1965. One-third of the amount was to be earmarked for "non-traditional import products" (TAS 1973, pp. 65-69). From that time onwards the Dutch development assistance to India has increased steadily, particularly since the early seventies. It grew from Fl. 75 million in 1972 to Fl. 238 million in 1982 and thereafter dropped to Fl. 190 million in 1984. The funds allocated to India account for around one-fifth of Dutch development aid under the bilateral country-wise programme. Although India has thus moved forward as the focal country, in terms of per capita aid, the allocation is very small. In 1982 for example, it represented 0.09 US dollar per capital per year or approximately 4 per cent of the ODA aid to India. By comparison, the other countries in South Asia received considerably more. Sri Lanka received as much as $ 27.43 per capita of which 1.40 from the Netherlands and Pakistan $ 8.59 and $ 0.43 respectively (Bruinsma 1986, p. 57).

From the initial stages of the Dutch "development cooperation" onwards, the subsequent Dutch governments have stressed the important role for Dutch (multinational) corporations in development activities. According to the various policy documents of the Ministry for Development Cooperation, Dutch corporations are expected to play an important role especially with regard to the delivery of goods, the transfer of technological know-how and the concrete implementation of projects (see e.g. Nota Bilaterale Ontwikkelingssamenwerking, 1976; Nota Ontwikkelingssamenwerking in Wereldeconomisch Perspectief, 1979).*

This policy has led to the situation that in the 1970s, between 70 and 90 per cent of all Dutch development aid was spent with Dutch corporations in the Netherlands itself (Internationale Samenwerking 1978, p. 289; also Louisse 1979). In the case of India, till recently approximately 70 per cent of the Dutch financing was related to the delivery of fertilizers. A rather small percentage of the total aid is being used for water supply schemes in Kerala, Himachal Pradesh, Rajasthan and Uttar Pradesh; and for various educational and artisanal projects, which are usually managed by non-governmental organisations.

One of the projects which has received public attention was the delivery of 17 trawlers, which after it was stopped following protest in defence of the traditional Indian coastal prawn fishers by the National India Committee (LIW 1981), was replaced by the commercial sale of an increased number of trawlers. The other projects which have come in for solid questioning are the development aid given to the Operation Flood (LIW 1985), the delivery of fertilisers at prices around 33 per cent above the market prices (LIW 1982), and the participation in the Ganga project, of which the Dutch minister of transport in an interview in January 1986 said: "Development aid will help us to get some of the huge orders. There are too many other rivals in the field".

The calculations of Dutch development aid which have been made by Sam Bruinsma show that, although only 36 per cent of the aid is officially tied to Dutch export, close to 70 per cent is spent in the Netherlands and that between 1970 and 1984 between 29 and 44 per cent of Dutch export to India materialised because of ODA allocations (Bruinsma 1986, p. 103). The

*The trends in the Dutch official development aid policy can be found in TAS (1973), Beerends (1980), Van der Velden (1980) and Bol (1983).

beneficiaries of the aid were mainly the bigger companies (Shell, Philips, Sluis, Vicon, Organon, Haskoning, Holec, IHC, Century Enka, Damen, etc.).

Recent developments indicate that even more stress than in the past should be laid on the role of private companies and banks, and that through the public development aid funds, private investments by Dutch companies in India should be encouraged (Schoo 1984). Various delegations from the Netherlands, working in this spirit, have visited India over the last few years. A delegation led by His Royal Highness Prince Claus, visited India in the beginning of 1981, and held talks with an Indian delegation led by the then Minister of Commerce Pranab Mukherjee. They signed a protocol for improving the cooperation on the plane of bilateral relations in the industrial, commercial, financial, agricultural, technological, scientific and cultural fields. In February 1982, a delegation led by the Mayor of Rotterdam visited India to study the transport and port facilities, to promote the Port of Rotterdam as a gateway to Europe and to study possibilities of cooperation with Indian ports. In February 1982, a joint Business Council Agreement was signed between the Federation of Indian Chambers of Commerce and Industry (FICCI) and Dutch representatives of Trade and Industry. In February 1983 the Dutch Deputy Minister of Economic Affairs, Mr. F. Bolkestein, paid an official visit to India on an invitation of Mr. Shivraj V. Patil, the Minister of Commerce. During this visit an agreement for economic cooperation was signed.

The crowning piece was in January 1986 the first visit to a developing country of Queen Beatrix and her husband, accompanied by an invited planeload of 22 Dutch businessmen. One of them, the chairman of the Dutch Chambers of Commerce and Industry VNO, declared his reasons for accepting the invitation: "The Indians are in need of improving the infrastructure, but decisions on these matters are ultimately taken by the state. So when you are in a position to present yourself in the company of your own head of state, then it is enormously important for the confidence that is created in India in the supplier of goods" (NRC, 22-01-1986). Minister of Foreign Affairs Van den Broek, in a more diplomatic language, conveyed the same message: "Although the royal visit is not in the first instance meant to sell Holland Ltd., there is indeed a happy coincidence" (NRC, 21-01-1986).

Holland Ltd., as it stands, is actually already doing well in its trading contacts with India. The balance of trade in recent years for India has turned from a fairly positive into an alarmingly negative position, amounting to a deficit of close to two billion rupees or five hundred million guilders in 1984-85. The most prominent Indian export items in the early eighties were clothes (26 per cent of the exports in 1981), fabrics (18 per cent) and gems. The decrease in the export volume after 1979 was on account of a sharp drop in the export of gems. Agricultural exports, particularly cattle feed, an area in which Unilever is particularly active, have accordingly become more important. In 1981-82, they accounted for 35 per cent of the Indian exports to the Netherlands. On the other hand, notwithstanding the sudden drop in the import of fertilizers (from Fl. 225 million in 1981 to Fl. 42 million in 1982), imports from the Netherlands have increased very sharply, resulting in a growing deficit on the trade balance account.

There does not seem to be any direct prospect for the balance to turn into a positive direction. The seventeen-member strong mission of the Dutch section of the Indo-Dutch Joint Business Council, which visited India short after the official signing of an economic and technical collaboration agreement in early 1983, expressed its helplessness with regard to India's balance of trade deficit. Mr. Van Veen, the chairman of the Dutch section of the Joint Business Council, and at that time also the Chairman of the Dutch Chambers of Commerce and Industry, declared on behalf of the delegation that his country was an open market economy, and that hence no guarantees could be given. The Indian exporters were welcome "to try their strength" on the basis of the quality of their products and the competitiveness of their prices. The Deputy-Director of the Dutch Ministry of Economic Affairs used literally the same argument (*Economic Times*, 23 and 26 March 1983).

Dutch trade statistics, however, do show that the tide appears to be turning in favour of India. According to the Dutch figures, India in 1984 had a positive trading balance of Fl 30 million. The explanation for the difference is probably the sharp increase in the export of crude oil (Fl 526 million out of Fl 862 million total imports into the Netherlands) which in the Indian trade statistics are not assigned to any particular region because, as the government indicates in its *Economic Survey* (1985-86), "details regarding destination are not available". Clothes, garments and fabrics, which in the early eighties still made for the bulk of Indian exports, have now been relegated to the third position, after foodstuffs, which in fact means that presently in the Netherlands more Indian products are eaten than worn.

Indian entrepreneurs may not in the first place be interested in changing this state of affairs. The message of Ashok Garware, the president of the Bombay Chambers of Commerce, during his visit to the Netherlands in October 1985 was outspoken about his intention to mainly look for Dutch products and collaboration agreements : "We are in the first instance not interested in the export of our products to the Netherlands". In this respect, there is a similarity of expectations, *Export Magazine* (18-09-1985), the journal of the Dutch Ministry of Economic Affairs, indeed sees ample scope for joining in the effort to open the Indian market: "At least seventy to eighty million (of the 750 million) represent a market of sophisticated, modern consumers with great purchasing power".

## 3.1. Dutch Private Investments in India

The involvement of Dutch companies in the Indian economy can be categorized under three headings: 1. branches, 2. companies with equity share participation, and 3. companies with only technical collaboration or licensee status. This section will deal with the second category.*

Our attempt in this section is to present a picture of the overall position of the Dutch companies in terms of assets,

*Since the five branches of Dutch companies in India do not have any manufacturing activities and since no separate data are available regarding the character of their activities in India, no attention will be paid to them in the rest of this report (The three major companies operate in the banking sector—ABN and AMRO—or in the airlines—KLM). In chapter 7, some consideration shall be given to companies with only technical collaboration.

**Table 3.1 : Trade between India and the Netherlands (1970-1971 to 1984-1985 ; Rs million)**

| Year | Exports | As % of total Indian exports | Imports | As % of total Indian imports | Balance |
|---|---|---|---|---|---|
| 1970-71 | 139.8 | 0.9 | 190.0 | 1.2 | —51.1 |
| 1974-75 | 717.4 | 2.2 | 549.3 | 1.2 | +168.1 |
| 1975-76 | 822.3 | 2.0 | 638.2 | 1.2 | +184.1 |
| 1976-77 | 1945.6 | 3.7 | 654.3 | 1.3 | +1291.3 |
| 1977-78 | 1371.3 | 2.5 | 821.5 | 1.4 | +549.8 |
| 1978-79 | 1793.5 | 3.1 | 1585.0 | 2.3 | +208.4 |
| 1979-80 | 2204.6 | 3.4 | 1451.9 | 1.6 | +752.7 |
| 1980-81 | 1520.4 | 2.3 | 2145.0 | 1.7 | —624.6 |
| 1981-82 | 1101.0 | 1.4 | 2785.7 | 2.4 | —1684.7 |
| 1982-83 | 1110.5 | 1.3 | 2486.9 | 1.8 | —1376.6 |
| 1983-84* | 2026.8 | 2.0 | 2787.1 | 1.6 | —760.3 |
| 1984-85* | 1946.0 | 1.6 | 3646.9 | 2.1 | —1700.9 |
| 1985-86* | 1714.2 | 1.4 | 2921.6 | 1.5 | —1207.4 |

*Provisional.

*Source* : Government of India, *Economic Survey*.

turnover and profits as well as in terms of import substitution and export performance. We shall make some broad references to the Indian industrial sector as a whole but should stress the point that the calculations are done on the basis of the official annual reports of the companies. It should be understood that the figures are the official visiting card of the companies with an eye on the reaction of the government and the share market. They may therefore not reveal the exact picture and may overstate or understate the company results. We shall, however, argue our case on the basis of the published results at their face value.

Although the annual reports are produced as public documents, there were a number of companies, including Philips India, from which the reports were not forthcoming despite repeated requests. In our final data, we shall, for this reason, not include the results of Music India (Philips), Maschmeyer Aromatics (India), Naarden (Chemicals) and WEBEL, a joint enterprise of Philips and the West Bengal state government. Burmah Shell Refineries Ltd., a 100 per cent subsidiary of the Royal Dutch Shell group from the Netherlands and U.K., was fully taken over by the Indian Government in 1976 against compensation (for the background, see e.g. Soumitro Chaudhury, 1979), and is not included in the analysis.

All the companies which we have listed can be assumed to be under the direct overall control of the foreign partner, with the possible exception of Das Repographics. The Calcutta-based company, in which Océ Van der Grinten has acquired a fifteen per cent equity share on account of the sale of technology, is run without non-resident directors. The dividend remitted to the foreign company is insignificantly small (Rs 129,326 over the period 1977-1980). Royalties were slightly higher, but remained less than half a per cent of sales.

The share of non-residential equity as well as the number of expatriates on the Board of Directors has been listed in Table 3.2. Hindustan Lever, which is by far the biggest Dutch-owned company operating in India, is an interesting case for two reasons. On the one hand, it had insisted on maintaining a foreign majority in the share capital, and in 1982 ultimately got the governmental approval. On the other hand it has reached an advanced stage of indigenisation of management. Prakash Tandon, who became the chairman of HL in 1961, was the first Indian chairman of a foreign company. The last but one chairman, T. Thomas, has even been elevated to the Board of Directors of the international Unilever concern. In the words of the present chairman, Dr. A. Ganguly, the development of local managerial manpower at a time when the managerial culture was still in its infancy in India, "was possibly Unilever's single most significant contribution to industry in this country. It is this measure which has resulted in the contrywide recognition of Hindustan Lever as being synonymous with professional management" (Ganguly 1981, p.4; see also Tandon 1971 and Thomas 1981).

The indigenisation of management and to some extent of the capital holding does not automatically lead to the indigenous control over the company, as we have argued in chapters one and two. As a matter of fact the parent company of Hindustan Lever, Unilever Ltd., is under the secure control of

Leverhulme Trust which owns only eighteen per cent of the shares.

**Table 3.2: Composition of the Board of Directors and Equity Participation of Indo-Dutch Firms**

| S. N. | Name of the company | 1975 | | 1982 | | Percentage Foreign Equity |
|---|---|---|---|---|---|---|
| | | Directors | Foreign Directors | Directors | Foreign directors | |
| 1. | Hindustan Lever | 7 | 3 | 7 | 1 | 51 |
| 2. | Peico | 8 | 3 | 5 | 2 | 40 |
| 3. | NOCIL | 17 | 4 | 18 | 2 | 33 |
| 4. | Lipton | 6 | 2 | 5 | 1 | 40 |
| 5. | Century Enka | 4 | 2 | 8 | 3 | 40 |
| 6. | Organon | 7 | 3 | 9 | 3 | 49 |
| 7. | ELMI | 4 | 1 | 3 | 1 | 100x |
| 8. | Hind Lamps | 8 | 1 | 6 | 1 | 50x |
| 9. | Stovec Screens | 7 | 2 | 12 | 3 | 40 |
| 10. | Stormac | n.a. | n.a. | 11 | 2 | 40 |
| 11. | Vicon | 8 | 5 | 7 | 5 | 49 |
| 12. | Wavin | 8 | 3 | 11 | 3 | 13 |
| 13. | Kinetics Technology | 6 | 1 | 6 | 1 | 35 |
| 14. | Das Reprographics | n.a. | n.a. | 7 | 2 | 15 |
| 15. | Duphar Interfran | 7 | 3 | 8 | 1 | 39 |
| 16. | Hazemeyer Elcon | — | — | 8 | 5 | 75 |

*Source* : Van der Velden, Lieten and Mitra, 1983.

*Since the foreign equity is not directly held by the non-resident company (Philips N.V.) but by its Indian subsidiary (Peico), the maximum ceilings as per the FERA guidelines do not apply.

The parent companies as well as the daughter companies make it a point to stress the independent position of the regional units in a federal set-up.* The managements in India,

*The argument often used by the companies in both the Netherlands and India in their correspondence with the project staff was that they should not be included in the survey since, after all, the companies operating in India were Indian.

moreover, have laid considerable stress on appearances to suit the local sentiments. The adoption of *swadeshi* names like Hindustan Lever, National Organic Chemicals India Ltd. and Peico, fit in with this endeavour. The company's house journals like *Parichay* (Peico), *Hamara* (Unilever) and *Taza* (Lipton) play a calculated role in blending the loyalties to the company with nationalist feelings and aspirations for the economic development of the country. *Parichay*, the house journal of Philips India, did possibly not overstress the point when it praised the "unity amongst the people to fight the *British imperialism* and to gain the political independence for the country". The reference to the nationalist movement (*Parichay*, September 1981) was accompanied by another reference which smacks of Hindu fundamentalism. Praise was showered on Tilak, a nationalist Maratha leader in the first quarter of the century who stood by all the less savoury social practices of Hinduism and on the god Ganesh, "the symbol of wisdom, strength, unity and prosperity". The editorial in *Parichay* ended by stating: "Needless to say that for centuries to come, Lord Ganesh will be the hope of the people for strength and prosperity. Let us invoke the blessings of Lord Ganesh to give us knowledge and strength to work hard so as to bring prosperity to all the members of the Philips family".*

The policy of a nationalist image-building towards the public at large, is supplemented by an endeavour at generating goodwill directly aimed at the political authorities. One example may illustrate the modus operandi. Wavin, co-owned by the Shell concern, decided to allocate Fl. 250,000 for a development project, inclusive of a water supply scheme with the company's PVC pipes. After "extensive scouting. . . the rural district Zaheerabad, Taluk Medak in the state of Andhra Pradesh, was selected. It is one of the poorest districts of India" (Shell Venster, January 1981, p. 16). The company failed to add one significant detail: Medak was the parliamentary constituency of

*Trade union officials in Peico and Hindustan Lever complained that workers were given ample facilities for religious activities by the management, thereby accentuating the ethno-religious borderline between the communities. On the other hand, trade union work, which the officials claim to be one of the most potent forces of communal integration, finds hostile reception.

**Table 3.3: Survey of the Factories of Indo-Dutch Companies in India**

| Name of the Company | Controlling Dutch Company | Factories of the Company | | Products | Totol Employment (1983) |
|---|---|---|---|---|---|
| | | City | State | | |
| 1 | 2 | 3 | 4 | 5 | 6 |
| 1. Century Enka | Akzo | Bhosari (Pune) | Maharashtra | — Plastic polymer resin<br>— Nylon Filament Yarn<br>— Polyester Filament Yarn | 750 |
| 2. Das Reprographics | Ocê | Taratalla, Calcutta | West Bengal | — Diazao Printing Machines and Paper | 620 |
| | | 24 Parganas Behala | West Bengal | — Electrostatic Copier Machines and Paper<br>— Drafting Machines | |
| 3. Hindustan Lever & Indexport | Unilever | Bombay | Maharashtra | — Hydrogenated Oils | 9360 |
| | | Calcutta | West Bengal | — Infant Milk Food & Milk Powder | |
| | | Shyamnagar | West Bengal | — Soap & Synthetic Detergents | |
| | | Ghaziabad | Uttar pradesh | — Sodium Tripoly Phosphate | |
| | | Etah | Uttar Pradesh | — Cosmetic and Toiletries | |

| | | | | | |
|---|---|---|---|---|---|
| | | Bari Brahmana | Jammu & Kashmir | — Industrial Machinery | |
| | | Twelve Animal Feed Centres | | — Animal Feed<br>— Glycerine | |
| | | Kandla | Gujarat | | |
| 4. Hind Lamps | Philips | Shikohabad | Uttar Pradesh | — Electric Lamps<br>— Lams Components | |
| 5. Duphar Interfran | Philips<br>(Solvay after 1982) | Thane | Maharashtra | — Drugs and Pharmaceuticals<br>— Cosmetics and Toiletries | 650 |
| 6. Kinetics Technology | Kinetics International | Okhla | New Delhi | — Burners & Generators<br>— Liquid Chlorine Storage Tank<br>— Chemical Plant Engineering | 180 |
| 7. NOCIL | Shell | Thane | Maharashtra | — Petro Chemicals & Utilities | 1600 |
| | | Lote Parshuram | Maharashtra | — Detergents<br>— Pesticides<br>— Plastics | |

(*Contd.*)

**Table 3.3** (*Contd.*)

| 1 | 2 | 3 | 4 | 5 | 6 |
|---|---|---|---|---|---|
| 8. Organon-Chefaro (Infer India Ltd.) | Akzo | Calcutta | West Bengal | — Hormones, tablets & Elixirs | 550 |
| | | Calcutta Ganganagar | West Bengal | | |
| 9. Peico | Philips | Calcutta Kalwa (Thane) | West Bengal Maharashtra | — Electric Components, Lamps and Glass Tubings | 8950 |
| | | Loni Kalbhor (Pune) | Maharashtra | — Radio Sets, Record Players, Tape Recorders, etc. | |
| | | Pimpri and Pela | Maharashtra | — Microphones & Intercom App. | |
| | | Administrative Centre at Delhi, Madras, Bombay, Calcutta | | — Electronic Measuring Instruments & Radioreceivers<br>— Specialized Tools, etc.<br>— Welding | |

| | | | | | |
|---|---|---|---|---|---|
| 10. Stormac | Stork | Lamba Village, Narol | Gujarat | — Automatic Rotary Screen Printing Machine<br>— High Pressure Continuous Loop Steamer<br>— Special Lacquers | n.a. |
| 11. Stovec Screens | Stork | Lamba Village, Narol | Gujerat | — Perforted Rotary Screens | n.a. |
| 12. Lipton | Unilever | Calcutta | West Bengal | — Blended Tea including Bulk | 2050 |
| | | Madras | Tamil Nadu | — Packets and Tea Bags | |
| 13. Elmi | Philips | Calcutta | West Bengal | — Lamps<br>— Glass Shells & Tubes<br>— Aerodrome Runways & High Volting Lamps | 600 |
| 14. Vicon | Thyssen | Bangalore | Karnataka | Agricultural Machinery | 125 |
| 15. Wavin | Shell | Madras<br>Ghaziabad<br>Nagpur | Tamil Nadu<br>Uttar Pradesh<br>Maharashtra | Hard PVC Pipes, etc. | 175 |
| 16. Maschmeyer | Maschmeyer Aromatics | Madras | Tamil Nadu | Aromatic Chemicals | n.a. |
| 17. Naarden Chemical Works | Naarden NV (Unilever after 1984) | Saki Naka | Maharashtra | Chemicals | n.a. |
| 18. Elcon | Hazemeyer | Kandla | Gujerat | Fuses | n.a. |

the late prime minister Indira Gandhi who may not have been unsympathetically predisposed towards such an initiative.

The total number of plants, thus excluding workhouses and local units, in which there is Dutch financial participation, amounts to thirty-five (Table 3.3.). The factories which are spread all over India with a concentration in and around Delhi, Calcutta, Puna and Bombay, are engaged in a rather limited range of industries. The products manufactured by the Dutch subsidiaries can be broadly classified under food and toilet products (Hindustan Lever, Lipton and Maschmeyer); electronic and electrical goods (Peico, ELMI, Hind Lamps); drugs (Organon and Duphar); petrochemical products (NOCIL, Hindustan Lever, Wavin and Naarden) and machinery (Vicon, Stormac, Stovec and KTI). Peico and especially Hindustan Lever have diversified their production packet considerably, albeit within their respective traditional areas. As can be observed from Table 3.4 which provides a ranking according to assets, turnover and profits for the Dutch subsidiaries in India, *Hindustan Lever* is by far the biggest one. *Peico*, the other important Dutch company, unlike Hindustan Lever, has diluted the non-residential equity share in accordance with FERA to less than half. A block of 40 per cent is held by Philips N.V. which thereby retains actual control over the Indian subsidiary. Hindustan Lever and Peico shall be dealt with in more detail in the following two chapters. In this section we shall briefly deal with the remaining companies.

*Nocil* (*National Organic Chemical Industries Ltd.*) for some time has been the second biggest Dutch company in India. The company is a collaboration venture of the Arvind Mafatlal group and the Royal Dutch Shell company which holds 33 per cent of the equity shares and, through its subsidiaries Shell Internationale Research Maatschappij and the Bataafse Internationale Chemie Maatschappij, provides the major technology. The company which was set up in the early sixties for the production of petrochemicals and plastics, during the last couple of years has been growing extremely fast. In five years, from 1980 to 1985, total income more than doubled from 1.1 billion to 2.3 billion and gross profits increased from Rs. 40 million to Rs. 344 million leaving, after the payment of taxes

(Rs. 40 million) and depreciation, a net profit of Rs. 191 million. Net profits in 1986 increased to Rs. 276 million.

Part of the success was contributed by the commissioning in 1983 of a new plant at Lote Parshuram in Ratnagiri district (Maharashtra) for the production of agrochemicals. The technology for the manufacture of the insecticide monocrotophos had been developed by the state-owned Regional Research Laboratory at Hyderabad and not by Shell, one of the world leaders in agrochemical research.

In the other production unit, commissioned in 1967 in the then equally undeveloped Thane village in Maharashtra, a number of modernisation and diversification programmes have been taken at hand for the production of, among other things, naphtha, ethylene, propylene and butylene which, in reaction with other chemicals, yield a wide range of products such as polyvinyl, synthetic rubber, filament yarn, etc. The two competitors in the field are Union Carbide and the public sector undertaking IPCL. The latter which had been the largest manufacturers of petrochemicals in India, despite its own expansion programme for the setting up of a 300,000 tonnes per annum gas-based ethylene plant, is likely to be overtaken by Nocil in the near future. Nocil has indeed decided to go in for a massive Rs. 13 billion modernisation programme which by 1990 should lead to a five-fold increase in the production of ethylene and propylene and to a more than ten-fold increase of benzene production.

The quadrupling of the total petrochemical capacity and the diversification into a whole range of agrochemicals will be linked to an increase of the Royal Dutch Shell in the equity structure to forty per cent. The Shell group appears to be attracted by the future prospects in India. In addition to the substantial increase in the equity capital of Nocil, it committed itself to take a forty per cent participation in the Rs. 15 billion joint sector refinery at Karnal in the Punjab. The injection of Shell finances was advanced by the NOCIL managers as a strong point in favour of the government approval when it is confronted with a foreign exchange crunch (*Business World*, 21 July 1986, pp. 43-57). In May 1987, the government, however, decided to grant the license to the Tatas.

The Mafatlal group presently holds twenty per cent of equity The rest is divided over financial institutions and around 30,000 shareholders who incidentally saw the prices of their shares move up from Rs. 150 in 1984 to Rs. 775 in 1986, and received a one for two bonus share and a dividened of 18 per cent, Nocil in this respect is one of the toppers in the share market, not very far behind the other Indo-Dutch company, Century Enka.

*Century Enka*, a collaboration started in 1965 between the foremost Indian monopoly house of Birla, and Akzo-Enka, has been the fourth biggest Dutch controlled company in India and will probably remain so despite the sharp advances made by Lipton. Lipton's advances, however, as we shall see in a moment, are almost exclusively on account of the transfers made by its sister company Hindustan Lever. Century Enka is doing extremely well. Its turnover spurted from Rs. 486 million in 1980-81 to Rs. 1692 million in 1984-85 which amounts to a growth of 83 per cent per year. During the same period, profits have risen at more or less the same rate, from Rs. 122 million to Rs. 371 million. After providing for depreciation and investment allowance reserves (together Rs. 130 million) and taxation, the company in 1985 was left with a net profit of Rs. 179.6 million, or 22.9 of the net worth of the company. As a ratio to total invested capital, net profits rates have been consistently above twenty per cent. This compares very well with the income performance of the world-wide AKZO concern, which is not surprising. The developing countries in general, who represent four per cent of the invested capital of the multinational corporation, in normal years account for more than twenty per cent of the profits. The parent company, by the way, is the result of a merger between the Dutch Koninklijke Zout Organon and Algemene Kunstzijde Unie and the German Enka and Glanzstoff.

The foreign partner controls around 40 per cent of the equity shares. Two out of the five directors of the company represent AKZO International. Till 1979 the President also was Dutch, drawing a salary of Rs. 320,432 a year. His successor, an Indian, in 1983 drew a salary of "only" Rs. 144,551. The Indian President is being assisted by a Dutch

**Table 3.4 : Assets, Turnover and Profits of Dutch Companies in India 1979-1980 (in brackets) and 1984-85 (Rs. Million)**

| Company | Net Assets* | Turnover | Gross Profit Net of Depreciation and Interest | Gross Profit/ Net Asset Ratio** |
|---|---|---|---|---|
| 1. Hindustan Lever | 1945 (822) | 6119 (3557) | 465 (295) | 32.2 |
| 2. Nocil | 1437 (609) | 2160 (1113) | 269 (40) | 14.2 |
| 3. Peico | 1288 (464) | 2268 (1216) | 187 (155) | 30.5 |
| 4. Century Enka | 675 (215)@ | 1621 (437) | 305 (93) | 26.6 |
| 5. Lipton India Ltd. | 485 (130)@ | 2779 (603) | 69 (—9) | n.a |
| 6. Duphar Interfran | 91 (27) | 153 (80) | 16 (7) | 22.4 |
| 7. Elmi | 81 (28) | 203 (138) | —5 (68) | 9.3 |
| 8. Organon (Infar) | 77 (49) | 167 (86) | 32 (14) | 19.9 |
| 9. Hind Lamps | n.a. (70) | n.a. (96) | n.a. (6) | 11.9 |
| 10. Wavin | 37 (44) | 200 (136) | —10 (9) | 0.7 |
| 11. Stoves | 42 (25) | 31 (23) | 2.3 (8) | 27.9 |
| 12. Stormac | 45 (27) | 38 (39) | 3.2 (5) | n.a. |
| 13. Vicon | 25 (2) | 28 (23) | n.a. (2) | loss |
| 14. Das Repographics | n.a. (16) | n.a. (36) | n.a. (2) | 49.3 |
| 15. Hazemeyer Elcon | n.a. (7) | n.a. (7) | n.a. (—0.6) | n.a. |
| 16. Kinetics | n.a. (4) | n.a. (10) | n.a. (0.4) | 29.7 |

*Notes* : *Net fixed assets represent the net fixed assets plus the net current assets exclusive of the carried over loss account.

**The long term ratio is calculated as a simple average of the profit-asset ratio over the years between 1970 and 1981 for which data were available.

@Figures refer to 1983-84.

*Source* : Annual Reports of the Companies.

Vice-President, who drew Rs. 336,568 net of Rs. 99,450 income tax and five Indian vice-presidents who received around 100,000. In order to prevent a possible exclusion of AKZO representatives on the Board of Directors, a special resolution was adopted by the shareholders meeting in 1981 to the effect that "AKZO NV shall have the right to appoint a special director who will not be liable to retire by rotation" even in case the foreign shareholding becomes "marginally less than 40 per cent in the event of issue of bonus shares" (Annual Report 1980-81, p. 3).

The high profitability of the company, which allowed for a dividend of 32 Rs. per share and for the issue of a one-for-two bonus share, is reflected in the stock market where the price per share of Rs 100 in August 1986 had risen to Rs 1130. The company, which imports more than half of its materials from abroad, engages in the production of engineering plastics, and nylon and polyster yarn. The progress made by Century Enka can be gauged from Table 3.5 One significant factor, apart from the steep growth rates and the high ratio of net profits to invested capital, is the declining tax rate. During recent years, less than twenty per cent of gross profits were paid as direct taxes to the exchequer.

The above mentioned companies, who are top-ranking in the Indian private sector in terms of assets, turnover and profit, belong to the four major Dutch multinational corporations (Shell, Philips, Akzo and Unilever) who, if their other holdings in India are added, account for 98 per cent of Dutch investments in India.

Unilever controls three more companies, in addition to Hindustan Lever and its related firms Indexport and Sharpedge, namely Lipton India, Naarden Chemical Works and Brooke Bond. The world-wide interests of both the latter companies were taken over in 1986 and 1984, but shall not be dealt with in the further treatment of Unilever operations in India. The share capital of *Lipton India* underwent a sharp rise from Rs 37.5 million in 1982 to Rs 157.5 million in 1984. In the preceding years, the company had been struggling to minimise the rather serious losses. Apart from the reasons given by the company to explain the bad performance (labour unrest and floods in its main factory unit in Calcutta), the overhauling

**Table 3.5 : Century Enka : Long Term Trends, 1972-85 (Rs Million)**

| Year | Sales | Net Worth | Gross Profit | Taxes as % of 4 | Net Profit | 6/3 | 6 as % of equity |
|---|---|---|---|---|---|---|---|
| 1 | 2 | 3 | 4 | 5 | 6 | 7 | 8 |
| 1970-71 | 78 | 40 | 25 | 42 | 14 | 29.0 | 48.2 |
| 1971-72 | 78 | 50 | 21 | 53 | 10 | 16.6 | 32 3 |
| 1972-73 | 84 | 59 | 23 | 57 | 10 | 16.5 | 32.7 |
| 1973-74 | 106 | 81 | 43 | 61 | 17 | 20.7 | 39.5 |
| 1974-75 | 112 | 85 | 22 | 56 | 10 | 11.5 | 23.0 |
| 1975-76 | 146 | 104 | 26 | 35 | 25 | 23.4 | 56.1 |
| 1976-77 | 147 | 112 | 25 | 67 | 8 | 7.4 | 17.6 |
| 1977-78 | 208 | 141 | 43 | 15 | 39 | 27.6 | 67.3 |
| 1978-79 | 352 | 166 | 64 | 37 | 37 | 22.4 | 64.4 |
| 1979-80 | 438 | 213 | 93 | 35 | 57 | 26.2 | 97.0 |
| 1980-81 | 489 | 272 | 112 | 32 | 62 | 22.8 | 73.7 |
| 1981-82 | 665 | 333 | 105 | 29 | 58 | 17.4 | 69.0 |
| 1982-83 | 987 | na | na | na | na | na | na |
| 1983-84 | 1185 | 560 | 132 | 19 | 66 | 12.0 | 55.4 |
| 1984-85 | 1612 | 782 | 304 | 19 | 179 | 22.9 | 151.3 |

*Source* : Century Enka, *Annual Reports.*

of the marketing system in order to bring it in line with that of its sister concern Hindustan Lever, temporarily upset the normal functioning. During that period, a number of management cadre was mutually exchanged on deputation between the two companies in preparation of what ultimately in 1983 appeared as the take-over of some of the less profitable production branches of Hindustan Lever.

In its portfolio, Lipton got all the food stuff production, *i.e.*, the dairy unit at Etah, the vanaspati units at Ghaziabad, Tiruchirapally, Shamnagar and Sewri and the animal food centres at Pune, Nagpur, Surat, Ahmedabad, Rajpura, Ghaziabad, Bangalore, Hubli, Coimbatore, Tiruchirupalli and Tatanagar. In this deal, one significant exception was made. It was stipulated that at the multi-product factories at Shamnagar (Calcutta) and Sewri (Bombay), only the domestic business of edible oils would be leased. The implication would be that exports, if any, would continue to be added to those of Hindustan Lever. As we shall see later, for Unilever the export performance of Hindustan Lever is an important argument in defending its continuing foreign majority in the equity structure. As a consequence of the deal, the export performance as a ratio of total sales of Lipton has declined sharply (see Table 3.8 later).

With total assets of Rs 78 million in 1985, *Organon* is one of the more important medium-size companies. Another pharmaceutical company, *Duphar Interfran*, which is roughly of the same size, was till 1981 in the hands of Philips but, consequent upon the liquidation by Philips N.V. of its pharmaceutical activities, was then sold to Solvay of Belgium. Organon and its affiliate Chefaro, mainly an import house, belong to the pharmaceutical division of AKZO which in the early eighties has come under sharp criticism for its propagation of anabolic steroids for children in developing countries (Wolfers 1983; Ruigrok 1983). The adverse publicity may have been the reason for the change of name. Henceforth Organon operates under the name *Infar* (*India*) *Ltd.* Infar, which in the late sixties took over the British-owned Harris and Co. in Calcutta through the signing of a technical collaboration agreement and the participation in the equity, has been allowed to retain 49 per cent equity. It however, does not seem to have fulfilled the requirements in terms of a high export performance or the manufacture of essential drugs. In the mid-seventies, not unlikely with an eye on getting government's approval for a high foreign shareholding, export as a percentage of total sales went up quite fast to a significant 32 per cent, but afterwards it dropped as fast as it had risen. Exports have now stabilised at around ten per cent of sales, most of it to the Soviet Union which does not involve hard currency. Imports, on the other hand, against hard currencies, have risen dramatically. The profitability of the company has continued to increase from around 15 per cent of net worth in the early 1970s to 20-25 per cent in the early 1980s.

The sale of Duphar Interfran by Philips N.V. was balanced by the newly acquired control over two lamp manufacturing companies. The *Electric Lamp Manufacturers* (*India*), which used to be a firm jointly controlled by Philips, General Electric,

Crompton Greaves and Mazda, was taken over by Peico (Philips) in 1981. In accordance with FERA regulations, foreign subsidiaries which have diluted the foreign equity to the required level, are allowed to have fully-owned Indian subsidiaries. The dilution by Philips N.V. of its share in Peico eventually created the possibility for the take-over of ELMI in which Philips had acquired a managerial edge over its competitors. Moreover, another company, *Hind Lamps*, which used to be owned half by the Bajaj group and half by the former ELMI group, came under the controlling influence of Peico.

*Wavin* (*India*) *Ltd.*, which now has a 13 per cent minority shareholding by Shell (earlier 49 per cent), is one of the few companies which has not been doing well. It has remained relatively small although it started its activities in the second half of the 1960s with a plant in Madras, and later with two additional units in Northern India. Wavin is engaged in the production of PVC pipes and, as a vertical expansion of its production line, has gone into the contracting of drinking water and irrigation facilities. Some of this was done in World Bank projects. Since these deliveries are deemed as exports, it gave the company in some years fairly high export figures. Operating results during the last couple of years have been rather negative. Over the two years 1984 and 1985, the combined loss, after depreciation, amounted to Rs 35 million against a share capital of ten million and reserves of only 8. Two comparatively recently-started companies who have been doing visibly better are *Stormac India* and *Stovec Screens*. They are a joint effort of the giant textile concern Mafatlal and the Dutch machinery production company Stork B.V. The machinery produced in the units which are located near Ahmedabad are (textile) printing machinery and, as a new line of interest, dairy equipment. In the mid-1980s, ten years after they were set up, the two companies had combined assets of hundred million rupees.

The few remaining companies neither belong to a major Dutch multinational nor to an Indian monopoly house. *Kinetics Technology India* has the technological know-how and a forty per cent equity participation by the rather small but dynamic Kinetics Technology International. It has grown since its inception in 1971 into an integrated engineering organisation which supplies petro-chemical and fertiliser plants with cracking furnaces and gas generators. *Vicon Ltd.* on the other hand has, except for the years 1980-1982, produced serious losses and has not been able to put itself on a sound footing, despite the regular many-million soft loans by the Dutch FMO development aid bank. For its parent company, Thyssen Bornemisza, the losses may be less important than the experience which, as it states, will help them in setting up new ventures in other developing countries. After the setting up of a plant for the production of agricultural machinery in 1968 at Bangalore in South India, it has shown only marginal rates of growth. By 1978 sales had gone up to only six million rupees. Present trends (*e.g.* sales of 28 million in 1984) indicate that the company may have overcome its teething problems. The choice for Bangalore because of the absence of labour unions and because of the suitable climate (Geertsema 1981, p. 67) at a time that the Green Revolution was increasing the need for agricultural machinery elsewhere in the country, may be the single-most important cause for the bad performance in the past.

Finally, *Hazemeyer Elcon* was set up in 1978 in the Kandla Free Trade Zone for the production of fuses. The foreign equity of 75 per cent reflects the export oriented nature of the company. During its first years of operation it has been able to export the major part of its production, but due to recessionary trends in Europe, it is increasingly looking for an outlet in the Soviet market.

## 3.2 Comparative Behaviour

In their 1983 survey, the Economic Times Research Bureau ranked the 251 industrial gains in India according to the profitability ratio in 1982. For this purpose three profitability ratios were combined (gross profits to capital employed; gross profits to net sales and net profits to net worth)*. Century

*The paid-up capital of a company is the book value of the shares of a company at a certain date. The retained profit (together with the capital obtained through the sales of shares at a premium) form the shareholders' reserves which together with the paid-up capital (shareholders' capital) forms the net worth or shareholders' fund of a company.

Enka ranks 2nd in this list (7th in 1979), Peico 47th (67th), Hindustan Lever 41st (86th) and Nocil 147th (36th). The ranking indicates that within the Indian corporate sector, the (Dutch) multinational corporations do not seem to register an exceptional performance. The following comparisons with both the smaller and the bigger companies in the private sector do, however, show that the Dutch companies function well above the average.

Comparative calculations can only be done with considerable reservation. To the unreliability of annual reports and statistics should be added, as a disturbing factor, the qualitative differences between the various types and branches of industry. Dutch subsidiaries are generally public limited companies of which there are some 8000 in India and who in 1978-79 had an average gross profit—capital employed ratio of 22 per cent (Annual Survey of Industries, 1978-79, p. 11). Most of the Dutch companies operated above the national average. For both the years 1978-79 and 1979-80, the comparable average figures were considerably higher for Hindustan Lever (29.6 per cent), Peico (45.0 per cent), Duphar Interfran (39.6 per cent), Century Enka (40.9 per cent), Nocil (27.1 per cent), Organon (31.8 per cent), etc. Some of the companies (Lipton, Vicon and Wavin) have tended to operate below the national average for some of the years.

For comparative purposes, it would be more appropriate to compare the public limited companies of a similar size group. The Reserve Bank of India in its annual Report on Currency and Finance collects the aggregate results for 426 large companies and for 1720 medium and large companies separately. The overall average results for two years can be compared in Table 3.6. Practically all Dutch firms had by far a better performance in terms of gross profits and net profits.

In order to relate the Dutch subsidiaries to closely similar Indian companies, we have made an attempt at comparing them with enterprises operating in the same line of production. The insights to be drawn from such a comparison can only be indicative and not really conclusive, since a wide number of variables are involved. A majority of the Dutch subsidiaries had a higher profitability and had a higher percentage of profits retained out of profits after taxation compared to local companies (Sridhar Krishna, 1983).*

Although for foreign as well as for Indian companies, actual profits may be at variance with declared profits, foreign companies have the additional possibility of transferring profits to their parent companies in the form of transfer pricing, royalty payments and interests on loans. The general conclusion that the Dutch MNCs have an above average profitability would therefore be reinforced if all open and hidden transfers would be added.

Gross profits, it should be noted, do not include the whole surplus generated by the companies. Part of it is deducted for interest payments which may not flow to non-company related third parties. Another part is deducted on account of depreciation. While some of this will be legitimate, a number of companies make entries for depreciation which appear to be on the high side and contribute to a lowering of the gross profit results. Two examples of 1984-85 may suffice to establish this point: whereas Nocil deducted Rs 119 million and ended up with a gross profit of Rs 150 million, Century Enka deducted Rs 66 million, leaving a gross profit of Rs 304 million.

In view of the relatively higher rate of profitability, (Dutch) multinational corporation can be expected to show higher growth rates than the industry as a whole. We shall compare the companies which during the 1970's were firmly controlled by a foreign company, thereby excluding Hind Lamps and Elmi, and which were already well established so that the growth can be calculated on a mature basis. The growth in current prices, with 1970-71 as the basis, has been calculated in respect of turnover, gross capital assets, net worth and profits. Since the gross national aggregates and even the aggregates of the registered manufacturing industry are not appropriate for a useful comparison, we have taken the

*The following companies were compared: Hindustan Lever—Tata Oil Mills, Lipton Tea—Duncan Agro Industries, NOCIL—Hindustan Organic, Century Enka—National Rayon, Stovec Screens—Kunal Engineering, Peico—Elmi—Hind Lamps—Bengal Electric Lamp Works, Organon Duphar—Ranbaxy—Bengal Chemical and Pharmaceutical Ltd.

**Table 3.6: Profitability in the Private Corporate Sector (1978-80)**

| Company | Gross Profits to Sales | Gross Profits to Net Assets | Net Profits to Net Worth |
|---|---|---|---|
| Above Rs One Crore Paid-Up Capital | 10.7 | 12.3 | 13.2 |
| Of which | | | |
| Unilever | 9.8 | 29:6 | 20.8 |
| Peico | 13.1 | 45.0 | 15.3 |
| Nocil | 15.5 | 27.1 | 16.5 |
| Century Enka | 20.6 | 40.8 | 24.4 |
| Duphar | 9.8 | 39.6 | 16.6 |
| Organon | 17.3 | 31.8 | 19.5 |
| Hind Lamps | 7.7 | 34.3 | 24.5 |
| Lipton | 0.8 | 5.0 | (—) |
| Above Rs 5 Lakh Paid-Up Capital | 11.4 | 9.2 | 10.2 |
| Of which | | | |
| Elmi | 3.8 | 17.8 | 11.3 |
| Stovec | 36.8 | 24.3 | 32.8 |
| Stormac | 13.0 | 22.9 | 26.7 |
| Das | 6.6 | 13.1 | 23.6 |
| Vicon | 6.9 | 8.5 | 43.0 |
| Kinetics | 5.3 | 32.5 | 11.6 |

*Notes* 1. Gross profits are net of interest payments and depreciation.
2. Net assets, as elsewhere in this book, are defined as the net fixed assets plus the net current assets exclusive of the losses carried over.
3. The figures represent the averages for 1978 till 1980.

*Source*: RBI, *Report on Currency and Finance*, 1980-81, II, p. 73; Annual Reports of the companies.

Reserve Bank of India data on the corporate sector, i.e. 1720 listed companies with each a paid-up capital of at least Rs 0.5 million. It appears from the figures that in respect of sales and gross assets, the Dutch companies between 1970 and 1979 did not show growth rates in excess of the growth of the gross national product and of the gross capital formation. Without going into the reasons, the picture which emerges indicates that foreign capital is not immune to the impediments operating in the Indian economy. Government restrictions and a well-established indigenous sector in combination with the overall stagnation in the economy are probably at the basis of the low rate of growth, particularly in the immediate post-FERA period.

At the same time, the comparison brings out that in terms of gross profits and net worth, the companies in general have performed much better than the corporate sector in general. Despite the fact that, as we shall see in the next section, the transfer of profits abroad has been growing, the growth of net worth is significant. Many of the companies appear to have been stocking capital for future investment till a time when government policies would change in their full favour, as happened in the mid-eighties. The higher profits in the meantime had resulted in an above average increase in the shareholders' funds of practically all companies.

The export-import behaviour of multinational corporations has, for various reasons, attracted considerable attention, not in the last place because of the intrinsic scope for transfer pricing. Although it is a difficult area of research, transfer price practices have been discovered in a number of cases involving subsidiaries of Dutch companies. The Monopoly and Restrictive Trade Practices Commission in its two reports on Philips India Ltd., now Peico, has shown that the company undervalued the exports of its products to the parent company and its affiliates abroad (see Chapter 5). The exports of Century Enka in the late seventies, which were undertaken in order to fulfil some government requirements, to a great extent consisted of third party products, particularly fabrics, which were purchased for internal sales and exports. A close look at the export prices of the fabrics reveal that over a period of eight years (between 1974-1982), the company earned 11.6 million rupees less than what it paid for the products. Since all the purchases were actually exported, since the value of sales was not affected by adverse market fluctuations, and since the exports of fabrics was a very lucrative business in the second half of the 1970s, it would seem that Century Enka was involved in an obvious case of unhidden transfer pricing.

A plea often used in favour of foreign investments in

developing countries is that valuable foreign exchange can be earned through the exports of the companies with their world-wide marketing system. In the past, the policy of the government of India was directed more at import substitution than at exports. Hence, one could argue that the established companies as a rule were not export-oriented and consequently should not be assessed in terms of their export performance. Nevertheless the MNCs in their and that they fitted in with the new government strategy based on export promotion.

In the light of the importance which has been attached to the increase of exports by foreign companies, the data in Table 3.7 reveal an interesting picture. It appears that, contrary to official expectations, exports as a percentage of net sales have remained at a low level and that the trend is rather downward than upward. Lipton is actually the only company which exported a substantial part of its turnover, which is not surprising given the product line in which it operates. After 1983, its export ratio has come down substantially as a consequence of the take-over of the food production line of Hindustan Lever. The latter company, without the switch with Lipton, would have registered a more definite decline in exports than the table shows. Under the pressure of FERA regulations, HL's export had gone up to 14.9 per cent of sales in 1981. In retrospection, it would appear that the examplary performace in that period was linked to the impending government decision on whether Unilever would be allowed to retain the majority equity in view of its export record. Similar fluctuations have taken place in the case of Organon, prior to the government decision to allow a 49 per cent equity by AKZO-Organon, and in the case of Century Enka. The latter company was required to engage in exports as a repayment for the import of machinery in the mid-seventies. After the export obligation had been met, exports dropped to a very low level. Exports, it should be added, do not necessarily bring in hard currency. One-third of Hindustan Lever's exports and more than 90 per cent of Organon's went to the socialist bilateral rupee trade countries and do not really qualify as exports on account of the benefits of the world-wide trading mechanisms of the MNCs. They were rather the consequence of the preferential treatment which Indian products receive on the

**Table 3.7: Exports as Percentage of Net Sales (1974-1984)**

| Name of the company | 1974 | 1975 | 1976 | 1977 | 1978 | 1979 | 1980 | 1981 | 1982 | 1983 | 1984 |
|---|---|---|---|---|---|---|---|---|---|---|---|
| 1. Hindustan Lever | 9.5 | 7.2 | 8.0 | 6.8 | 6.3 | 9.9 | 10.8 | 14.9 | 9.9 | 8.8 | 10.9 |
| 2. Peico | 6.1 | 5.7 | 6.6 | 6.3 | 6.7 | 5.7 | 4.1 | 4.6 | 4.0 | 4.2 | 3.3 |
| 3. NOCIL | n.a. | 6.0 | 9.5 | 11.7 | 5.4 | n.a. | n.a. | 0.1 | 0.0 | 0.1 | 0.1 |
| 4. Lipton | n.a. | n.a. | n.a. | n.a. | 3.3 | 10.8 | 17.5 | 25.4 | 20.3 | 14.9 | 14.8 |
| 5. Century Enka | 5.2 | 4.0 | 3.3 | 8.9 | 2.4 | 2.7 | 1.5 | 0.4 | 0.6 | 0.5 | n.a. |
| 6. Organon (Infar) | 20.1 | 24.1 | 31.6 | 5.7 | 1.8 | 6.6 | 10.8 | 11.4 | n.a. | 14.3 | 8.4 |
| 7. Wavin | 2.4 | 4.5 | 23.2 | 27.7 | 18.6 | 8.2 | 2.5 | 4.6 | 3.2 | n.a. | n.a. |

*Source*: Annual Reports of the respective companies, as earlier tabulated by Van der Velden, Mitra and Lieten, 1983.

In the light of government stimulation, it is interesting to mention that as a reward for their exports, the MNCs received handsome subsidies, amounting to e.g. 20.0 per cent of the value of exports in the case of Peico and 25.6 per cent in the case of Century Enka in 1981. Export subsidies and duty drawback could possibly be treated as a new form of transfer pricing: the exporting company receives the normal price from the parent company but is compensated by the export subsidy which helps to increase the profits and, ultimately, the dividends transferred abroad.

In contrast to the rather low levels of exports of most companies, stands the overall increase in the import of raw materials, spares, components, etc. as a percentage of goods consumed during the production process (see Table 3.8). As important as the percentage of imports (Stovec: 70 per cent, Stormac: 48 per cent, Century Enka: 55 per cent, Organon: 30 per cent, Peico: 30 per cent in 1981) is the very substantial increase which has taken place during the last ten years. Recently, Hindustan Lever's imports appear to be diminishing, but most likely this is on account of the transfer of some business to Lipton India.

The rather high import content of the final output deserves some comment. Imports of capital goods and raw materials can make a necessary contribution to the developmental process in the sense that they initiate a value adding process of production.* In the case of our sample, all imports in 1980 and 1981 represented 15.1 per cent of the ultimate turnover which means that the imports had a multiplier effect of seven. In comparison with the period of a more strict economic regime of import substitution, the reliance on imports is definitely increasing. According to RBI figures, the import content in the total value of production between 1960 and 1970 decreased from 18.6 per cent to 6.5 per cent in the case of subsidiaries and from 23.1 per cent to 9.2 per cent in the

*The argument assumes that without the imports all or most industrial activities adding value to the particular imported materials would have fallen away. It also assumes that the resources employed in the project weve previously unused and do not replace resources previously employed in other seclors of the economy or even in the same product line.

**Table 3.8: Consumption of Imported Raw Materials, Spares and Components as Percentage of Total Inputs, Two Yearly Averages 1974-1984**

| Name of the Company | 1974-75 | 1976-77 | 1978-79 | 1980-81 | 1983-84 | Total Imports as % of output value, 1980-81 |
|---|---|---|---|---|---|---|
| 1. Hindustan Lever | 13 | 18 | 22 | 25 | 20 | 16.6 |
| 2. Peico | 17 | 21 | 22 | 30 | 33 | 7.4 |
| 3. Nocil | 4 | 6 | 6 | 9 | 14 | 5.4 |
| 4. Lipton | 1 | 1 | 2 | 1 | 3 | — |
| 5. Century Enka | 13 | 21 | 34 | 55 | 53 | 10.1 |
| 6. Organon (Infar) | 5 | 32 | 27 | 30 | 36 | 10.9 |
| 7. Elmi | 16 | 18 | 21 | 26 | 16 | 16.7 |
| 8. Hind lamps | 30 | 17 | 17 | 20 | n.a. | 9.3 |
| 9. Stovec Screens | 11 | 66 | 72 | 70 | n.a. | 25.7 |
| 10. Stormac | — | n.a. | 55 | 48 | n.a. | 25.1 |
| 11. Vicon | 30 | 9 | 16 | 23 | n.a. | 14.3 |
| 12. Wavin | 7 | 20 | 28 | 44 | n.a. | 39.0 |
| 13. Das Reprographics | n.a. | n.a. | 25 | 22 | n.a. | 9.3 |
| 14. Duphar Interfran | 23 | 29 | 33 | 18 | n.a. | 7.2 |
| 15. Kinetics Techn. | — | 3 | 5 | 3 | n.a. | 16.6 |

*Source*: Annual Reports of the Companies.

case of minority companies (RBI 1974, p. 14; see also RBI Bulletin 1984, April, p. 607). The new policy as reflected in Table 3.8 indicates that the trend since than has been reversed. Our conclusion would be that the activities of the MNC, in the absence of a strict import substitution regime, tie their local industrial production to the deliveries of semi-finished products from the Western world and push the fast growing sectors of Indian industry in the direction of the screwdriver-economy model.

### 3.3 Balance of Payment Implications

The concern with the balance of payment implications arises because of the scarcity of foreign exchange resources in developing countries and because of the financial reservoir in the hands of multinational corporations which could be diverted for productive purposes to countries in the third world.

While there are a number of advantages associated with the import of private foreign capital in the poorest non-industrialized countries of the world, the case in favour of import of foreign capital becomes rather complicated in a country like India. The latter not only has a vast industrial basis, but has also a reasonably high internal savings coefficient. Moreover, there is sufficient historical and recent evidence to show that India has paid a high price for the imported capital, and in the bargain, has lost precious foreign exchange reserves. This fact, as we have seen in chapter two, necessitated the government of India in 1973 to amend the Foreign Exchange Regulation Act (FERA) of 1947. The aim of the amendment to the Act was not only to regulate dealings in foreign exchange, as the 1947 act had aimed at, but to do this for "the conservation of foreign exchange resources of the country and the proper utilisation thereof in the interests of the economic development of the country" (Directorate of Enforcement 1977, p. 1).

It is not uncommon to look at the remittances by foreign companies on account of dividends, royalty and interest payments as the relevant headings revealing the foreign exchange losses. The remittances are, however, only one aspect of the balance of payment implications of foreign firms. The total effect is the aggregate of the current effect and the capital effect. These two effects correspond to the transactions occurring in the current and capital accounts of the country's balance of payments.*

*The current effect=f.o.b value of exports (X)—c.i.f. value of imports of capital goods, raw materials, and stores and spare parts (M)—transfer payments abroad (T) i.e., dividends, interest payments, royalties, technical know-how fees, technical service fees, etc., remitted abroad. The capital effect=inflow of equity capital net of capital liquidation (I)+inflow of loans, net of amortization (L).

The balance of payments account (X+I+L—M—T) will provide us with a neat idea of the yearly inflow or outflow of foreign exchange. The end result will have to be qualified in two ways. In the first place, since no figures are available for other multinational corporations or for indigenous industrial houses, the conclusions will not allow for comparisons.

Another factors qualifying our final results are the net savings accruing to the country on account of the import substituting effect. The substitution of imports by indigenous products may have been considerable in the case of some firms and of some products, although Table 3.8 earlier appears to suggest that import substitution has lost it momentum. Calculations of the effects are confronted with very tedious problems indeed, even if questions of the social relevance of the substituted imports would be excluded.

We have estimated the balance of payments effect for all the Dutch companies operating in India with an equity participation of at least twenty per cent. The Reserve Bank of India of considers this share ratio as the cut-off point sufficient for control. The annual reports of the companies, which contain the official accounting figures, were used as our source for computation. Information on the balance of payment effect was available for twelve companies for the period 1974-1978, including the four large companies Hindustan Lever, Peico, Century Enka and Nocil which accounted for 93 per cent of the the total assets. The remaining eight companies, with the exception of Lipton, with its two subsidiaries Brindavan and Heath, are relatively small (Organon Infar India and its subsidary Chefaro, Duphar, Wavin, Electric Lamp Manufacturers, Hind Lamps, Maschmeyer, Stovec Screens, Kinetics Technology and HL's subsidiary Indexport).

Over the period 1974-78, the twelve companies together appeared to produce a surplus on the current account of the order of Rs 7.39 crores (Rs 73.9 million). In this aggregation, the contribution of one company, Hindustan Lever, explains for the positive current effect. The foreign exchange loss in the trading operations of the other companies amounted to Rs 17.56 crores. The drain of surplus* totalled Rs 28 crores during the same period. The data in Table 3.9 indicate that the positive effect was only valid during the first years following on the enactment of FERA, and that towards the end of the 1970s, the balance started to become negative. In the next two chapters we shall investigate whether this negative trend has continued in case of the major companies Peico and Hindustan Lever. A very important caveat should however, already be introduced when interpreting these official figures. On the basis of a different set of official figures, we shall indeed come to a dramatically different conclusion.

The declared expenditure in foreign currency, generally, indicates *only the direct imports* at c.i.f. by the companies and excludes the imports which are routed through official canalising agencies, like the State Trading Corporation.** For information relating to these indirect imports, i.e. those routed through the canalising agencies, we have used the figures for the consumed value of imports, as reported in the balance sheets, for making the necessary adjustment.

We have calculated the imported value of consumption by the four largest companies (Hindustan Lever, Nocil, Peico and Century Enka) during the period 1974-1980. This works out to Rs 132.94 crores, which is considerably more than the direct exports during the same period, valued at Rs 61.84 crores. The four companies consumed Rs 78.10 crores indirect imports. If then, we include the indirect imports of just these four companies, *the apparent current account surplus of Rs 7.39 crores, turns into a real deficit of Rs 70.71 crores*. Hindustan Lever proudly advertised its foreign exchange performance and it indeed appeared to have had a positive contribution of Rs. 68.26 crores over the period 1973-80. The export earnings of Rs 141 crores compared favourably with the imports of Rs.

*The surplus (value) is value-added net of wage payments. This surplus can take different forms such as dividends, royalties, and technical know-how fees, technical service fees, interest payments and transfer pricing, as well as taxes. The total payments under these various heading constitute the drain of surplus.

**Public sector undertakings have the exclusive right to the import of a specified list of items, such as paper, petroleum products, fertilizers, drugs, oils, T.V. picture tubes, many chemicals, etc. In practice, the public sector agency purchases the goods abroad and sells them, often prior to import, to the purchasing company.

**Table 3.9: Direct Balance of Payment Effects of Dutch Investments in India, 1974-1978 (Rs million)**

| Year | Exports f.o.b. | Imports c.i.f. | | | | The Drain of Surplus | | | | | | Total Expenditure in foreign currency | Current effect |
|---|---|---|---|---|---|---|---|---|---|---|---|---|---|
| | | Raw materials | Spare parts | Capital Goods | Total direct imports | Dividend | Interest | Royalty | Commission Service Fees | Others | Total | | |
| 1974 | 181 | 87 | 9 | 20 | 118 | 20 | 9 | 6 | 6 | 2 | 43 | 162 | 20 |
| 1975 | 187 | 72 | 9 | 9 | 91 | 12 | 7 | 6 | 6 | 2 | 33 | 125 | 62 |
| 1976 | 253 | 76 | 17 | 34 | 127 | 48 | 2 | 7 | 12 | 3 | 71 | 199 | 54 |
| 1977 | 238 | 164 | 24 | 28 | 206 | 46 | 3 | 8 | 3 | 8 | 68 | 274 | —36 |
| 1978 | 247 | 143 | 25 | 37 | 205 | 47 | 4 | 6 | 7 | 3 | 67 | 272 | —26 |
| Total | 1106 | 542 | 83 | 119 | 748 | 173 | 25 | 33 | 34 | 18 | 284 | 1032 | 74 |

*Notes* : 1. The aggregate figure for imports includes miscellaneous imports also.
2. Imports include only the direct foreign transactions and are thus exclusive of the imported material purchased through government agencies and third parties.
3. Due to rounding, the aggregate may not tally.

*Source* : Sridhar Krishna et al., 1982.

59 crores and the drain of surplus of 20 crores. The positive current effect of Rs 69 crores, however, turns into a deficit if the indirect imports routed through the canalising agencies are included as well.

Summing up the various trends emerging from the individual firms and from the aggregate figures, it seems clear that the productive operations of multinational cooperations have a negative impact on the balance of payment situation. One could argue that this was to be expected since, after all, their presence in India did not originate as active export-oriented foreign exchange agents. Throughout the 1970s they were still functioning within the established import substitution policy as passive foreign exchange savers. The local production for the domestic market was supposed to replace the hitherto imported end products. Since more domestic value-added was expected to be created on the basis of imports of necessary raw materials and components, the balance between imports and exports should not necessarily be regarded as the decisive criterion for judging the performance. While we do recognize the logic of the argument, we have a number of reservations on the legitimacy of its application.

In the first place, there is the overriding question of the product mix of multinational corporations. A detailed investigation of the various consumer products, which are now indigenously produced, would establish that in most cases they were not quite necessary for development purposes. The ongoing addition of new products, imported or otherwise, is an open-ended process and turns the argument on import substitution into an open-ended discussion. Actually, Professor Paranjape, with specific reference to the two major products of Hindustan Lever, hydrogenated oils and non-soapy detergents, has argued that the government of India was induced to accept a permanent import liability for the indigenous production of items which were not needed. They actually replaced traditional local products (Indu Emencee 1983, p. 26).

In the second place, the natural evolution under conditions of a strict policy of import substitution, after the initial phase, would have to lead to a decreasing import content. As we have shown in Table 3.8 an opposite trend has been emerging in the 1970s. This reverse development need not necessarily be ascribed to the malintentions of the MNCs concerned. The gradual waning of government initiatives in building up an indigenous industrial infrastructure in combination with a pronounced liberalisation in the import policy have enabled firms to set up a production network without providing for the indigenisation of the inputs.

In the third place, the import substitution strategy would necessarily entail a relative increase in the share of imported capital goods in relation to raw materials and components. In Table 3.10, the aggregate share of the different components in the foreign exchange expenditure has been calculated for the period 1974-1978. The share of capital goods in the total imports turns out to be slightly less than sixteen per cent, with sharp fluctuation between the lowest point of around nine per cent in 1975 and 1977 and the highest peak of twenty-seven per cent in 1976. Although the time period is rather short, it seems to suggest that the import of capital goods is not growing in importance.

In the fourth place, as long as the closing of the foreign exchange gap is one of the benefits assigned to the operations of multinational corporations in developing countries, a gross foreign exchange evaluation as we have attempted remains a valid exercise.

The final point to be considered in this subsection is the capital account effect, which could not be properly estimated. Often the equity was acquired against the sale of goods or technical know-how without any payment of cash. Even if we would know what proportion of the equity has peen acquired in this manner, and decided to consider total capital flow rather than only the money flows, an accurate estimate of the inflow, would remain difficult. The equity may have been acquired at inflated prices of the goods sold or the technology transferred. We shall have to content ourselves with the figures as reported by the companies.

For most of the companies, the shareholdings have increased in this period, not because of additional inflow from abroad, but on account of bonus issues. Relative to the existing foreign equity share, part of the bonus shares were added to the foreign ownership.

Hindustan Lever's foreign contribution to equity, net of

**Table 3.10 : Share of the Different Components in the Foreign Exchange Expenditure of Dutch Companies in India 1974-1978 (%)**

| Year | Raw Materials | Spare parts & components | Capital goods | Total imports | Dividend | Interest | Royalty | Interest, Commission & Technical Fees | Others |
|---|---|---|---|---|---|---|---|---|---|
| 1974 | 53.9 | 5.3 | 12.5 | 73.0 | 12.4 | 5.6 | 3.7 | 3.8 | 1.4 |
| 1975 | 57.6 | 7.3 | 6.7 | 72.9 | 9.9 | 5.8 | 4.9 | 4.8 | 1.7 |
| 1976 | 38.3 | 8.3 | 17.3 | 63.9 | 23.9 | 1.0 | 3.5 | 6.0 | 1.6 |
| 1977 | 59.8 | 8.9 | 6.5 | 75.3 | 17.0 | 1.0 | 2.8 | 0.9 | 2.9 |
| 1978 | 52.5 | 9.1 | 13.8 | 75.3 | 17.1 | 1.6 | 2.2 | 2.5 | 1.1 |
| Total | 52.5 | 8.1 | 11.5 | 72.3 | 16.8 | 2.5 | 3.1 | 3.2 | 1.9 |

*Source* : Sridhar Krishna et al., 1982.

bonus issues, in 1980 stood at Rs 42.3 million. This could be taken to be the inflow of capital from Unilever over the lifespan of the company. During the 1970s the total flow of fresh equity from abroad amounted to Rs 14.4 million. The return cash-flow in the form of dividends was significantly higher, namely Rs 164.6 million. During the eight-year period 1973-1980, the total drain of surplus (including royalty payments and service fees) was Rs 203.2 million, i. e. around fifteen times higher than the net inflow of capital during the same period. In the case of Nocil the total capital inflow over the lifespan of the company was Rs 30.2 million. During the period 1974-1980 alone, four times more cash (Rs 111.8 million) was expatriated on account of dividends and technical service payments. This was also the case with Peico, which since its start in the early thirties had a total capital inflow of Rs 18.5 million and a drain of surplus of Rs. 90.5 million in the restricted period 1973-1979.

It is clear that the remittance of dividend has continued to grow after the enactment of the FERA in 1974. The total return flow on account of dividends remitted abroad is conditioned by the profitability of the company, the percentage of non-residential shareholding and the ratio of profits retained to the profits transferred abroad. The latter, as a percentage of the non-residential contribution to the paid-up capital has been on the increase. In 1974, the remittances amounted to 22.7 per cent of the total Dutch equity, net of bonus issues, in the concerned companies. The ratio gradually increased to 39.2 per cent in 1977 and then went down to 32.8 per cent in 1980. For some of the individual companies separately, the ratio has been considerably higher. In 1977 Hindustan Lever set an all-time record by repatriating to its parent company Unilever profits equal to 75.6 per cent of its foreign equity stock. The ratio in relation to the total value of the foreign shareholding, i.e. including the bonus issues accruing to the parent company was less dramatic, but nevertheless fairly high, e.g. 21.8 per cent in the case of Hindustan Lever in 1977. The calculations of outflow of profits have been done on account of the payments of dividends only. The use of a broader definition of profit flows could include payments on royalty, interest and service and commission fees. These categories in the period 1974-1978 amounted to Rs 111 million as against Rs 173 million on account of dividend transfers by the companies in the sample. Lall and Streeten (1977, p. 141) have calculated this total drain of surplus (servicing costs in their terminology) net of fresh capital inflows in relation to sales, and arrived at a negative result of 0.3 per cent for their country sample in the late sixties. In our sample, the four major Dutch companies had a negative effect of between 0.9 per cent (Century Enka and HL) and 1.7 per cent (Philips and Nocil).

The figures can obviously be interpreted in two ways. One school of thought will tend to stress that the firms have indeed transferred sizeable amounts to their parent companies, but nevertheless have reinvested a significant percentage of the profits in the country. The result is seen as a reciprocal advantage for both the MNCs and for the Indian economy. The ploughing back of profits indicates that the operation of the corporate affiliates do follow a strategy of profit-use for local expansion, which is considered as being more advantage than a situation of a predominant drain of profit. The opposite school of thought, while recognising the advantage of re-investments for the national economy, stresses the absolute as well as relative drain of profits in itself. The argument concerns for example the profit repatriation by Hindustan Lever to Unilever equal to 75 per cent of its exported equity stock in HL rather than the high share of profits retained by HL for further local expansion, irrespective of the nature of that expansion.

We have preferred to concentrate on the transfer of foreign exchange because of the wider implications for economic policy. The widening of the foreign exchange gap indeed creates various kinds of problems. In a number of cases it has led to a change in policy towards a more liberal regime in line with the development strategy of the International Monetary Fund. Since multinational corporations may logically be expected to favour such an open border policy, it makes sense to establish whether the companies concerned are sharing the responsibility for the balance of payments deficit or not. In that case, the liberalisation of the economic regime would be a result of their own creation. From our analysis of the profits retained and the profits distributed, it does not follow that the foreign companies are shifting towards a policy of increasing re-investing instead of taking out profits. Both operations appear to go hand in hand. Some figures relating to Philips illustrate this point. In 1977, the company's remittances were equal to 12.9 of its own equity and 4.0 per cent of the net worth of the company. In 1982, the comparative figures were 13.5 per cent and 1.6 per cent. The latter figure was abnormally low on account of a steep increase which occurred in the reserves fund. What seems to have happened is that the non-resident shareholders continue to repatriate the returns on their share-capital, which are fixed at a rather high level, and at the same time expand the financial basis of the company through a growing volume of reinvested profits. In the next section, we shall have a closer look at the different sources of finance.

### 3.4. Financing Policies

As far as the financing policies of the Dutch companies are concerned, we have considered only one issue, namely the relative importance of the different sources of finance for investment by these companies. They have been divided in internal, local and foreign sources, and contain the following funds:

1. *internal*: reserves and surpluses (including bonus issues), and accumulated depreciation.* Retained profits and

*Is accumulated depreciation a source of finance, for the growth of the firm? There is one view (Chaudhury 1979b) that though depreciation is a provision for the replacement of the assets, the distinction between replacement and new investment is often vague. The worn-out machine might not actually be replaced, while the fund of accumulated depreciation, would be available for financing new investment. There is a second view (Manser 1973) that in an age of rapid technological obsolescence the old machine is never really replaced, but an entirely different machine takes its place (which could presumably happen before the machine wears out), embodying a superior and different technology. Either way, depreciation could be viewed as an additional source of finance for the growth of the firm.

that part of it which had been capitalised, have been treated as an internal source, even though there may be foreign claims over this in terms of ownership;

2. *local*: the issue of equity shares and borrowings from the local banks and financial institutions and from local capital markets, in the form of debentures and fixed deposits;
3. *foreign*: borrowings from international banks and financial institutions, from the parent company or its affiliates abroad and inflow of equity capital from the parent.

Virtually the entire finance of the eleven companies* during 1973-80 which have been tabulated in Table 3.11 came from local and internal sources. Reserves and surpluses, including bonus issues, accounted for 43.9 per cent of the total finance and accumulated depreciation for 42.3 per cent. Local banks and financial institutions provided approximately 6 per cent of total finance. Debentures and fixed deposits accounted for about 7.5 per cent and the local equity shares about 3.6 per cent. The annual reports of the companies have been the only source of information on their finance, and not all the foreign loans incurred by these companies are reported in these reports. The limited inflow of foreign equity and the repayment of foreign loans caused a negative foreign contribution to the gross investment over the period under consideration. The flow position indicates that the cash transfer was particularly significant in the year 1975-76, following on the enactment of the FERA in 1973. If we consider the stock position, which

*Information on finances was available for 18 companies, over varying periods. Information for the period 1973-80 was available for the following 11 companies: Hindustan Lever, NOCIL, Peico, Century Enka, ELMI, Kinetics Technology India Ltd., Duphar Interfran, Organon, Indexport, Wavin India and Chefaro Pharmaceuticals. Information was also available for Burmah Shell, Hind Lamps, Maschmeyer, Stovec Screens, Lipton, Brindavan Properties and Heath and Company, but for different periods. The data on these companies have therefore not been included in the aggregate data of Table 3.11.

**Table 3.11 : Sources of Funds of Indo-Dutch Multinationals (Flow Position, 1973-1980, Rs. 1000)**

| Period | Reserves and surpluses incl. bonus issues | Col. 2 Col. 24 % | Depreciation | Col. 4 Col. 24 % | Total internal | Local Banks & Financial Institutions | Col. 7 Col. 24 % | ICICI |
|---|---|---|---|---|---|---|---|---|
| 1 | 2 | 3 | 4 | 5 | 6 | 7 | 8 | 9 |
| 1973-74 | 201746 | 81.16 | 77874 | 31.40 | 112.76 | —2163 | —.87 | —2913 |
| 1974-75 | 17129 | 21.36 | 85066 | 106.38 | 127.44 | —13932 | —17.33 | 752 |
| 1975-76 | 23165 | 12.72 | 91510 | 129.25 | 161.97 | —30192 | —42.64 | —842 |
| 1976-77 | 86025 | 35.86 | 93228 | 38.87 | 74.33 | 38009 | 15.84 | 3470 |
| 1977-78 | 162768 | 56.69 | 107117 | 17.32 | 93.91 | 10711 | 3.72 | 9335 |
| 1978-79 | 181641 | 46.14 | 126678 | 32.32 | 78.66 | 38087 | 14.82 | —1333 |
| 1979-80 | 193742 | 33.53 | 252231 | 43.66 | 77.19 | 56776 | 9.83 | —4423 |
| 1973-80 | 866216 | 43.95 | 833924 | 42.11 | 86.26 | 117296 | 5.95 | 4046 |

(*Contd.*)

*Notes*:

1. The individual percentages may not, when added, amount to 100% because of rounding.
2. The companies included are Hindustan Lever, NOCIL, PEICO, Century Enka, ELMI, Kinetics Technology India Ltd., Duphar Interfran, Organon, Indexport, Wavin India and Chefaro-Pharmaceutical Private Ltd.

*Source* : Annual Reports of the respective companies; Sridhar Krishna, 1982.

**Table 3. 11 : (*Contd.*)**

| Period | Col. 9 Col. 24 % | Borrowing from local capital | Col. 11 Col. 24 % | Local contribution to equity net of bonus issues | Col. 13 Col. 24 % | Total local | Local & internal | Foreign Banks & Financial Institutions |
|---|---|---|---|---|---|---|---|---|
| 1 | 10 | 11 | 12 | 13 | 14 | 15 | 16 | 17 |
| 1973-74 | 0.5 | 1298 | 0.52 | —630 | —0.26 | —1.77 | 110.92 | —4022 |
| 1974-75 | 21.0 | 16854 | 21.02 | —30 | —0.04 | 4.67 | 132.11 | —1824 |
| 1975-76 | —17.8 | —12624 | —17.83 | 14361 | 20.28 | —41.38 | 120.59 | —2828 |
| 1976-77 | 5.8 | 13978 | 5.83 | 669 | 0.28 | 23.40 | 98.13 | 1953 |
| 1977-78 | —1.5 | —4561 | —1.58 | 13731 | 4.77 | 10.15 | 104.06 | —2302 |
| 1978-79 | 4.9 | 19389 | 4.95 | 11385 | 3.41 | 22.85 | 101.50 | —1701 |
| 1979-80 | 19.7 | 114295 | 19.78 | 29926 | 5.18 | 14.03 | 111.22 | —7859 |
| 1973-80 | 7.5 | 148629 | 7.54 | 71412 | 3.62 | 17.32 | 103.58 | —2053 |

(*Contd.*)

**Table 3.11 : (*Contd.*)**

| Period | Col. 17 Col. 24 % | Loans from Parent | Col. 19 Col. 24 % | Foreign contribution to equity net of bonus issues | Col. 21 Col. 24 % | Foreign % | Finance for gross investment |
|---|---|---|---|---|---|---|---|
| 1 | 18 | 19 | 20 | 21 | 22 | 23 | 24 |
| 1973-74 | —1.62 | —23852 | —9.61 | 630 | 0.25 | —10.98 | 247768 |
| 1974-75 | —2.27 | —23851 | —29.74 | 30 | 0.04 | —31.97 | 80194 |
| 1975-76 | —3.99 | —23852 | —33.69 | —13148 | —18.57 | —56.25 | 70798 |
| 1976-77 | 0.81 | —23855 | —9.35 | 26351 | 10.99 | 1.85 | 239831 |
| 1977-78 | —0.8 | —23852 | —8.12 | 14440 | 5.02 | —3.90 | 287607 |
| 1978-79 | —0.94 | — | — | —2162 | —0.35 | 1.49 | 391984 |
| 1979-80 | 1.36 | 61159 | 10.59 | —18103 | —3.13 | 8.82 | 577744 |
| 1973-80 | —1.04 | —58101 | —2.94 | 8038 | 0.40 | —3.58 | 1896126 |

contains the different sources of funds used before 1973 as well, the impact of the present trend stands out clearly. Whereas internal sources in 1973 represented only 67 per cent of the gross investments, in 1980 it had gone up to 76 per cent. Since the average share of local funds remained at the same level, a corresponding fall in the share of foreign sources has occurred. The fall looks quite dramatic, from 13.7 per cent in 1973 to 4.9 per cent in 1980, but is less on account of a decreasing share of equity (from 6 per cent to3.2 per cent) than on account of dwindling loans. The latter development could signify a run on local sources of finance. From the flow position in Table 3.11 it appears that during the last couple of years, this has been very much the case. In the years 1978-79 and 1979-80 the total loan fund from the local finance market, exclusive of the Industrial Credit and Investment Corporation of India which reroutes largely foreign loans, provided for respectively 19.8 and 29.6 per cent of the total additional funds. Although the net call on indigenous resources does not yet amount to a drain of local savings, the present trend, if it continues, could go in that direction.

We shall presently look at some of the major companies in somewhat more detaial on the basis of Sridhar Krishna et al., 1982 and 1982a. Over the period 1969-80, 92 per cent of the funds of Hindustan Lever accrued from local and internal sources, and the remaining 8 per cent accrued from foreign sources. Internal sources accounted for 85.6 per cent of the total finances. For the period as a whole, the borrowings from the local capital markets in the form of debentures and fixed deposits, were generally insignificant, but during particular years, for example in 1974-75, this source accounted for 18.7 per cent of the total finance. Hindustan Lever borrowed from the local banks and institutions only during 1978-79 and 1979-80. During the former year, this source accounted for 10 per cent of the total finance. It incurred a loan from its parent only in one year, 1979-80, of Rs 6.1 crores. The gross investment during the period under review was Rs 95.7 crores, 79 per cent of which was accounted for by additions to gross fixed assets, 21 per cent by net current assets and 0.14 per cent by investment in subsidiaries and other companies.

The entire finance of NOCIL during the period 1971-80 came from local and internal sources. Reserves and surpluses, including bonus issues, accounted for 52 per cent of the total finance. The borrowings from local capital markets provided 17 per cent of the total finance during the entire period 1971-80. In particular years, the local banks and financial institutions, were another important source of finance: around 40 per cent of the total finance during 1976-77, 15.5 per cent of the total finance during 1978-79, and a little over 30 per cent of the total finance during 1979-80. The gross investment during this period was Rs. 59.9 crores, of which 57 per cent was accounted for by gross fixed asset formation, 43 per cent by net current assets, and only 0. 4 per cent by investments in subsidiaries and other companies.

Virtually, the entire finance of Peico during the period 1971-80 accrued from local and internal sources. Internal sources accounted for 77 per cent of the total finances. Reserves and surpluses, including bonus issues, accounted for 42 per cent approximately and accumulated depreciation for 35 per cent. During the entire period 1971-80, the borrowings from local capital markets accounted for 16.7 per cent of the total finance, particularly on account of borrowings durings 1979-80, when this source accounted for 59 per cent of the funds of that year. Foreign sources provided only 0.1 per cent of the total finance during the entire period 1971-80. Gross investment during the period 1971-80 was Rs 42.9 crores, 57 per cent of which went into gross fixed asset formation; net current assets took up 41 per cent and investments in subsidiaries and other companies only 1 per cent.

During 1973-81, Century Enka's finances came entirely from local and internal sources. Reserves and surpluses, including bonus issues, accounted for 76 per cent and accumulated depreciation accounted for 27.7 per cent. Whereas borrowings from local banks and financial institutions occurred only in one year (1975-76) it borrowed consistently from the local capital markets during 1974-81. For the entire period 1973-81, this source, however, provided only 2.3 per cent of the total finance. The gross investment during this period was Rs 26 crores, which was entirely accounted for by additions to gross fixed assets.

**Table 3.12: Profit Allocations (1973-1985)**

| Name of the company | 1973-74 | | 1977-78 | | 1981-1982 | | 1984-85 | |
|---|---|---|---|---|---|---|---|---|
| | Distributed | Retained | Distributed | Retained | Distributed | Retained | Distributed | Retained |
| Hindustan Lever | 67 | 33 | 44 | 56 | 37 | 63 | 53 | 47 |
| Peico | 26 | 74 | 61 | 39 | 51 | 49 | 79 | 21 |
| Nocil | 150 | —50 | 47 | 53 | 44 | 56 | 28 | 72 |
| Century Enka | 33 | 77 | 92 | 8 | 29 | 71 | 27 | 73 |
| Organon | 48 | 52 | 42 | 58 | 33 | 67 | 52 | 48 |
| Duphar Interfran | 40 | 60 | 43 | 57 | 47 | 53 | 45 | 55 |
| Hind lamps | 53 | 47 | 33 | 66 | 43 | 57 | n.a. | n.a. |
| ELMI | 89 | 11 | 0 | 100 | 0 | 100 | n.r. | n.r. |
| Wavin | 18 | 82 | n.a. | n.a. | 13 | 87 | n.r. | n.r. |
| Stovec Screens | — | — | 0 | 100 | 33 | 67 | n.a. | n.a. |
| Stormac | — | — | n.a. | n.a. | 38 | 62 | 31 | 69 |

*Note* : n.r. : not relevant in view of losses (either before or after allocation for investment allowance reserves).

*Source* : Annual Reports of the companies, in Van der Velden et al. 1983.

The ploughing back of profits into the business instead of distributiong it leads directly to the productive application of the surplus generated. In countries like India, where money resources are still to a large extent channelled into conspicuous consumption and merchant-cum-lending activities, such a policy has a positive impact on development. The transfer of the resources to the investment allowance reserve funds within the company before declaring the profits, on the other hand depresses the profits considerably and thereby reduces the tax liabilities. In other words, it allocates to the private enterprises resources which otherwise would have accrued to the public government fund and could be applied for general purposes.

We have in this section observed that Dutch MNCs acquire their resources largely through internal funds, i.e. depreciation and ploughing back of profits. In Table 3.12 some more details are given on the profit allocation by the various companies. All of them appear to apply fluctuating ratios, in some cases retaining as much as hundred per cent of the profits and in some cases distributing most of it. In the majority of cases, particularly in recent years, at least half of the profits after tax and after deductions for the investment allowance reserve, were retained by the companies. This seems to be generally on the high side, particularly in comparison with the aggregate results for the corporate seetor.* As a consequence, the share of the shareholders' reserves has become more important than the paid-up capital. In 1985, ratio was 71 to 28 for Hindustan Lever, 69 to 31 for Peico, 66 34 for Nocil, and 71 to 29 for Century Enka.

On the basis of the data on the working of the Dutch multinational corporations in India, it can be concluded that in terms of growth and profitability, the results tend to

*In 1978-79 there were 7515 public limited companies (Rs 126 billion assets; 2.8 million employees), 8367 private limited companies (Rs 18 billion assets; 0.9 million employees) and 1676 public corporations (Rs. 68 million assets; 0.7 million employees). In the industrial sector as a whole, they account for slightly more than two-thirds of the assets and slightly less of the generated employment (Annual Survey of Industries 1979, pp. 10-11).

move above the industrial averages. This in itself is a certificate of successful performance potentially beneficial to the economy. The question can be posed whether on the other hand, a number of costs associated with the operations, like e.g. the foreign exchange loss, will be matched with sufficient advantages in order to advocate the existing arrangement on economic grounds. On the basis of a close study of two specific companies operating in India—Unilever and Philips—we shall in the following chapters attempt to draw a more detailed picture of the issues at stake.

# 4

# *Hindustan Lever*

Hindustan Lever is the Indian affiliate of a double-structured parent company operating with an identical Board of Management from Rotterdam and London. The parent company, Unilever, was formed in 1929, and, as a leading manufacturer of margarine, soaps, detergents, and other consumer products, has grown into one of the top multinational corporations in the world.

The soap export business to India by Lever Brothers, the British branch of the later Unilever company, started in the last decade of the nineteenth century. In 1913, Levers registered its Indian trade business as Lever Brothers (India) Ltd. By then, together with Gossages and Crossfields, it had wrested almost total control of soap export to India. The latter company eventually was taken over by Levers which still had to confront a competition from two local companies, the North West Soap Factory and the Premier Soap Factory. Both these companies, who provided the Indian market with soap of a lower quality than the imported Lever soaps, were acquired from their owners, the Boulton Bank, during the early twenties. A new factory was commissioned in 1934 at Sewree (Bombay) at an estimated cost of £ 1.5 lakh. The original plan to start the new company, merging the three above-mentioned divisions, on the basis of sixty per cent Indian share capital and involving Indians in the management, was ultimately shelved in favour of a fully-owned subsidiary (Fieldhouse 1978, pp. 148-149).

By the end of the second world war, Lever Brothers (India) commanded more than half of the soap market. After independence, the Indian Soap Manufacturers Association, which united some major indigenous entrepreneurs like Godrej and

Tata, started a movement against the continuing presence of Levers on the Indian market. The reaction, in the form of a price cut, brought about the fizzling out of the movement.

In the meantime, Unilever had started another subsidiary, namely Hindustan Vanaspati Manufacturing Company Ltd. The story of HVM dates back to the end of the first world war, when Margarine Unie, the Dutch manufacturers of vegetable ghee (*vanaspati*) entered the Indian market. Their product, a substitute for *desi ghee* (melted butter), because of its low price, frequently came to be used by Indian traders for purposes of adulteration.

In 1931, a factory with a nominal capital of hundred thousand pounds was started at Bombay. The erection of tariff barriers for hydrogenated vegetable oil (although not for edible oil), and for soaps may have induced the English and Dutch companies to move the production process to India. As a matter of fact, as Fieldhouse (1978, pp. 170-172) seems to suggest, the decision to increase the tariff was taken by the government in London in 1930, after managers of Van Den Bergh's Margarine Unie had concluded that the decision to set up a factory in India would depend upon "an assurance" from a reliable government source that an increase in duty would be granted. The emerging evidence that an Indian-owned firm, Ganesh Flour Mills, was planning to set up a vegetable ghee plant, and the threat of a new alternative source of imports for adulterative purposes, namely whale oil from Japan, were other important considerations why local production should be started.

The growing Indian market made the new enterprise into a lucrative undertaking. The sales of ghee grew from 11,000 tonnes in 1935 to 43,000 tonnes in 1940, but stagnated afterwards. Whereas the profitability of LB (I) remained rather low at around ten per cent on capital employed, the earnings of HVM grew from a mere 11.8% in 1935 to 79% in 1938 (Fieldhouse 1978, p. 177). Unfortunately for HVM, the government during the war years took some steps unfavourable for the growth of the vanaspati industry. It declared that vanaspati was an essential item, and that its production and price should be regulated. Afterwards, the profitability of HVM temporarily declined. The shortage of and the high price to be paid for imported edible oil induced the company to change over to the use of mutton tallow—at least so went the rumour—which resulted in a Hindu aversion for the products of HVM. Its share in the total vanaspati market dropped from 64% in 1940 to 24% ten years later.

With the emergence of the independent Republic of India, some measures were taken to control the operations of foreign and local business houses. Fieldhouse (1978, pp. 186-189) has argued that a number of these measures hindered the further development of HVM and Lever Brothers. Some of the measures, like the foreign exchange control, price control, the industrial licensing policy, the tax policy, etc., have become basic elements of the policy framework in India and will be discussed at a later stage. Suffice it to mention that the high tariff walls erected by the government were in fact beneficial to the company. Both soaps and vanaspati were insulated from foreign competition, and since the two subsidiaries of Unilever had already attained a strong position in both product lines, it profited fully from the import restriction measures (Usha Menon 1986).

The two separate production branches of Unilever, LB and HVM, together with United Traders Ltd, a trading company, were, at the management level, integrated in 1944. The second phase of integration came just before going public in 1956 when the amalgamation of the three subsidiaries into one public company was approved by the government. So was the Memorandum of Association. The Company Law Administration, despite the then apparent nationalist bias in the Indian policy framework, approved of the various clauses in the memorandum, and thereby put an official stamp on Unilever's intention to engage in all possible production, trading, financing and consulting activities in the fields of soaps, oils, food products, printing, etc.

It shored up Unilever's confidence in the pliability of the Nehru government : "This confidence in the basic moderation of Indian nationalists proved fully justified...; and during the early 1950s the hostility of Indian private capital gradually evaporated" (Fieldhouse 1978, p. 186).

The approval was not accidental. Even after the enactment of the Monopoly and Restrictive Trade Practices (MRTP) Act in 1969, the company was allowed to expand its activities by further including two more clauses in its memorandum :

(i) Manufacturing, assembling, designing, constructing, servings and dealing in all kinds of plants, machinery, instrument, appliances apparatus, utensils and tools for commercial, scientific, industrial and other purposes. Manufacture of accessories, requisites, facilities and supplies of necessary or useful items in connection with any of them.

(ii) to carry on business as manufacturer and dealer in paper, pulp board of all kinds, synthetic fibre, plastic and rubber goods of all kinds, metal etc." (Amendment of memorandum, 1973).

## 4.1 Related Interests

With the memorandum approved by the government of India, the company had prepared the legal groundwork for its further expansion. In the next pages, we shall analyse how that expansion and modification took place. That assessment, however, cannot be complete without a reference to the direct linkages with other companies of which the most important are the advertising agency Lintas (sold in 1981), Indexport, Lipton India Ltd., Naarden Chemical Works (taken over in 1986), Brooke Bond (taken over in 1984 after an equity participation of 4.5% equity was established earlier) and a number of small-scale soap units which remain formally independent. In addition, HL exercises indirect control over *Sharpedge Ltd*. The concern is engaged in the production of Erasmic brand razor blades, a product which is actually reserved for the small-scale sector. The technology was brought from a Unilever subsidiary in France in the mid-sixties, and was first proposed to the Indian company Escorts, which had the necessary machinery know-how. The anxiety of HL to bring the Erasmic blades to India should be traced to its own production of Erasmic shaving cream. HL, which has got a Rs. 3.5 Lakh equity participation, claims not to exercise any control over the company, but cannot deny a quite direct personal involvement : the Delhi branch manager of HL (R.S. Talwar) in December 1980 moved over to Sharpedge Ltd as its general manager (*Hamara*, January 1981).

*Indexport Limited* has been registered as a company trading third party products and handling HL's exports. The capital employed and fixed assets in 1981 were as low as Rs. 2.2 and Rs. 0.9 lakh respectively. Till 1975, Indexport was the vehicle of the HL export trade. As a consequence of a change in the government policy on export houses, HL took over the export activities directly. Indexport was, however, kept alive "because the question of what export will be recognised as the company's own export and what export will not be allowed was left a little big vague.... So we kept Indexport alive in order to decide our course of action, depending on how the government's attitude develops" (Dutta 1982, p. 31). In 1979, the activities of Indexport were rekindled. The exports of animal feed, detergents, textiles, agricultural commodities, engineering goods, etc., which had formed the mainstay of activities till 1974 (when Rs. 94 million was traded) were stopped and replaced by the export of marine products (Rs. 13 million in 1981). The percentage of Indexport's foreign exchange earnings to the total of HL has come down from 61% in 1974 (at the time of the FERA enactment) to less than 2% in 1981. The development indicates that a considerable part of the exports of HL, for which it has received FERA relaxations, derives from the earlier Indexport business. An interesting feature of the subsidiary company is that, despite the fact that it is involved in admittedly lucrative foreign trade sectors, there was only one single year between 1973 and 1982 in which it did not suffer losses.

From 1982 onwards, the performance of Indexport has changed dramatically. Sales went up steeply and reached a record level of more than Rs. 303 million in 1983 of which only roughly two-thirds was exported. A comparison with the export data of HL itself (Table 4.2) shows that exports of the daughter company are valued at between one-fifth and two-fifth of the exports by the parent company. This would seem strange in view of the fact that the mother company is still very far removed from attaining its export obligation as a FERA company. Since gross profits remain low, Indexport is not useful to HL as a source of dividends either. Why then is an increasing percentage of exports routed through its subsidiary? A closer look at the exported products (margarine, marine products, carpets, textile sheetings, cashew nuts and footwear) may suggest an answer. In one year, the textile sheeting was purchased at Rs. 116 million and sold at Rs. 115 million. Marine products were purchased at Rs. 82 million and, after processing, sold at Rs. 84 million. Cashew kernels were sold at a loss. Footwear and carpets were exported at a price hardly fifteen per cent above the purchasing price. Since Indexport, unlike Levindra Trust Ltd. and Hindlever Trust Ltd., is not a charitable organisation and since no capital has been sunk (paid-up capital is 3 lakh) so as to make sales even at break-even rate compulsory, serious doubts emerge as to where the operation becomes profitable. The foreign trading partner is most likely the beneficiary of a transfer pricing mechanism.

*Lipton India Limited* is the major sister concern of HL. Formally it is directly related to Unilever, which holds forty per cent of the Rs. 157.5 million equity. After 1979, with the appointment of C.R. Shah, a director of HL as an additional director to Lipton, the interaction between the two managements was initiated, ultimately leading to the shuffling of business in 1983, as was already mentioned in Chapter 3. The company controls 30% of the Indian packaged tea market (together with the other Unilever company Brooke Bond 80%), and 10% of the total tea market. Lipton India (earlier Lipton Tea) is one of the oldest tea companies in India. Thomas Lipton started his tea operations in India as far back as 1883, and today, together with its two subsidiaries, Heath & Co. and Brindavan Properties, constitutes the single biggest tea business of Lipton International (Blend 1978, p. 6), which is a consolidated company under Unilever. Lipton (India) Ltd. became a fully-owned subsidiary of Unilever in 1972. The company till 1983 had two tea blending and packaging factories at Kidderpore (Calcutta) and at Ambattur (Madras), employing 1800 people, including 250 people in the fifteen years' old sophisticated plant at Ambattur. Since the mid-seventies, the company has started laying off workers and has started shifting some of its production to small-scale units.*

Hindustan Lever, apart from the above-mentioned cases, has also a number of direct linkages with fisheries and agricultural activities. HL directly or indirectly manages a dozen prawn farms in coastal western and eastern India (For the requirements of Indexport), and the milk production around Etah for the local HL milk factory. It is now planning to promote oil palm plantations in coastal Andhra, Kerala and parts of Tamil Nadu, besides the Andaman and Nicobar Islands which, according to the present chairman of the company, Dr. Ganguly, offer "excellent and practically unlimited posssibilities" (Economic Times, 26 June 1982).

In the seventies, HL had received great praise and, besides tax concessions, the goodwill of the government of India for processing sal seed as a substitute for cocoa butter. Sal seed is a forest product in eastern India. In the early seventies, HL claimed the credit for developing the use of the seed commercially : "Sal seed which has been rotting on the forest floor for centuries, has now changed the health of the tribal economy" (HL, annual report, 1972). The seed, apart from earning foreign exchange through exports, was used as a substitute for imported tallow in the production of soaps.

A cursory look at the claims put forward raises a number of questions. In the first place, the technology for extracting sal seeds was not developed by the Andheri research centre of the company, but by the state-run Regional Research Centre at

*The employment in the Calcutta factory has come down from 2100 in 1971 to 1500 in 1982. Drawn-out strikes, like the 5 months in 1979, were directed against the installation of the Electronic Data Processing Machinery, which has been postponed for the time being, and the decentralisation process. The company indeed, as the second best alternative to the process of automation, has been shifting part of its business to small-scale units in Pune, Nellore and Hyderabad (Medchal and Uppal). The wage levels (Rs. 10 per day minus deductions), educational levels, working conditions and degree of organisation fall far behind those of the official factories.

Hyderabad* (Usha Menon 1982). The technology was handed over to the Orissa Joineries and Contractors Private Ltd. who was probably the first to extract the sal seed commercially. Afterwards HL came in and contracted a number of firms to deliver to them directly. In the second place, the utilisation of the seed for oil production was first undertaken by the industries run by the Khadi and Village Gramodyog Commission. The excellent public relations and advertisement strategy of HL rather than its well equipped research centre ensured that, however, the company got all the praise for the technological breakthrough.

In the third place, the question should be asked whether and to what extent the tribal economy thrived on the new sal seed economy. HL claims the credit for giving employment to hundreds of *adivasis* (tribals) in the interior of Orissa. Our investigations have delivered a somewhat different picture. The sal seeds were certainly not "rotting on the forest floor for centuries". Sal seed collection has taken place since time immemorial during the two months' procurement season just before the onset of the monsoon. Nowadays the traders during those couple of weeks come to the village *hats* (weekly markets), and offer 50 to 75 paise a kilo for raw seeds and 25 paise for extracted seeds. The tribals have their own traditional system of extraction, which after all leaves enough oil behind to be further processed industrially. From our survey in 12 villages in three districts, we gathered that many tribals do not prefer to exchange their seeds for either salt or money. It is mainly young adivasis who take their collections to the traders, often

*The first patent relating to the purification of sal seed oil was submitted in June 1970 by four researchers of the Oil Technology Research Institute at Anantapur (Patent Office Calcutta, nr. 127314). Its claim was accepted within one year. A somewhat different process with a similar aim, the decolorisation of sal fat in order to make it suitable for soap production, was submitted by HL in July 1972 (nr. 137097). It took almost three years before it was accepted by the patent office. The Anantapur researchers had developed the process and had indicated the usefulness of the solvent extraction :

"The property of sal seed oil makes it eminently suitable in the raw state itself for soap preparation. The fatty acid moiety of sal seed oil or fat is indicative of its suitability as a substitute for cocao butter in chocolates and other confections."

for thriftful spending. As A.K. Rath (1982, p. 136) reports: "Sal oil, being their only cooking medium is collected by the adivasis mainly for that purpose. . . . In this way it can be said that the commercialisation has rather hampered the tribal economy than doing any good to it. In some cases, it was noticed that the young adivasis physically confront the elderly one for the collection of the seeds".

Indeed, before the commercialisation of the sal seed, an adivasi family would extract about thirty kilo of oil per season which would suffice for their cooking purposes. Nowadays, to compensate for their shortfall, they have to purchase from the market *Dalda* cooking oil, a product of Hindustan Lever, at a price which is at least the twentyfold of the price they get for one kilo of unextracted sal seed. One can therefore hardly conclude that the sal chapter of HL has helped either the tribal economy or the individual adivasi households.

## 4.2 The Process of Indianisation

The formation of Hindustan Lever Ltd. in 1956 heralded the beginning of the so-called process of Indianisation of the company. At that time, ten per cent equity shares were offered to the Indian public. In the meantime, the Indianisation of management had also started. This was done partially in response to an official circular requesting all foreign companies to start recruiting Indians at the decision-making levels. The process, however, had started well before independence and was particularly speeded up by the wartime shortage of trained European managers. In 1942, the company decided that "Indians who prove themselves qualified to do so should enjoy privileges equal to the Europeans they substitute" (Fieldhouse 1978, pp. 192-193). By 1944 there were 15 Indians at the management level out of the total of 57. At the time of the amalgamation of the different business lines under one company in 1956, there were three Indians on the eight-member Board of Directors. Prakash Tandon, the first Indian to be appointed at the junior (sales) management level in 1937, thereafter gradually made his way to the top till he was finally appointed the chairman of the company in 1961. By the early eighties, the number of expatriate members on the Board had been reduced to just one vice-chairman. Consecutive chairmen like Tandon, T. Thomas and A.S. Ganguli, have furbished the company with an Indian image. In the eyes of many Indians, the company, which moreover had adopted an indigenous name, appear as a truly *swadeshi* company.*

The Indianisation of capital was less pronounced and took many more years to materialise, despite repeated requests by the government. After independence, the first minister of Finance, T.T. Krishnamachari, attempted to persuade the then chairman of Lever Brothers Private Ltd. to sell part of its shares, and thereby set a good example as a progressive organisation. The negotiations between Krishnamachari, who earlier actually had been a marketing agent for Lever Brothers, ended in an agreement to sell only ten per cent of the shares in exchange for the promise of a free flow of profit remittances and of no increase in taxation.

Afterwards more requests were made to Hindustan Lever with the argument that, although the government would not take legal measures and would not otherwise discriminate against the company if it would dilute its foreign shareholding, the company's position would be strengthened in the eyes of the public and in its negotiations with the government. Only in 1977, the government of India made a serious effort to reduce the foregin equity to less than fifty per cent. In the meantime, the Foreign Exchange Regulation Act (FERA) had been introduced, instructing foreign companies to sell the majority of shares. The act, however, had a number of provisions allowing for the continuation of a majority foreign equity. Whereas companies like IBM and Coca Cola left the country, Hindustan Lever got a special treatment.

*In an evaluation report of Unilever in 1955, this long-term development was favoured: "Altogether, apart from current nationalist sentimants, I believe it to be in our interests, as well as in accord with our declared policy, to Indianize in the true meaning of the word, i.e. the uttermost practical extent. . . If our Indianized company is to remain a Unilever company the men and women in it will have to be Unilever people first and foremost. . ." (quoted in Fieldhouse 1978, pp. 194-5). It may be assumed that the policy of close personal contacts and excellent term of employment indeed has turned the Indian managers into trustworthy corporate citizens.

We shall look at the dilution issue in somewhat more detail since it throws interesting light on the holding power of a company vis a vis the government, particulariy if in the enacted legislation loopholes can be found. Informal discussions with government officials and the running for time strategy may have helped Hindustan Lever to find solutions which are actually within the purview of the legislation, but at the same time raise a number of important questions. Whenever the company allowed Indianization of equity, it was followed by a further expansion of the lines of production and of other non-manufacturing activities. In 1956, when 10 per cent equity shares were offered to the Indian public, the company had a plan of entering into another line of production, i.e. synthetic detergents, production of which started in 1959. At the same time, an application of Tata Oil Mills Company was rejected by the licensing authority of the government (MRTPC, Dissenting Report of HL, 1973, p. 60).*

The next government move in 1960 to raise the question of the sale of shares was connected with Hindustan Lever's plan to raise new capital for expansion and diversification. The suggestion by the concerned minister that import licenses would be granted more easily if the extent of indigenous shareholding were increased, finally led to the second dilution of shares in 1965. The diversification programme went in the direction of foodstuffs, particularly cattle food, milk products, dehydrated peas and onions, and cotton seeds processing. In the end only animals feeds, largely for export, proved to be reasonably successful. In 1969, the company entered into the production of the Hima range of food products, luxury toilet soaps, personal products (Erasmic brand), talcum powder and Signal tooth paste.

The pressure from the government to bring the company in line with the FERA resulted in a third phase of dilution. In 1977, Hindustan Lever indeed brought down the foreign equity participation to 65.5 per cent, but at the same time increased

*For licensing capacity expansion, HL had made 9 applications during 1958-73 out of which 7 were granted, whereas for Swastik only 5 out of 13 applications were granted during 1952-73 and for Tomco only 3 out of 15 applications.

Unilever's paid-up capital in HL from Rs. 799.64 lakhs in 1965 to Rs. 1153.45 lakhs in 1977. So, although the ratio of Indian shares increased, the financial stake of the foreign company was further increased in absolute terms. In 1979 a further expansion of HL took place with the commissioning of the Taloja factory for the production of fine chemicals. The last phase of dilution took place in 1980 when the foreign share holding was brought down to 51 per cent, and the paid-up capital of Unliever went up to Rs. 1487.16 lakhs. Whereas the company in 1976 had only sixteen thousand shareholders (hardly three thousand more than in 1960), during the next years the number increased to well over ninety thousand. It thereby strengthened its social anchorage within the Indian society without at the same time creating a shareholders' power block.

The Government in 1982 approved Hindustan Lever's application to retain 51 per cent majority share on the claims that Hindustan Lever was exporting more than 10 per cent of its product value, and was producing more than 60 per cent in sophisticated product lines. The FERA guidelines put the condition that a foreign company in order to hold a majority share has to export a minimum 60 per cent of its products. So, it is difficult to understand how a 10 per cent export performance satisfied the government. The sophisticated product lines in the core sector were explicitly listed in the Appendix I to the FERA Guidelines.*

Hindustan Lever operates in three of these product lines (synthetic detergents, industrial machinery and fine chemicals). Table 4.1 shows the contribution of these products in value terms to the total value of products of Hindustan Lever for the last 5 years before the approval of the majority foreign equity participation. The Table shows that the maximum value of the products in Appendix I product lines as a percentage of the

*According to the industrial policy announcement of the government in 1973, foreign companies were allowed to invest in the so-called "Core industries" set forth in Appendix I of the announcement. This excluded soaps, vanaspati, toothpaste, etc. and included industries like metallurgical, electrical equipments, synthetic detergents, fine chemicals, etc.

**Table 4.1 : Value of Core Sector Products of Hindustan Lever**

(Rs. million)

| Products | 1977 | 1978 | 1979 | 1980 | 1981 |
|---|---|---|---|---|---|
| a. Synthetic detergents | 393 | 477 | 662 | 1009 | 1180 |
| b. Industrial machinery | — | 0.2 | 0.1 | 0.3 | 0.6 |
| c. Fine Chemicals | 1 | 2 | 2 | 3 | 2 |
| a+b+c | 394 | 479 | 664 | 1012 | 1182 |
| d. Total value of products | 2617 | 2765 | 3326 | 4042 | 4808 |
| %age of (a+b+c) to (d) | 15.09% | 17.30% | 19.96% | 25.02% | 24.57% |

*Source* : Annual Reports of HL, in A.K. Rath, 1982.

total production of Hindustan Lever accounted for only 25.02% in 1980. In late 1983, a shortcut for increasing the ratio was found by transferring a number of food items to Lipton India which is not subject to the FERA regulations. The core sector production of Hindustan Lever accordingly went up to 33.88%, which was still far short of the minimum requirement of sixty per cent which the government imposed in 1982. In the view of Hindustan Lever, the situation was not ideal because it meant that some consumer parts of the business would remain restricted in their growth so as not to stray too far away from the minimum requirements of export and core sector obligations. The reorganisation which took place in the early eighties, in the view of the parent Unilever company, "was, in its way, a master stroke", although those who ferried Hindustan Lever and Lipton through the operation "say fervently that it was almost impossible to believe that they would ever emerge with the permissions they needed from the government" (Unilever Magazine 1985, nr 57, p. 22).

The idea to transfer the food business was born in the late 1970s, after Lipton had gone public and had reduced its foreign equity to 40%. Hence, as the Unilever house journal reflects, there was no compulsion to stay in the core sector or the advanced technology sector, nor anxiety about export commitments. What happened next, reads like an industrial thriller. Rather than spoil the lucidity of the thriller by trying to interpret the developments in our own words, we shall take recourse to a lenghty quotation from a document in which the headquarters of the Unilever concern describe the unfolding of the operation :

> As time passed the merits of the proposal to sell some of the HLL businesses to Lipton grew and flourished in people's mind—and so did the feeling that it would never be allowed. All those involved knew only too well, the hurdles were many and high—the idea would involve permissions obtained from many ministries and would also mean persuading the press, opinion formers, shareholders and company employees that the proposed solution to both companies' problems would be in everybody's interests.
>
> Having decided that the reorganisation was the right answer a programme of campaign was developed which was of a complexity that defies description. No department of HLL was left untouched by the need to project the right image of the change.
>
> The key problem was getting ahead with the move through effective communication with the numerous agencies of the government. Dr. Ganguly and other board members regularly came to Delhi to make their explanations. Bharat Mahay, stationed in the capital to liaise with the officials, soon realised that as many as 600 permissions were going to be necessary to achieve the transfer : 'This is a vast bureaucracy involving several ministries... copies travel from one department to another, gathering comments. We feared it might take too long, but that it was all through in a year and a half now seems incredible'.
>
> Of the 600 permissions, three were crucial : The Foreign Exchange Regulation Act, which determines shareholding levels and spheres of activities; that under the Monopolies and Restrictive Trade Practices Act, which aims to prevent large companies becoming too powerful; and that covering the issue of shares. The fear with FERA was that HLL would not be allowed to behave as it did even though it was not changing its already agreed status. With the MRTP it

was thought that perhaps the Lipton business was becoming too large, but as Chandrapal Mahimker, company secretary, argued with the Law Minister for an hour and forty minutes, the essence of the reorganisation was moving marbles from one pocket to another, not introducing new marbles. The drama was tense and until the paper was signed, Mahimker could hardly believe his arguments had prevailed.

The third permission was perhaps the most dicey.... How could a purchase of Rs. 15.62 (£10 million) crore be financed by a company with a share capital standing of Rs 3.75 (£3 million) crore? The only way was to offer a rights issue to the shareholders or HLL and Lipton India Limited—an unprecedented move" (Unilever Magazine 1985, nr 57, p. 23).

The skilful conjuring—the expression is Unilevers'—ultimately gave Hindustan Lever plenty of latitude in expanding its remaining consumer goods business and silenced the guardians of the law of the country and its plenty of investigative journalists. It established a foreign controlled corporate power which, through three separate companies, Hindustan Lever, Lipton India and Brooke Bond, occupies a dominating position in the field of detergents, soaps, tea and, to a lesser extent, hydrogenated oil.

On the basis of this short description of the behaviour of HL in response to government's restrictions on foreign capital, some valuable lessons on the possible consequences of this type of action by multinationals can be drawn. In the first place, the company has greatly increased its capital stock. In the second place, it has succeeded in trading a dilution of shares against licenses which led to an expansion and a diversification of its business. Thirdly, the host government has been induced to officially proclaim the special contribution of the company to the economic development of the country. In the fourth place, the financial control by the parent company remains as firm as before, particularly in view of the fact that the Indian shares are dispersed over ninety thousand shareholders.*

The insufficient, often lukewarm and even inappropriate application of government regulations can be illustrated in respect of the licensed capacity regulations. According to the MRTP act, Hindustan Lever was not supposed to expand its production capacity in production lines like soap, detergents, glycerine, etc. in which it had a substantial market share. There are, however, three ways in which the company has managed to expand its production and, although it does not necessarily violate the letter of the act, it has circumvented the restrictive government policies.

The first method is by making use of subcontracting. The company is allowed to engage in these activities (clause 17 of its memorandum of association), but has to record any such subcontracting with the Registrar of Companies in Bombay. No such registration has taken place in the case of soap contracting to at least three small scale industrial units in Aurangabad (Maharashtra), Pune and Bangalore. In 1977, the concerned ministry put laundry soap on the so-called reserve list of products exclusively restricted to the small units. Big houses, like HL, were accordingly not allowed to expand their production. Thereupon, HL approached the government to allow it to help increase the overall production of laundry soap in the country by setting up an industrial machinery unit. The HL plant in Bombay is now engaged in the production of such machinery which can be used by the small scale units. HL's control over some of these units is almost total. The above-mentioned units were earlier stockists and agents for HL soaps. The raw materials they now use for the production of soap are soap nuddles processed at the Sewree plant of HL. The nuddles are fed into the machine, a product of HL, and are extruded as HL Sunlight soap. Even the stamping machine is provided by HL, who also deputes technicians and quality control personnel for regular check-ups and streamlining of

*As a matter of fact, the Leverhulme Trust, which controls the parent Unilever company, owns only 18% of the shares, which is apparently much less than the 51% which Unilever owns in Hindustan Lever, and of which actually only 14% has been contributed in the form of export of capital. The rest has been appropriated through the issue of bonus shares.

the production process. The employees in these units (few in number, mostly women and children) are paid wages hovering at around one-fourth of the wages paid at the Sewree factory. Probably one-tenth of the total soap nuddle production at Sewree gets distributed to these units, where it is processed into the final product which is then marketed by Hindustan Lever. This system of subcontracting, of which we have located three cases and of which there are probably more, increases the monopoly position of the company without adding capital or labour risks and without formally cutting across the government poilcy aimed at the protection of the small scale industry.

The second method for circumventing the production ceilings is by statistically entering laundry soap as toilet soap for which the legal restrictions are not applicable in the same form. For revenue purposes, toilet soap attracts a basic excise duty of 15% as against 7% for laundry soap. HL nevertheless pays the government 15% on Lifebuoy which, given its proportion of fatty matter, caustic soda, etc., should be treated and, by and large, is actually used as a laundry soap.

The third method is by openly producing more than the licensed capacity. The production of the various brands of soaps in 1981 was 270% higher than the permitted capacity which, for technical reasons, is 25% higher than the licensed capacity. In the same year, surplus production took place in twelve out of the fourteen product lines. Underutilisation of capacity occurred only in the case of oils and machinery.

The policy which the company has followed in respect of the dilution of capital, namely playing for time and lobbying for a change in government guidelines, has proved successful in the case of production ceilings as well. Regularly, ceilings have been raised. In 1982, through an amendment of the MRTP Act, the government has revised all licensed capacities upward by 33.3% above the best production level in the years 1977-82. Part of the previous surplus production has thus become legalised. Most applications for new licenses have been approved, albeit with some delays. The allegedly slow and bureaucratic government machinery does not seem to have detracted the company from starting new production lines in the expectation that it afterwards would be honoured by the government (e.g. the case of clinic shampoo).

The export performance of Hindustan Lever seem to fit in well with the export orientation in government policy. The total value of exports increased from Rs. 180 million in 1978 to Rs. 685 million in 1981, prior to the FERA approval, but then dropped sharply to Rs. 465 million in 1983. On account of what the company does not get tired of advertising as "impressive successes", amounting to hardly ten per cent of sales, HL has been recognised by the government as a Trading House. In addition to its own products, it exports footwear, garments, carpets and other small-scale sector products, which actually constitute one-third of the exports.

FERA exports requirements are actually to be fulfilled from its own production. This may have been an additional reason why a number of projects have been taken at hand in order to increase this type of exports. A carpet washing plant has been constructed in Varanasi for the removal of the toil from the carpets which are purchased in Kashmir and Varanasi. At Muttukudu in Tamil Nadu a prawn hatchery has been in operation for a number of years, and new ponds for growing the post-larval species have been acquired, among others, in the marshy Sunderbans area in West Bengal. Others are exported to neighbouring countries or find their way to local farmers through a putting-out system. In Kandla, a one million polycotton shirt factory has been started, with the aim, as Unilever put it, of "helping India to fulfil her quota in the international garment market" (*Unilever Magazine* 1985, nr 57, p. 26). Production at Kandla proceeds on the basis of fabrics imported from the Far East. The garments made from Indian fabrics, however, are not made by HL : the company only undertakes the marketing, albeit while maintaining a close check on the producers (HL, Hindustan Lever Exports, n.d.). Furthermore, a license has been requested for a footwear factory at Kanpur.

The biggest contribution to the exports in the coming years will, however, be made by tea which will be blended and packed at Pune. HL expects the tea component to go up to around 30 per cent of exports, mostly to the Middle East. This planned development again raises the issue of the monopoly position which Unilever has acquired : it will now be able to purchase tea from Brooke Bonds, and from Lipton, which is not expected to export, do some final packing and export the same as its contribution under the FERA requirements. It only reinforces the idea that, in terms of core sector production and export performance, the total turnover of all Unilever companies in India should be taken as the yardstick.

Moreover, the exports of Hindustan Lever have to be set against the imports in order to assess the impact on the foreign exchange front. The picture which will emerge (Table 4.2) is somewhat blurred in view of the fact that, whereas all the imports are against hard currency, around one-fourth of the exports, mainly to East European countries, are transacted in Rupee terms. In the last years, the foreign exchange contribution has been negative throughout (Table 4.2.) The value of the imported raw materials has doubled between 1979 and 1981, thereby offsetting the expected salutary effect of increasing exports. The reversal to an export boom is unlikely, given a number of worldwide developments, and given the fact that with the government approval in 1982 of the 51% foreign equity holding, the pressure to export has been reduced. This may again lead to a widening of the foreign exchange gap. In the import-export business, more drain of foreign exchange takes place than through the repatriation of dividend, which is only a trickle of the amount involved in the total flow. Whereas dividends amount to between 14 and 39 million Rs. a year, the net foreign exchange drain, as computed in Table 4.2., reaches an average of around Rs. 200 million a year, albeit with sharp fluctuation.*

One final remark on the foreign exchange contribution should be added. The directors of Hindustan Lever readily agree that the parent company has not transferred much capital for fresh investments. Since the 1950s, the flow has

*We have not taken account of transfer pricing. The practices of over-invoicing the imports or underinvoicing the exports are difficult to detect, particularly since the departmental offices of the ministry concerned seem unwilling to disclose the unit prices of exports and imports. One clear example, the export of Liril soap to Australia in 1981 at Rs. 0.91 although the ex-factory price is Rs. 1.95, may indicate that other export products are priced similarly.

**Table 4.2: Net Drain of Foreign Exchange from India by Hindustan Lever**

(Rs. Million)

| Year | Value of imported raw materials & spare parts consumed | Value of imports of capital goods | Other payments in foreign exchange | Dividend Remitted | Total F.E. payment | Expprt F.O.B. & other Earning | Net Drain of Foreign Exchange |
|---|---|---|---|---|---|---|---|
| 1977 | 374 | 0.3 | 2 | 31 | 407 | 181 | 225 |
| 1978 | 386 | 24 | 6 | 25 | 441 | 181 | 260 |
| 1979 | 380 | 6 | 9 | 32 | 427 | 323 | 104 |
| 1980 | 697 | 8 | 17 | 14 | 36 | 426 | 309 |
| 1981 | 748 | 3 | 37 | 32 | 820 | 686 | 134 |
| 1982 | 632 | 12 | 28 | 28 | 700 | 455 | 245 |
| 1983 | 598 | 30 | 7 | 39 | 674 | 465 | 209 |
| 1984 | 682 | 9 | 13 | 42 | 743 | 616 | 127 |
| 1985 | 930 | 17 | 44 | 47 | 1038 | 738 | 300 |

*Note* : The figures after 1982 exclude the transactions which have been transferred to Lipton.
*Source* : Annual Report of the company; A.K. Rath 1982, Sridhar Krishna 1982.

practically dried up. HL argues that the bonus shares are actually a hidden from of capital transfer "because Unilever as a shareholder did not repatriate hundred per cent of the profits that it made in the country" (Dutta 1982, p. 17). The fact, however, remains that in just fifteen years (1969-1984) the company repatriated Rs. 350 million, which annually amounted to a repatriation more or less equal to the total capital transfer which took place around and before independence. It is significant to note that after the enactment of the FERA, the net dividend remittance has almost trebled.

## 4.3 Company Finances

The financial history of Hindustan Lever contains some interesting features. It has already been mentioned that the retained profits have been profusely used for re-investment in the form of bonus shares. In 1937, when the paid-up capital was increased to Rs. 3.4 million, capitalisation of profits through the issue of bonus shares was practised for the first time. The practice was continued after independence. Apart from widening the capital resources of the company, the procedure had as an added advantage that instead of proportionately high taxes to be paid on the profits, bonus shares escape the tax net. From 1962 onwards, when the new government tax policy was introduced, HL adapted its profit management to the new situation. Today, the paid-up capital is to a very high degree (85%) made up of bonus shares. It is probably no coincidence that the taxes paid as a percentage of the gross profit have come down significantly. From the early sixties till the early eighties, the gross profit as a percentage of the capital has risen from an average of fifty per cent to an average of hundred and fifty per cent. The dramatic increase, it should be noted, is not necessarily a reflection of the growing profitability of the company. Since in the company balance sheets, shares remain fixed at their original price tag, profits as a percentage of paid-up capital are bound to increase in the long run. Even then, the rise after 1974 (from 58% to 155% at the end of the decade) as well as the growth of profits as a percentage of total capital employed reflect a more than buoyant rate of profitability. The ratio of profits to sales, which does not suffer from inflationary disturbances has increased from an average of 7.0% in the five year period 1962-66 to 8.9% in the period 1977-84. For a further analysis we refer to Table 4.3.

The time series of a number of data relating to the profit structure of the company corroborate the suspicion that less and less of the surplus generated in the labour process flows to the exchequer. It may not have been the intention of the government that a company which in the sixties had an average profit on capital employed (net worth) of less than thirty per cent, during the more recent period manages average figures of above 35% and, despite the more radical legislation on monopoly houses and foreign companies, has succeeded in gradually decreasing its tax ratio. Whereas taxes in the early sixties amounted to 58.82% of gross profits (after depreciation and interest), and then increased to 60.62% in the period 1970-74, by 1980-84 the annual average had come down to 48.78%. During the same period, the percentage of profits which has been retained by the company for further investments has more than doubled, as column 5 in Table 4.3 indicates. This practice, instead of dishing out the profits as dividends, will in the end lead to new investments and expansion of economic activities. The significance of the opposite development of tax ratio and retention ratio is twofold. On the one hand, it indicates that the management of the foreign controlled company is committed to expand its investment in the country, instead of only skimming off the profits in the form of higher dividends. The latter, it may be added, have grown from an average of Rs. 12 million in the early sixties to Rs. 23 million in the early seventies and ultimately to an average of Rs. 87 million in the first half of the 1980s. The balance sheets on the other hand reveal that the surplus which is generated in production does not so much accrue to the government as to the private company. The inference is that the steering role which government had assigned to the public sector will be devoid of finances and that the private companies like Hindustan Lever will grow accordingly relatively faster.

Before we shall have a closer look at the various product lines, let us have a look at the income and expenditure

**Table 4.3: Profit and Tax Ratios of Hindusian Lever, 1962-84**

| Year | Gross Profit as % of Turnover | Taxes as % of Gross Profit | Profit Retained (Rs Million) | Profit Retained as % of Gross Profit | Profit Retained as % of Profit available for Distribution | Gross Profit as % of Paid-up Capital | Gross Profit as % of Net Worth | Dividend Declared (Rs. Million) |
|---|---|---|---|---|---|---|---|---|
| 1962 | 8.9 | 60.70 | 4.6 | 9.56 | 31.72 | 58.35 | 38.38 | 10 |
| 1963 | 7.3 | 64.76 | 3.3 | 7.55 | 22.29 | 53.01 | 32.75 | 12 |
| 1964 | 6.3 | 53.32 | 5.5 | 14.03 | 32.35 | 47.55 | 28.78 | 12 |
| 1965 | 6.3 | 58.63 | 7.0 | 15.49 | 36.27 | 57.83 | 28.83 | 12 |
| 1966 | 6.2 | 54.86 | 8.0 | 15.24 | 35.09 | 48.34 | 30.66 | 15 |
| 1967 | 5.7 | 48.03 | 3.8 | 7.13 | 19.00 | 49.08 | 26.37 | 16 |
| 1968 | 6.2 | 47.72 | 5.4 | 8.76 | 25.00 | 56.72 | 29.45 | 16 |
| 1969 | 5.8 | 52.54 | 9.0 | 14.29 | 32.73 | 58.01 | 28.64 | 18 |
| 1970 | 4.5 | 52.12 | 3.2 | 5.96 | 13.67 | 39.66 | 23.95 | 20 |
| 1971 | 5.5 | 61.48 | 5.8 | 7.78 | 21.09 | 54 88 | 32.24 | 22 |
| 1972 | 6.9 | 62.23 | 9.4 | 9.70 | 28.92 | 71.38 | 23.14 | 23 |
| 1973 | 6.9 | 64.79 | 13.2 | 14.30 | 33.67 | 67.99 | 21.41 | 26 |
| 1974 | 6.2 | 62.90 | 10.2 | 11.06 | 28 09 | 58.22 | 19.78 | 26 |
| 1975 | 7.3 | 68.35 | 17.8 | 11.81 | 37.00 | 95.16 | 30.43 | 30 |
| 1976 | 9.2 | 64.72 | 35.6 | 18.12 | 51.51 | 124.39 | 39.29 | 34 |
| 1977 | 8.3 | 64.03 | 44.6 | 20.51 | 56.38 | 137.27 | 37.99 | 34 |

| | | | | | | | | |
|---|---|---|---|---|---|---|---|---|
| 1978 | 8.6 | 63.91 | 49.3 | 19.10 | 50.35 | 162.91 | 37.58 | 49 |
| 1979 | 8.6 | 42.50 | 72.6 | 23.71 | 49.89 | 144.96 | 37.23 | 73 |
| 1980 | 8.1 | 48.66 | 88.7 | 27.55 | 54.89 | 155.62 | 33.40 | 73 |
| 1981 | 8.6 | 49.73 | 125.8 | 30.51 | 63.31 | 141.35 | 34.77 | 73 |
| 1982 | 9.7 | 50.16 | 160.2 | 35.95 | 68.72 | 152.92 | 38.77 | 73 |
| 1983 | 9.4 | 49.59 | 86.3 | 18.06 | 45.11 | 102.12 | 42.00 | 105 |
| 1984 | 8.6 | 47.95 | 100.8 | 21.6 | 47.37 | 99.82 | 37.50 | 112 |

*Source* : Annual Reports of the company.

*Note* : 1. The percentages in column 6 have been calculated after proper adjustments between gross and net profit, i.e. including deductions or addition for taxation claims in the previous years, taxation rebate allowances, etc.

2. The capital employed used for the calculations in column 8 represents the revalued fixed assets and the net current assets.

3. Gross profit is net of depreciation and interest.

behaviour of the company. In Table 4.4, we have aggregated a number of key data relating to the sales, assets, expenditure and profits. Sales have increased at a very rapid speed. If we limit our analysis to the fifteen years' period 1970-1984, we notice that the turnover has increased fivefold. If deflated against the wholesale prices of edible oils and chemical products, which is the closest available approximation to Hindustan Lever's product range, value of sales has still doubled.

The spurt in the absolute profit figures was even bigger, leading to an almost tenfold increase in the same period. The relative faster increase in the volume of profits obviously follows from an increase in productivity. The declining relative expenditure (see column 5 of Table 4.4 and column 1 of Table 4.3) is related to economic measures affecting some of the items of expenditure. The major part of the expenditure is involved in the purchase of raw materials of which, as we mentioned earlier, around one-fourth is being imported. If anything, the outlay on raw materials has proportionately shown a rising trend since the early sixties. It rose from 66% of income in the five year period 1961-65 to slightly less than 70% in the five year period 1976-80. The share of sales promotion (between 1.1% and 3.1%) also has grown significantly. On advertising, there may have been an even bigger increase in spending, but since the company in its balance sheets prefers to club this type of expenditure (as well as other sensitive items which are subject to a legal maximum and which are monitored by government machinery) under the general head of miscellaneous spending, it is difficult to arrive at a clear picture.

The two major items on which the company has been able to economise are tax expenditure and salaries. The latter is somewhat surprising since it is generally agreed that Hindustan Lever pays its workers quite well compared to Indian standards. While assessing the total wage fund, due consideration should be given to the fact that HL workers are more skilled and much more productive than workers in the average indigenous plants. Productivity increases have indeed taken such a huge stride that, as one of the senior supervisors in the soaps department reminisces, "work that used to take days and

**Table 4.4 : Hindustan Lever Ltd. Key Data on Income and Expenditure (1962-1986)**

(Rs. million)

| Year | Total Asset | Total Sales | Expenditure % of income | Profit before Tax | Net Profit |
|---|---|---|---|---|---|
| 1962 | 125 | 536 | n.a. | 48 | n.a. |
| 1964 | 136 | 619 | n.a. | 39 | n.a. |
| 1966 | 171 | 847 | n.a. | 53 | n.a. |
| 1968 | 209 | 996 | n.a. | 61 | n a. |
| 1969 | 220 | 1088 | 94.0 | 63 | 27 |
| 1970 | 224 | 1192 | 94.3 | 54 | 23 |
| 1971 | 213 | 1341 | 93.8 | 74 | 27 |
| 1972 | 419 | 1404 | 92.6 | 96 | 32 |
| 1973 | 431 | 1327 | 92.7 | 92 | 39 |
| 1974 | 466 | 1487 | 92.9 | 92 | 36 |
| 1975 | 495 | 2059 | 91.9 | 151 | 48 |
| 1976 | 501 | 2130 | 90.0 | 197 | 69 |
| 1977 | 572 | 2617 | 91.6 | 217 | 79 |
| 1978 | 687 | 3010 | 91.4 | 258 | 98 |
| 1979 | 822 | 3557 | 89.8 | 306 | 146 |
| 1980 | 1064 | 4463 | 91.6 | 322 | 162 |
| 1981 | 1376 | 5336 | 91.5 | 412 | 199 |
| 1982 | 1676 | 4850 | n.a. | 455 | 233 |
| 1983 | 1664 | 5651 | 90.16 | 476 | 191 |
| 1984 | 1945 | 6169 | 90.82 | 465 | 213 |
| 1985 | 2242 | 7069 | 89.04 | 555 | 325 |
| 1986 | 2281 | 8239 | 88.85 | 651 | 391 |

*Note* : 1. For comparative purposes in growth rates, reference should be made to deflationary factors. The index number for whole-sale prices of manufactured products stood at 308 in 1984 (1970: 100).

2. Sales is exclusive of excise duty and exclusive of miscellaneous income.

*Sonrce* : Annual reports of the company and A.K. Rath 1982.

weeks, now takes minutes" (*Hamara*, March 1981, p. 2).* The data which are available in the annual reports of HL, show that salaries and other social benefits (including those accruing to the three hundred odd employees earning more than thirty thousand Rs. a year), as a percentage of the total expenditure, have declined from 7.2% in the period 1961-66 to 6.5% in the period 1976-80 and to 5.9% in the period 1983-1985. There have been some variations, however, particularly in the mid-seventies. In the year before the emergency, salaries represented 10.7% of the expenditure. During the three consecutive years, total salaries increased by less than one per cent a year. Profits on the other hand in that period rose annually by 31%. Important for the ultimate profitability on capital employed is the distributional aspect of the income of the company. We have made a comparison between Unilever and Hindustan Lever. Normally, the biggest share of the value-added goes to the salaries and the wages' component. That at least is the picture prevailing in Unilever. Over the last decade on an average 67 per cent of the value-added of Unilever went to the salaries, wages, etc. In the case of Hindustan Lever, the share of salaries, wages, etc., in the value-added has been declining throughout the last decade. In 1970, the share of total labour costs in the value-added was 60 per cent. By the year 1981 the share had gone down to as low as 35 per cent. The only break in the continuing downward trend occurred during the two years preceding the emergency.

Since on the other hand over the last decade, the share of value-added going to the government has been stagnant at a level of around 32.5 per cent, the share of value-added going to profits has been rising consistently. The implication is that the increasing relative exploitation of labour is progressively being channelled into the private accumulation fund of a foreign company rather than into the resource fund of the state sector. This observation is of great importance. In view of the high

*The generation of direct employment by the company has practically ceased since 1977, although there has been some recruitment of casual workers and contract workers. Indirectly employment has also been created in the ancillary industry. The wages of the latter group of workers are, however, miserably low.

productivity of labour and in view of the generally depressed wage levels, from which the modern private sector cannot be expected to deviate with too wide margins, multinational corporations are bound to control ever vaster funds of capital.

It would be interesting to have a closer look at the financial importance of the Indian subsidiary to the worldwide concern. Although Hindustan Lever is just one among the more than 800 controlled companies of Unilever Ltd., it is of great importance to the parent enterprise.

Before dealing with the specific comparison between Unilever and Hindustan Lever, a general idea will be presented of the spread of the Unilever concern over the world. In Table 4.5 we have made some aggregate calculations of the share of the developed and the developing countries in the overall asset structure, profit generation and employment position. The Table has to be treated with some reservation since the developing countries are not strictly identical with the category Rest Of the World which we were forced to use since Unilever in its reports does not separate the figures on New Zealand, Australia and Japan from the figures relating to the Asian continent.

If we first look at the changes, we notice pre-eminently the growing share of the United States and Canada in terms of assets and profits. Although its share of the total employment has remained more or less stagnant at around six per cent, assets have doubled in the period between 1976 and 1984. The growth of profits (see also Table 4.6) indicates that business in the North American area is more attractive than in Europe where assets, profits and employment have declined considerably. Operations in the developing countries appear to be growing. The growth is partially accounted for by the consolidation of previously unconsolidated companies, as happened with the operations in Zaire in 1977 and the oil palm plantations in Thailand in 1983. Subsidiaries in the developing countries contribute considerably more to the overall profits than their share in the asset structure would account for. The contribution of the developing countries in terms of employment continues to be twice as high as the share in the assets. Employment which on the basis of Table 4.5 appears to have risen, has actually declined after 1977. In that year, due to the

**Table 4.5: Geographical Distribution of Assets, Profits and Employment of Unilever, 1976-1984**

| | 1976 | | | 1981 | | | 1984 | | |
|---|---|---|---|---|---|---|---|---|---|
| | Assets | Profits | Employment | Assets | Profits | Employment | Assets | Profits | Employment |
| | % | % | % | % | % | % | % | % | % |
| Europe | 71.1 | 55.2 | 57.9 | 67.7 | 53.6 | 49.6 | 57.4 | 44.4 | 49.5 |
| North America | 10.3 | 8.3 | 5.8 | 14.5 | 10 8 | 6.1 | 19.2 | 20.4 | 6.6 |
| Rest of the World | 18.6 | 36.5 | 36.3 | 17.8 | 35.6 | 44.3 | 23.8 | 35.2 | 43.9 |
| Total Magnitude | 12.444 | 2.602 | 342 | 20.044 | 3.325 | 343 | 24.044 | 3.841 | 301 |

*Source* : Annual Reports of Unilever N.V.

*Notes* : 1. The magnitude is expressed in million florins for assets and profits and thousand numbers for employment.

2. The take-over of Brooke Bonds by Unilever is not expressed in the 1984 figures. The inclusion from 1985 onwards (for example an additional 65,000 employees) may bring about significant shifts in the geographical distribution.

**Table 4.6 : Spatial Distribution of Share of Profits of Unilcver**

| Year | E.E.C. | Other European Countries | North America | Central & South America | Africa | Asia, Australia including India |
|---|---|---|---|---|---|---|
| 1971 | 55.17 | 5.91 | 12.80 | 2.46 | 15.76 | 7.88 |
| 1972 | 56.42 | 8.17 | 9.12 | 3.50 | 12.06 | 10,11 |
| 1973 | 56.80 | 8.57 | 8.57 | 3.25 | 13.01 | 9.76 |
| 1974 | 52.10 | 7.00 | 11.20 | 2.24 | 16.24 | 11.20 |
| 1975 | 40.98 | 6.55 | 10.10 | 2.73 | 26.50 | 13.11 |
| 1976 | 49.11 | 6.11 | 8.30 | 2.72 | 23.86 | 9.87 |
| 1977 | 56.13 | 8.54 | 7.85 | 4.79 | 11.09 | 11.57 |
| 1978 | 62.37 | 6.43 | 6.43 | 4.77 | 9.20 | 10.77 |
| 1979 | 57.96 | 7.47 | 9.69 | 3.58 | 9.34 | 11.95 |
| 1980 | 50.48 | 8.64 | 8.92 | 5.25 | 11.63 | 15.06 |
| 1981 | 44.27 | 9.35 | 10.82 | 6.88 | 11.21 | 17.44 |
| 1982 | 36.41 | 9.04 | 14.27 | 7.27 | 13.54 | 19.47 |
| 1983 | 34.49 | 9.84 | 18.72 | 7.07 | 12.01 | 17,86 |
| 1984 | 35.12 | 9.32 | 20.41 | 6.12 | 10.44 | 18.59 |

*Source* : Annual Reports of Unilever.

unusually fast expansion of business in Africa, which was caused by the consolidation of hitherto unconsolidated operations, employment in the developing countries went up to 160,000. By 1984, the figure (without Brooke Bond) had come down to 132,000, a decline which was of the same relative order as the decline in Europe. A significant aspect of the global employment situation is the constant share of the contribution of the North American operations despite the fact that their share in assets has doubled in the relatively short period. Profits in the OECD countries generally tend to be much below the profit ratio achieved in the developing countries.

The importance of the various regions in the profit generation of the corporate structure can be studied in some more detail after disaggregating the figures in smaller geographical areas (Table 4.6). The figures relating to the European Economic Community reveal a fast diminishing share in the profit volume of the concern. Whereas the share of the units operating in the EEC in 1971 was as high as 55%, by 1984 it had come down to 35%. The decline has not been gradual, but the trend is obvious anyway. The rather sharp fluctuations indicate three periods. The sharp fall in 1975 was followed by a new temporary peak in 1978 when the share in overall profits went up to 62%, followed by a declining phase which is still continuing. The cycle happens to coincide with the crisis cycle in the OECD countries. The data on the Asian continent show a gradual increase in the profit share from less than eight per cent in 1971 to more than double that ratio in the early eighties. The increase, unlike the equally fast rising North American share, does not follow from a commensurate growth of assets. The figures for Hindustan Lever separately confirm the general trend of a higher share in profits as compared to assets. For example, in 1981, HL accounted for 1.69% of the assets and for 3.55% of the profits.

The comparative analysis of profitability could be undertaken in one more way. Taking Unilever as a whole on one side and Hindustan Lever on the other, we have made a comparison of profitability in terms of profit before tax as a percentage of capital employed. It is significant to note that in not even a single year between 1970 and 1981, has Unilever as a whole had a higher rate of profitability than Hindustan Lever. As a matter of fact, in most of the years, profitability rates were twice as high (Table 4.7). Similar results will be obtained if we compare the gross profit--net worth ratio, in which case we find averages of around 20% (Unilever) and 40% (Hindustan Lever). It should be kept in mind that the profit rates are studied in isolation of other factors which may directly have caused an increase in the profit volume of the parent company and a concomitant decrease in the profit volume of the daughter company, such as the payment of royalties and the sales of products and materials, either with or without transfer pricing. After deduction of taxes, the net profitability on net worth of the daughter company moves around 5% above the ultimate result of the corporate group as a whole.

**Table 4.7 : Gross Profit—Net Assets Ratio of Unilever and Hindustan Lever, 1970-1984**

| Years | Unilever | Hidustan Lever |
|---|---|---|
| 1970 | 13.65 | 23.75 |
| 1971 | 16 30 | 32.33 |
| 1972 | 17.75 | 23.13 |
| 1973 | 20.49 | 21.41 |
| 1974 | 17.24 | 19.94 |
| 1975 | 14.86 | 30.43 |
| 1976 | 20.51 | 25.42 |
| 1977 | 18.02 | 37.98 |
| 1978 | 17.28 | 37.57 |
| 1979 | 16.75 | 37.22 |
| 1980 | 15.87 | 33.40 |
| 1981 | 16.69 | 34.77 |
| 1982 | 15.11 | 26.54 |
| 1983 | 15.16 | 28.59 |
| 1984 | 15.91 | 23.91 |

*Source* : Annual Reports of Unilever and Hindustan Lever.

## 4.4 Product-wise Analysis

When Hindustan Lever was first registered in India in 1934 as Lever Brothers, it was engaged in the production of soap, vanaspati, toilet preparations and chemicals. Today, the company produces many more different commodities than half a century ago, but the product mix remains by and large similar. In addition to soaps (Lux, Pears, Sunlight, Liril, Taj, Vim, Lifebuoy, Rin, etc.), vanaspati (Dalda, and Aneek), toilet preparations (Signal and Close-up tooth paste, Sunsilk and Clinic shampoo, skin cream, toilet powder, talcum powder, etc.) and related chemicals, the company since around 1970 has gone into the production of food products (Hima range of products) and animal feed products. In the product mix of the company the predominance of soaps, detergents and vanaspati, in that order, remains unaltered.

The three products in 1983 together represented 95% of the total turnover of the company. The importance of the three rather unsophisticated consumer products during the 1970s rather increased than decreased. We shall deal with some of the products in greater detail.

The production figures on soap show that between 1974 and 1984, output doubled, and that the licensed capacity of 96,000 tonnes was overstepped by more than hundred per cent. The commissioning of the new soap plant in the Kandla Free Trade Zone in 1983 stimulated a 25% increase in soap production in just two years' time, and has likely led to a further strengthening of HL's position in the soap market. At least during the period up to 1984, for which information was available, the company has managed to keep its share of around fifty per cent of the registered soap market intact, despite the entry of numerous small scale and large scale soap producers in recent years (Usha Menon, 1986). The domination of HL is particularly strong in the market segment of popular brands. Lux, Hamam, Rexona and Lifebuoy are reported to have cornered more than two-thirds of the popular brand market (*India Today*, 15 March 1985). Although sales figures continue to rise (from 0.6 billion in 1974 to 3.0 billion in 1984), synthetic detergents have come in as a major competitor for some of its products. Before looking into the detergent production, we shall first deal with the second important product, vanaspati.

The production of hydrogenated vegetable oil (vanaspati) was started in 1932. The installed production capacity rapidly increased to 52000 tonnes by the beginning of the second world war. By that time, however, Indian competition had come up and the market share of HL decreased from 64% in 1940 to 24% in 1950. The restrictive government measures—quality control and price control—continued to operate after independence. This may be regarded as one of the major reasons for the slowdown in the production increase and for the diminishing market share, unlike in the case of soaps. By the early seventies, the market share had come down to around 15%, and stagnated at that level afterwards. The plants at Shamnagar (Calcutta), Trichurappali (Tamil Nadu) and Ghaziabad (Delhi) for most of the time have been producing well below their capacity, and have been running at a low rate of profit or at

**Table 4.8: Product-wise Output of Hindustan Lever (1974-84)**

| | Soaps | | | Hydrogenated Oils | | | Synthetic Detergents** |
|---|---|---|---|---|---|---|---|
| | Sales Rs. Mill. | Production Metric Tonnes | Market Share | Market Sales Rs. Mill | Prod.* Metric Tonnes | Prod. Share* | Sales Volume Rs. Mill |
| 1974 | 635 | 94 | 46.8 | 157 | 50 | 14.1 | 352 |
| 1975 | 1030 | 130 | 48.5 | 333 | 76 | 16.5 | 380 |
| 1976 | 1069 | 151 | 56.5 | 280 | 83 | 15.2 | 355 |
| 1977 | 1240 | 159 | 54.4 | 507 | 89 | 15.4 | 416 |
| 1978 | 1305 | 162 | 53.6 | 569 | 101 | 15.7 | 477 |
| 1979 | 1425 | 162 | 49.8 | 554 | 107 | 15.8 | 663 |
| 1980 | 1775 | 164 | 54.9 | 569 | 92 | 14.9 | 1009 |
| 1981 | 1920 | 166 | 52.4 | 865 | 109 | 16.5 | 1140 |
| 1982 | 1684 | 154 | 48.6 | 833 | 108 | n.a. | 1208 |
| 1983 | 2373 | 179 | 49.0 | 810 | 107 | n.a. | 1162 |
| 1984 | 2980 | 200 | 54.1 | 231 | 67 | n.a. | 1406 |

*Notes* : *The production of hydrogenated oils includes around one-fourth of output for HL's own captive consumption. The market share in the total hydrogenated oil market would therefore be lower than its share in production.

**More detailed figures on the detergent industry will be given in a later section.

*Source* : Hindustan Lever and Indexport annual reports; Central Statistical Organisation, Basic Statistics Relating to the Indian Economy 1950-1981, New Delhi; Usha Menon 1986.

a loss. This, however, has changed in recent years. In 1984 production was sixty per cent above the permitted quantity.

The government-sanctioned increase in the sales price per tonne (Rs. 11030 in 1975; Rs 9335 in 1978 and Rs. 13886 in 1981) may have moved HL to increase its production substantially. The volume of sales in 1981 increased with twenty per cent over the preceding year. Increases of an even higher order took place after the government sanctioned a big increase in the regulated prices in 1975 and 1977. The reaction seems to indicate that price regulation by the government, under the prevailing conditions, may result in a hold back in production, even if the dominant company thereby loses its market share.

In November 1983, the vanaspati business was transferred to Lipton India Ltd. We have already mentioned before that two of the considerations for the corporate group Unilever to take this step may be assigned to the statutory obligation on HL, in view of its majority foreign equity, to have a high export performance and a high percentage of production in the core sector, which includes detergents but excludes edibles. Another consideration, apart from streamlining management into two different sectors, may have been the constant pressure which the price regulation exerts on profitability. Higher profits will be directly more beneficial to Unilever in the case of HL than in the case of Lipton in which it has only a forty per cent shareholding interest.

In 1972, Hindustan Lever applied for a license to produce STPP (sodium tripoly phosphate). The proposal for a new product line was vigorously opposed by a number of Indian industrialists. The opponents of the application argued that there was already one existing firm and a number of potential producers in the country, and that, if the HL plant would go on steam, its domination in the production of detergents would be strengthened. The new plant of HL, which was approved and eventually came up at Haldia in West-Bengal, indeed did not represent a diversification programme into a new, core sector as the company had submitted. STPP is namely the raw material for the production of non-soapy detergents which HL, through the vertical integration of production, would now be able to secure at cost price and thereby put its competitors at a distance (Paranjape

1982, MRTP 1976). One of the most important consequences of the entry of HL was that the potential offtake from other producers fell away, and that a number of indigenous entrepreneurs had to give up their own proposal to venture into the production of STPP. The Monopoly and Restrictive Trade Practices Commission, by approving of HL's application, gave a new push in strengthening the dominant market position. In STPP production, HL acquired one-fourth of the licensed capacity. Moreover, production in 1985 exceeded the liberalised capacity license by 75%, As much 80% was used for internal captive consumption. This single fact gave HL, as the detractors had argued at the time prior to the government approval of the STPP diversification, an added advantage over its immediate competitors in the field of detergent production to which we shall now turn.

The Indian industrial structure is generally characterised by a growing concentration of production in large corporate groups. We shall investigate this process in the case of the detergent industry which, for various reasons, is the most interesting division of the company with such leading market products as Surf, Sunlight and Rin.

Detergents rank highest in terms of sales of Hindustan Lever, although sales value of all soaps together is higher than that of detergents. But since soaps refer to a multi-product including laundry soaps of different qualities it would be difficult to study them as a single product line. Secondly, there has been a steep increase in the production of detergents which in fact are replacing the laundry soaps. The fact that numerous small scale units have entered this product line in recent years make it into an interesting field for comparison. The entry of small scale units started as a consequence of the scarce supply and rising prices of non-edible oils which made the running of small scale laundry soap units cumbersome.

Swastik Oil Mills was the first to enter the detergent industry in 1957 on the basis of indigenous technology. Hindustan Lever thereupon negotiated with the government for a license on the basis of imported technology, and was granted one for the production of 4300 tonnes a year. Production started in December 1959. In 1966, the third unit in the field, Tata Oil Mills Company (TOMCO) went on steam, six years after having received its license. Godrej Soap Limited entered the industry in 1976. At the moment there are sixteen units in the organised sector, including the government soap factory at Bangalore which produces the brandname Point.

During the period 1974-1984, the production of HL in terms of value went up by 339%, reaching a turnover of Rs. 1406 million in 1984. The production and sales figures show some stagnation in the early eighties is a new jump in 1984 when, in the wake of the completion of the new synthetic detergent plant at Chindhwara in Madhya Pradesh, production shot up from 82 million to 110 million tonnes. TOMCO, the most immediate competitor in the organised sector, experienced a much lower growth. Its market share, which had been 19% in 1977 consequently dropped to well below ten per cent. The market share of HL, in terms of volume, which is generally lower than the market share in terms of value, has been hovering at around fifty per cent, as Table 4.9. shows. Whereas the installed capacity of the organised detergent industry has gone up with 108% over the period 1974-81, HL's installed capacity went up from around fifteen thousand tonnes to around thirty-four thousand tonnes, showing an overall increase of 122%. In terms of capacity utilisation, however, HL breaks all records. In 1981, its capacity utilisation in terms of officially licensed capacity went up to 418%, which is considerably more than the 75% of the industry as a whole. If we exclude HL's performance from the industrial aggregate figure, the capacity utilisation of the rest of the industry drops to below 45%. Table 4.10. shows that during the last couple of years there has been an improvement in the capacity utilisation by the other firms. which brought it back to the level reached in 1974. A more detailed look at some of the major plants (TOMCO, Godrej, Detergent India, Swastik) confirms this picture. Only TOMCO succeeded in a limited number of years to have more than hundred per cent capacity utilisation.

The high degree of capacity utilisation by HL, even to a degree which seems impossible on the basis of the officially declared installed capacity, completely distorts the licensing

**Table 4.9 : The Share of Hindustan Lever in the Detergent Industry**

| Year | Production (1000 tonnes) | | Share of HL in Industry | | |
|---|---|---|---|---|---|
| | HL | Organised Sector | Production | Sales Value | Registered Capacity |
| 1974 | 40.2 | 84.5 | 47.6 | 44.4 | 13 |
| 1975 | 35.8 | 75.2 | 47.6 | 65.6 | 11 |
| 1976 | 36.0 | 78.8 | 45.7 | 50.7 | 12 |
| 1977 | 47.6 | 103.9 | 45.7 | 53.4 | 12 |
| 1978 | 59.0 | 122.0 | 48.4 | 52.0 | 12 |
| 1979 | 67.8 | 154.3 | 43.9 | 53.9 | 10 |
| 1980 | 83.5 | 180.2 | 46.3 | 45.1 | 10 |
| 1981 | 92.1 | 179.6 | 51.2 | n.a. | 14 |

*Source* : Annual Reports of Hindustan Lever and Annual Reports of DGTD, as tabulated by A.K. Rath, 1983, pp. 24-29.

**Table 4.10 : Hindustan Lever and the Capacity Utilisation in the Detergent Industry in India**

| Year | Industrial Average | Industry minus HL | HL Utilisation as % of | |
|---|---|---|---|---|
| | | | Licenced Capacity | Installed Capacity |
| 1974 | 73 | 44 | 263 | 263 |
| 1975 | 52 | 30 | 234 | 234 |
| 1976 | 51 | 32 | 193 | 138 |
| 1977 | 52 | 32 | 255 | 204 |
| 1978 | 61 | 36 | 317 | 253 |
| 1979 | 64 | 40 | 363 | 291 |
| 1980 | 75 | 45 | 447 | 358 |
| 1981 | 74 | 43 | 419 | 270 |

*Source* : Annual Reports of Hindustan Lever and Annual Reports of DGTD, as tabulated by A.K. Rath, 1983, pp. 25-27.

policy of the government. The registered installed of HL indeed in 1981 represented only 14.23% of the total installed capacity in the organised sector. The fact that it nevertheless has acquired a monopoly position necessitates a fundamental debate on the adequacy of the legislative process. The question should be asked, therefore, how Hindustan Lever has managed to capture fifty per cent of the detergent market and has kept its production plant running at full speed, while the other companies have showed a dismal performance. The quality of the end product does not seem to play a significant role. As a matter of fact, the government-produced soap Point is superior to HL's Surf in terms of the active ingredient component. The other major detergent makes are of a quality similar to Surf. HL's market network, and its aggressive advertisement policy (the company tops the list of advertising expenditure in the country) may represent one set of explanations. Another explanation may be provided by the access to the raw materials, particularly to Sodium Tripoly Phosphate.

The opening of its own STPP captive unit in 1979, the second such unit in India, has made the access to the major raw material input both cheaper and secure, and has allowed for a continuing increase in production and capacity utilisation. The other companies, to which the HL STPP factory as per the government orders was required to sell its surplus production for the first five years of production, are likely to face more difficulties than they have alredy faced in the past.*

The general conclusion on the position of Hindustan Lever in the organised detergent industry seems to be that

*The government has sanctioned a new STPP captive unit and the setting up of new detergent units in Jammu and in Madhya Pradesh. It has taken a very liberal attitude to the continuing excess production. The benevolent government attitude is not of recent origin. Paranjape (1982, pp. 10-11; also his dissenting report in MRTP, 1973) has shown conclusively how already in the fifties, applications for either expansion or entering the detergent industry made by Swastik and TOMCO were not approved by the licensing authorities, whereas HL was allowed to set up a new soap unit at Calcutta, in addition to its Bombay unit. Swastik's application for a STPP plant in 1960 was discouraged by the licensing authorities.

its dominance is anything but threatened, and that the new production licenses as well as the regularisation of part of its excess production will actually strengthen its dominant position. The other danger to the quasi monopolistic position of the multinational corporation in the field of non-soapy detergents, seems to come from the small scale units. To that sector we shall now turn our attention.

The detergent industry in the small scale sector has grown both in numbers and in size, particularly in the Ahmedabad region, where around eighty per cent of the country's small scale units are concentrated. There are locally some six hundred units ranging from plants with a production of only one tonne per day to 300 tonnes a day. In addition, numerous units in the household sector produce a few kilos a day. The other major region of small scale detergent production is Delhi, where some ten odd manufacturing units operate, albeit with a considerable larger capacity then the units in Ahmedabad.

Most of the units came into operation during the 1970s, and originally started as tiny production units. For example, Nirma Chemical Works at Ahmedabad, the most successful venture, started with a production of seventy kilo per day in 1969. The proprietor, Karshan Bhai Patel, a chemistry graduate, formulated his own formula and has gradually made his Nirma washing powder into a famous brandname with a turnover of over Rs. 400 million. Its production in terms of volume has surpassed the level of the HL product Surf. In 1984, it commanded a turnover of 180,000 tonnes valued as Rs. 100 crores, and registered an annual growth rate of 40%. The emerging war between the two producing companies in 1982 even resulted in a court case. HL was taken to court for allegedly sabotaging the marketing of Nirma washing powder. Marketing officials of the company were found tampering with the content of the Nirma washing powder which they had offloaded at HL's Sewree factory in Bombay (*India Today*, 16-30 September 1982).*

*More concrete measures to counteract Nirma were taken in 1983 by introducing Sunlight powder at half the price of Surf but which double the soda ash content.

A number of factors can be mentioned to explain the growth of the small scale detergent units. We shall list some of them.* The low capital needed and the high rates of return, calculated at 25% on the capital investments (*Chemical Digest*, February 1979), in combination with a rather simple technology, based on the drymixing process, make it possible for many prospective investors to take their chance in this field of industry. The risks are minimal, since no electric power is needed and the raw materials are readily available, namely soda ash and alkyl benzene (STPP is partically not used by the Ahmedabad units). There is only a need for unskilled labourers, who are not only cheap but are also more vulnerable in their bargaining power. Government concessions, e.g. on excise duty for units not using electric power, make it possible to charge a still cheaper price for the end product.

Whereas HL's Surf was sold at Rs 21 per kilo, Nirma could be obtained for Rs. 5.75 per kilo. The huge price difference has induced many people to change over to the small scale products. In many cases the shift has taken place from the earlier use of low-priced laundry soap or soda ash.

Some differences can be observed between the units in Delhi and Ahmedabad. In respect of the workforce, the social conditions in Delhi, where the bigger industries operate, seem to be better. None of the few thousand workers in Ahmedabad are officially on the payroll of the manufacturers. The factory owners confess that in order to avoid labour problems, they engage all their workforce through labour contractors. Hence, the expenditure on wages as a percentage of total expenses varies between three and five per cent in Ahmedabad and five and seven per cent in Delhi.

It is quite possible that in view of the low quality of the small scale products, namely the low level of active detergency component, the absence of water softening agents and the high margins of the acid level which affects the skin of the user,

*The information was collected by A.K. Rath during a field investigation in Ahmedabad and New Delhi between November 1982 and January 1983.

there is not likely to be a real and lasting competition with the high quality products like Point, Surf, Tej, Key, etc. It is quite possible that the small scale units have either cut into the market of laundry soaps or have created an altogether different market.*

The substitution effect in the detergent market my have had some effect on the sales of premium brands, although the increase in production by the large scale sector has gone on unabated, except for a stagnation in 1982. The slowdown in the latter year may have been due to other variables, and not necessarily on account of the increasing sales of small scale detergents.

The further growth of small scale units seems to be hampered by recent developments. One of the most attractive incentives for the non-power units was the exemption from excise duty. This exemption has come to an end in July 1985 when the government slapped a 15% duty on small scale detergent manufacturers, i.e. units not using electric power. The use of power and the concomitant changeover to a more complicated and capital intensive technology may be within the reach of the bigger informal units (Nirma, Narayan Soaps and Syndet), who actually have already made investments in acid slurry plants, but may also cause them to increase their prices. This would confront them with a serious competition from the big companies.

The small scale producers express their apprehension of a further hardening in the government attitude as a result of the lobbying by the big companies in the organised sector. Hindustan Lever is often named by the small scale proprietors as the leader of the move. They complain that as a consequence of the lobby, the government has already circulated notices to the small units inquiring about environmental pollution. A task force report by the ministerial department in

*A similar situation has actually been noticed in the case of the lamp production. For example, whereas the West Bengal market is covered by the major lamp producing companies, particularly by Philips (Peico and ELMI), the 200 odd small scale units in and around Calcutta cater to the cheaper markets in Orissa and Bihar (*Economic Times*, 22.03.83).

New Delhi has argued that the small scale units indeed cause pollution and labour health hazards. If on this basis further restrictions were to be imposed on the non-power units, then the future of the non-organised sector would be bleak.*

The product of HL is protected by a strong financial basis, an improved technology, good government contacts, a good marketing network, big sales promotion resources and an established trade name. The new units, if they wish to enter the market segment of HL will have to give up the advantages they enjoy now (excise concessions, small investments, simple technology, unskilled labour force, etc.). The few companies who have tried to do so in the past (e.g. Haryana Detergents, Stepan Detergents, etc.) have failed to take off, and finally had to close down. Moreover, at least one of these companies, Stepan Chemicals, a joint-sector unit of the Punjab State Government, has been given on lease to Hindustan Lever (Lok Sabha Debates, 14 April 1984). High quality detergent powder can enter the more lucrative market provided it can be sold cheap. Attaining a higher quality (e.g. through the use of the spray drying method, the control of the acid levels and the inclusion of STPP) will, however, lead to a prohibitive increase in the price of production. It is therefore not likely that HL will lose its hold over the high-priced detergent market. On the contrary, one may expect the company to expand into the cheap detergent market, possibly while establishing direct forward linkages with the small scale units.

The activities of Hindustan Lever, as they have been assessed in the previous pages, bear witness to a well-established company with considerable power to withstand adverse political winds. That power seems related to a number of factors, in addition to the characteristics of the Indian state which may not be genuine in the execution of the anti-monopoly and anti-MNC legislation which it has occasionally enacted. HL has a monopoly position in a number of product lines. In addition to the commanding influence it has on the soap and detergent

*The disaster in the Union Carbide factory at Bhopal has made the plea for a check on environmental hazards more imperative. In a report which got ready after the disaster, the Garg Report on 18 chemical plants, Hindustan Lever's detergent unit was actually named as one of the nine polluting factories in Bombay.

sectors as a whole, it has established a number of direct backward and forward linkages which enables it to add activities in the small scale sector to its advantages. The company has vast funds of capital in addition to a vast fund of public sympathy, both in terms of the consumer market and in terms of the share market. The vast funds of capital are partially generated by the considerable profit volume, for example Rs. 325 million net profits in 1985 of which Rs. 186 million were added to the general reserves. In additon, the transfer of the dairy products, animal feeds and cooking oils to the sister concern Lipton India has not only provided the company with additional investible surplus, but has also opened new possibilities for further expansion into both priority and non-priority areas.

The transfer of non-priority activities to Lipton has given HL a new lease of life as a FERA company, and the recent investments indicate that the company knows that its interests in India are safe. The commissioning during the last three years of a synthetic detergent plant at Chhindwara in Madhya Pradesh, a fine chemicals unit, a drug intermediary unit and an expanded detergent bar unit at Jammu in Jammu and Kashmir, a soap and personal products plant, a garment manufacturing as well as a herbicides unit at Kandla in Gujarat, a sal upgrading plant at Taloja in Maharashtra, and a DAP fertiliser plant at Haldia in West Bengal are pointers to the ambitious and self-assured programme of expansion the company has taken at hand.

A decisive legitimisation for its further development in the country may be provided by its activities in the field of agriculture, in addition to the prawn farms which it already manages. The coordinated trials with the Indian Council of Agricultural Research stations and agricultural universities as to the efficacy of its Plant Growth Nutrient have fructified in an industrial license. The various research efforts at its Research Centre, in combination with a number of government institutes all over the country, have a strong emphasis on agriculture. Although the research efforts may have an important global component, as we shall further argue in chapter six, developments are likely to lead to a more direct involvement of the company in agrarian production. One immediate objective appears to be the government approval for the opening up of the (oil palm) plantation sector, particularly on the Andamans, a move which from an ecological perspective may turn out to have devastating consequences for the islands.

Hindustan Lever, after many decades of anti-monopoly legislation, still holds the reins. The combination of a more liberal government policy and the skilful manoeuvring of a corporate group within the permissible elasticity of that policy, may imply that HL will be out in front for some time to come.

# 5

# *Philips-Peico*

The Philips family in the small Dutch town of Eindhoven in 1891 bought a small disused factory, invested a small amount of money and started the production of lightbulbs. The technical know-how was imported by one of the sons of the family who had gained experience while working for the German lightbulb producer AEG. The start of the production of the metal filament lamp in 1906, which gave the company an edge over its European competitors, was also done on the basis of borrowed know-how, this time under a licensing agreement with the American giant General Electric.

The growth of the company (600 workers and a production of two million carbon filament bulbs by the end of the century) went hand in hand with growing profits. Particularly the war years brought windfall profits : 37 million guilders on a total capital of six million guilders between 1913 and 1919 (TIE 12). The takeover of other Dutch firms in the field was, after World War I, followed by the acquisition and the establishment of new firms in other countries of Europe, and, starting with the 1924 venture in Brazil, in the southern part of the hemisphere. The regional expansion was in 1927 followed by a product diversification. The venture into the production of radios was supported by grants to the radio broadcasting system.

By the time of the second world war, Philips had subsidiaries in 38 different countries and employed more than 25,000 workers abroad, almost double the number of employees in the Netherlands. The war years were particularly useful in expanding the business to the USA, more often than not under an agreement with General Electric. In the 1950s, the company entered into a number of new production areas. With the production of black and white television sets and the acquisition of the armaments factory HSA (Holland Signaal Apparaten), the stage was set for a further and rapid expansion. The latter development signalled the entry into the non-consumer sector. Telecommunications and defense systems were followed by the diversification into data systems, medical systems, scientific and industrial equipment, pharmaceutical products, grammophones, etc.

The several product divisions have now been grouped under six broad categories. The share of the different categories in the total production can be seen to have undergone some changes (Table 5.1). Except for home electronics, which is falling behind, the other product divisions either maintained a constant share or improved it over the last five years. The group of products and systems for professional applications has grown very rapidly from 24 per cent to 32 per cent. The share of this sector in the new investments is even bigger. The fastest growing component in this sector are the telecommunication and defense systems.

**Table 5.1 : The Production Structure of Philips N.V. (1977-1984)**

| Products | 1977 | 1981 | 1984 | Change (%) |
|---|---|---|---|---|
| Lighting and batteries | 10.0 | 10.6 | 13.9 | +3.9 |
| Home eletronics for sound and vision | 31.3 | 27.9 | 23.1 | —8.2 |
| Domestic appliances and personal care products | 10.7 | 12.0 | 11.4 | +0.7 |
| Products and systems of professional applications | 24.4 | 29.6 | 29.6 | +5.2 |
| Industrlal supplies | 12.6 | 13.3 | 15.9 | +3.3 |
| Miscellaneous activities | 10.8 | 6.7 | 6,2 | —4.6 |
| Total | 100.0 | 100.0 | 100.0 | |

*Source* : Annual Reports of the Company.

The operations of Philips in several individual countries are much bigger than the volume of business in the home country market. Actually, the share of sales in the Netherlands is steadily going down. At the same time, the volume of business in the USA and Canada has been growing rapidly since the beginning of the seventies. Currently around sixty thousand people are employed in Philips plants in the USA, as compared to a mere four thousand in 1967 (Tamineau 1982, p. 47). Despite the declining trend of Philips' sales in the EEC countries, they still represent the largest market. In general, the existence of a big local market for mass production, which is typical of the multinational plant, is an added reason for the companies to invest in some developing countries. Philips N.V. when it justified its expansion in South East Asia in the early seventies, advocated as one of the reasons, apart from the availability of cheap labour for the specific labour processes, the possibility "to participate in the growth of the market" (Philips, Annual Report 1973, p. 12).

As long as the global trading network remains unaffected by restrictions based on a policy of import substitution, the corporation, however, prefers to continue exporting from its politically secure home base to those areas in the Third World which are not politically safe or which do not have a sufficiently developed market. This method of operation emerges clearly from the figures. Philips in 1982 had a sales figure of around fifteen billion dollars. As much as 23 per cent of the production originated in the Netherlands where, however, only 7 per cent of the overall production was sold at a loss. The rest of Europe and North America accounted for 63 per cent of output and 72 per cent of sales at an average profit rate of between 2.6 and 4.7 per cent. The countries in the Third World finally produced only 10 per cent of the worldwide output of Philips, but provided 18 per cent of the sales and 31.5 per cent of the profits at an average profit on sales of between 6.3 per cent in the case of Asia and 11.8 per cent in the case of Latin America (Philips N.V., Annual Report, 1982).

Philips, which after General Motors, Ford and ITT, is the largest private industrial employer in the world, reached its highest employment position in 1974 when it provided 418,000 jobs. By 1984, the figure had come down to 344,000 of which

212,000 in Europe. Presently, employment is expanding only in the United States where it has reached a level of employment almost equal to that in the Third World, namely 61,000.

**Table 5.2 : Philips N.V. : Geograpbical Distribution of Assets, Profits and Sales (%) in 1982[1]**

| Areas | Assets | Out-put | Sales[2] | Profits | Profits on Sales |
|---|---|---|---|---|---|
| Netherlands | 24 (29) | 23.4 | 7 | —2.4 | —1.8 |
| Rest of EEC | 35 (37) | 35.6 | 39 | 45.4 | 5.8 |
| Rest of Europe | 9 ( 6) | 10.1 | 10 | 16.2 | 7.7 |
| USA & Canada | 16 (11) | 17.4 | 23 | 10.4 | 6.5 |
| Latin America | 7 ( 6) | 5.5 | 8 | 18.8 | 11.8 |
| Africa | 2 ( 1) | 1.4 | 3 | 4.1 | 6.7 |
| Asia | 5 ( 4) | 3.1 | 7 | 8.6 | 6.3 |
| Australia & New Zealand | 2 ( 3) | 2.5 | 3 | 0.1 | 0.2 |
| Total | 100 (100) | 100 | 100 | 100 | 4.9 |

*Notes* : 1. Between brackets the comparative figures for 1977 have been added.

2. Sales figures represent the deliveries to third parties and do therefore not include that part of the output which has been transferred to associated or owned companies.

*Source* : Annual Reports of Philips N.V.

Philips N.V. has approximately 1,800 plants spread over around eighty countries. The expansion of production into other countries is not only generated by the compulsion to overcome trade barriers and to penetrate in this way into new markets. It has to be noted that the production lines of Philips are mainly in the consumer sector. A typical feature of this industry is that it is not safe from local competition. To overcome this situation, Philips probably opted for a wide network of manufacturing activity all over the globe. The adaptation of products to local needs and the security of supply necessitated production of these consumer articles in the area of its consumption.*

The electronic goods of Philips have during the last decade encountered stiff competition from the Japanese competitors. The situation has led to a large reorganisation of plants, including the discarding of some of the product divisions which were not showing sufficient returns. In this connection we can mention the pharmaceutical-chemical sector, known as Philips Duphar, of which the component parts were sold to Solvay of Belgium, Schering and Hoechst of Germany, and others.

Philips N.V. is presently changing its strategy of plant allocation. The trend seems to be in the direction of a declining number of highly automated, large scale production centres rather than spreading production units all over the world. The consequences for employment are felt most severely in Europe where the number of jobs has fallen sharply from 318,000 in 1973 to 209,000 in 1985. The amalgamation of the European market has made it possible to manufacture the goods in a limited number of specialised centres and has led to the closure of many plants (Bouwman 1982, p. 180).

The Philips 1981 Annual Report says, regarding products and systems for professional applications, that in view of the rapidly developing process of technical innovation in this sector, great flexibility is required in order to continue operating successfully in a highly competitive climate :

> To achieve greater flexibility, the arrangement and organisation of activities is being adjusted in some operating units. In addition, in a number of these units capacity is being geared to the reduced labour content of the products and systems which they produce.

Takeovers (e.g. of the West Germany Grundig) and joint ventures (e.g. with the American Telephone and Telegraph, the

*Many other multinationals in the same electrico-technical field, like Siemens and General Electric have gone in for a diversification to the heavy electrical sector. The structure of this sector is such that the production is concentrated in Western Europe and the United States, and that the entry by newcomers is practically sealed off by export cartels and the exclusive control over technology (Helms 1979, pp. 41-42). In the light electrical sector, a different picture prevails.

German Siemens and the French CII and Thomson) form an important aspect of its recent activities. Through the process of takeovers and mergers Philips is internationalising its capital. It at the same time is not relinquishing its national character. The Philips family remains firmly entrenched as the highest controlling authority. The share capital of the corporate structure applies to the N.V. Gemeenschappelijk Bezit van Aandelen Philips Gloeilampenfabrieken, which acts as the holding company of N.V. Philips. The shares of N.V. Gemeenschappelijk Bezit are divided into ordinary shares and priority shares. The ordinary shares are held by shareholders all over the world; the majority of the ten priority shares are held by the Dr. A.F. Philips Stichting, a foundation incorporated and established in the Netherlands Antilles. The Board of Governors, consisting of 6 persons, are appointed (not elected) by the General Meeting of Shareholders from a list of nominees drawn up by the Meeting of the Priority Shareholders. This list is binding, unless two-thirds of the votes cast at a shareholders' meeting, together representing more than half of the issued capital, are opposed thereto. This explains why the ten priority shareholders, the majority of which belong to the Philips family, control the Philips Multinational Corporation.*

## 5.1 General View of Philips Activities in India

Peico Electronics and Electricals Limited, the present name of the Philips subsidiary in India, was initially incorporated on January 31, 1930 as a private limited company under the Indian Companies Act 1913 as Philips Electrical Company (India) Limited. In its early years, Philips India was engaged in the marketing of the products of its parent company as a small

*The operating company NV Philips has two boards. One is the Supervisory Board and the other is the Board of Management. The statutory powers of the Supervisory Board are minimal. It cannot appoint or dismiss members of the Board of Management which looks after the day to day management of the operating company, and which is the highest decision-making body of NV Philips. The directors of the Board of Management are controlled by the Board of Governors of NV Bezit.

import and sales organisation. The products marketed were mainly electrical lamps and radio receivers.

The company in its further history changed its name several times. In September 1956, its original name, Philips Electrical Company, was changed to Philips India Private Limited, and in October 1967 to Philips India Limited. Its present name PEICO Electronics and Electricals Limited was acquired with effect from 20th April 1979.* The changes in its name reflect the change in its activity. It started as an electrical products trading company, and later turned into a huge industrial manufacturing company, producing several dozens of components, raw materials and finished end products. After starting with lamps and radio manufacturing, it diversified into electronic components, tape recorders, stereo towers, intercom system, dry battery cells, domestic appliances, welding equipment, computers, hearing aids, medical apparatus, telecommunication systems, etc.

Until 1948, Philips India operated without any manufacturing unit of its own, although it was involved in electric lamp manufacturing since 1938. The strategy of the company during almost two decades of its pre-Independence period was not to expand under its own banner. In 1938, the Electric Lamp Manufacturers (India) Limited (ELMI) was established. The sponsors of ELMI were all U.K. companies, and Philips, which operated through its U.K. branch. Apart from Philips U.K., the other companies were General Electric Company (GEC) Limited, Crompton Parkison Limited, Mazda Lamps and Associated Electrical Industries (AEI). Later the Mazda Lamps withdrew its membership from ELMI. All these companies were till then engaged in the import of lamps (Kidron, 1965

*In order to save its brand name, PHILIPS changed its corporate name to Peico Electronics and Electricals, just before its 'Indianisation' in 1979. Peico reduced the foreign equity participation to just below forty per cent, and thereby became an Indian company according to the FERA legislation. As an 'Indianised' company it enjoys the benefit of the use of its brand name after changing the corporate name and further maintains the right to have one-third of the directors appointed by its parent body. With a view to dropping the name PHILIPS from the corporate title, Philips regulated the use of trade marks through a separate agreement with the government.

p. 204). Philips received 33.35 per cent equity shares of ELMI and the rest was divided among the other promoters. In 1982, Peico finally succeeded in becoming the sole proprietor of this company.

Another unit with a Philips connection, the Radio Lamp Works Ltd., was registered at Karachi in 1938. In 1947, as a result of the partition, Radio Lamps Works was shifted to Shikohabad in Uttar Pradesh, where it amalgamated with the local Kaycee Glass Works. Following the various financial difficulties faced by the unit in 1952-53, a new company called Hind Lamps Limited was formed on the basis of a collaboration between Radio Lamps Limited (later called Bajaj Electricals Limited) and the group of companies which had formed the ELMI. Both these groups, Radio Lamps and ELMI, contributed fifty per cent each of the equity capital of Hind Lamps Limited. The technical management of the new unit was entrusted to Philips N.V. (MRTP Memorandum 1975, p. 87). After the takeover of ELMI in 1982, Peico automatically established its control over Hind Lamps in which it acquired half of the equity and half of the directorships.

Whereas before independence, Philips had opted for a joint production with other firms, after independence it progressively expanded its own production network. The first unit to be set up was at Calcutta in 1948 for the production of radio receivers. Hitherto it used to import radios for trading purpose. The new unit could capture a substantial portion of the radio receivers market. By the mid-fifties, its production accounted for 35 per cent of total output in the country. Presently the company is controlling almost half of the organised sector's production. In 1960 the Company made another attempt to produce lamps after the failure of the first attempt in 1934. It is to be noted that Philips was not allowed to enter the electric lamp production activity. The company tried several times to get a licence to manufacture electric lamps, but it was not permitted. According to F.J. Philips

> the Indians would not give us a licence, so we had to wait until we were able to take over an existing factory. One day a small lamp factory in Bombay, with an annual output of

> 5 million bulbs, came up to sale. This gave us our chance. But what to offer for a run-down old factory? We badly wanted the factory and feared being outbid. So we offered a little above what we considered it to be worth (Philips 1978, pp. 191-192).

As the highest bidder Philips India Limited purchased this factory, the Osler Electric Lamps Factory, for Rs. 51 lakhs. The sanctioned capacity of the factory was 5 millions GLS lamps. The production of GLS lamps was started in 1962 after the renovation and installation of new machinery. In 1966, the factory was shifted to new premises, constructed by Philips at Kalwa near Bombay. The highly integrated ultra modern light factory was formally inaugurated in January 1967, and reached full production capacity by the end of the year.

Another major development of the company was the manufacturing at Calcutta of telecommunication equipment for the Defence Ministry in 1965. In order to ensure continuity of the operation, the company in the mid-seventies proposed a joint sector with West Bengal Electronics Industries Development Corporation (WBEIDC) for the manufacturing of trans-receivers. The WBEIDC had necessary industrial licence for the manufacture of trans-receivers and other telecommunication equipment. In 1980, this proposal materialised as Webel Telecommunication Industries Limited in which Philips acquired a forty per cent equity. The technology was supplied as per a contract with the Philips Telecom Manufacturing Company Ltd., Australia.

The project was not received without criticism. The Beliaghatta factory of Philips had to discontinue its production substantially following a setback in defense orders which went, as the law required, to the new public sector units. After the revival of the factory under the joint sector with the then still Congress-dominated West Bengal government, a fresh flow of orders from the Ministry of Defense started. It was duly approved by the then Janata government in New Delhi. When the new Congress-government came to power, the leader of the CPI (Marxist) parliamentary faction asked Prime Minister Indira Gandhi whether she would not review that decision. She answered in the negative, although she conceded that Philips

(India) had been given permission to produce one type of communication equipment in 1963 "to meet the urgent national requirements of communication equipment in the wake of the Chinese aggression, (but) not as a regular industrial activity" (Rajya Sabha, unstarred question nr 173, 13.03.1980). The decision to allow Philips both the entry and the continuation in the defense sector, as the *Economic Times* reported, were taken "on the quiet", despite the opposition of high placed persons like Dr. Bhabha and Dr. Vikram Sarabhai. It reported that "there have been pointed questions and criticism in parliament and also in a section of the press in Bombay in the matter of allowing the small Calcutta telecommunication factory to be the Trojan horse for Philips entry into the country's telecommunication industry" (ET, 29.07.1977).

Another activity in the non-consumer sector, and which presently accounts for around 4% of output, is the production of welding electrodes. The entry of Philips into this line of activity was again different from the previous ones. In 1963, the newly established WELMA company (Welding Electrodes and Metallic Alloys Pvt Ltd), which was linked to the Khatau House, was given a license for the production of sixty million running feet of welding electrodes. In the next year, a technical collaboration agreement was entered into with Philips Gloeilampenfabrieken of Eindhoven. The agreement, which would be valid for ten years, specified that documents regarding the manufacturing process would be supplied, but that this did not include the supply of drawings for the manufacture of tools, machinery and instruments. Production started in 1965, but four years later the company was taken over as a sick unit by the company which had earlier supplied the technology. Philips India Ltd. at that time agreed to the government condition that at least ten per cent of the production would be exported (ILPIC 1968, p. 133; Usha Menon, 1984).

The Loni Kalbhor factory near Pune came into existence in the year 1957. Initially it was set up for the production of radio sets. However, in the year 1970 when the company established another Factory at Pimpri near Pune, some of the activities of Loni Kalbhor factory, viz. manufacturing radio sets, were transferred to the Pimpri factory. The entire Loni Kalbhor factory became oriented to the manufacture of electronic components and plastic and metalware products. Loni Kalbhor as the biggest factory of Philips in India employs more than one-third of its total technical work-force.

In 1977 Philips-Peico added another unit to its credit, the Luminaire Centre at Calcutta. The production of lighting fittings and accessories has been shifted to this new luminaire centre in which around 400 workers are employed. After 1982, the company started expanding its activities at a hectic speed. A new research and development building was added to the Loni plant in 1982. In 1984, the Professional Electronic Equipment Factory for the production of a wide range of professional equipment (multi-meters, oscilloscopes; microphones, etc.) was inaugurated at Pimpri by the Union Minister of State for Communications. One year later, at Salt Lake in Calcutta, the Rs. 130 million electronic factory for the production of radio-recorder combinations became operational. At the same time, a start was made with the erection of a factory in the industrial area in Bangalore for the production of computer peripherals and medical equipment. At the Loni factory also, an expansion on the basis of a newly received license for the production of circuit boards has been initiated. The generation and sale of computer software in 1985 followed upon the constitution of a separate, fully-owned subsidiary, the Unique Dataware Systems and Consultants Limited. Philips N.V., it may be added, is the biggest European producer of chips with sales of over 1.5 billion dollars in 1985. In the field of research, it has a close cooperation with Siemens as well as common programmes with Intel, Motorola, RCA, Texas Instruments and others.

In addition to these units, Philips-Peico has a number of associated companies in which it has or until recently had financial participation, namely Music India, Duphar Interfran and Punjab Anand Batteries Ltd. The latter participation of only Rs. 40,000 may lead to an interesting development, comparable to what happened to the Osler lamp factory and the Welma welding equipment factory in the 1960s. Punjab Anand in 1985 commissioned its Punjab Anand Lamp Industries plant which, in due time could establish itself as a rival to Peico which, as we shall see later, has a quasi-monopoly control over the Indian Lamp market. Its success may depend very much on the cooperation, in return for a heavier involvement, of Peico. Alternatively it may have to follow the fate of the public-owned Hindustan Machine Tools lamp division, which is in the process of closing down its product line with 2000 odd workers (*Business India*, 25.08.1986).

The case of Punjab Anand, which was approved by the government in 1982, raises fundamental questions about the government declared intention to prevent the formation of monopoly power and to invite multinational corporations only on considerations of export prospects or transfer of high-tech. The production process of Anand Lamps is set up according to a technical collaboration agreement with the parent company of Peico, ELMI and Hind Lamps. In exchange for the supply of technology to Anand Lamps, mainly in the nature of advanced efficiency, Philips N.V. would get forty per cent equity in the company.

Peico also has had a number of arrangements with state-owned as well as private television companies (Tamil Nadu State Electronics Development Corporation, Solidaire, Beltek, etc.) for the supply of television components. A deal was also signed with the Andhra Pradesh Electronics Development Corporation, but is reported to be cancelled or modified in the wake of the government decision in August 1986 to provide Peico with a letter of intent for the manufacture of colour T.V. sets at its Salt Lake plant. The new government policy of March 1984, reversing its colour T.V. policy of 1983, allows companies with a foreign equity not exceeding 40% to manufacture T.V. receivers subject to the condition that they supply one-fourth of their production in kit form to small-scale units during the first five years. Peico had actually proposed to do more: in addition to its own 100,000 sets it would provide 50.000 kits to different companies.

The T.V. Manufacturers Association ITMA was, to put it mildly, not enamored with the proposals and sent a number of delegations to the government. The licensed production capacity in the country is already 15 million; actual production in 1984 was 1.8 million black and white and 6.6 million colour sets (*EPW*, 26.04.1986). The entry of Peico, the ITMA argues, is not needed, and may actually result in its acquiring a dominant position. The ITMA was particularly afraid that Peico would sweep the market on the strength of the Philips brand name (*India Today*, 15.10.1985). Its suspicion that the government was going to reverse its policy on this score was confirmed in August 1986 when the government decided to allow foreign companies to use the brand names of the parent company.

Prior to the receipts of an industrial license for T.V. sets, Peico used to have its sets produced by anciliary units, among others by Orient Vision Ltd. at Hosur in Tamil Nadu and HI-Bi Electronics at Madras. Whereas Peico in 1984 did not have any installed capacity for video products, it sold 11,000 sets. Since the sets were sold as Philips sets, and were actually supported by a massive advertisement campaign (a total budget of Rs. 33 million in 1984), some consumers felt duped, and in May 1985 filed a complaint with the Delhi magistrate (*India Today*, 31.07.1985). The license for the production of its own sets under the Philips brand name, which was finally awarded in 1986 for no obvious reason of economic or technological necessity, has removed the legal hurdles which had kept the expansion of Peico into the leading sector of the consumer electronics in check. It may also go some way in blending the accusation that Peico is thriving on selling third party products such as casette recorders, radios, refrigerators, casette tapes, etc. at high profits, as J. Dubashi illustrated in *India Today* (31.07.1985): "The margins are enormous and also raise the question of whether Peico is a predominantly manufacturing company or is turning into a trading firm intent on getting into as many segments of the fast-growing electronics market as possible. The Philips name is obviously the key factor in the sale". The accusations caused sufficient annoyance to the company, and made it appropriate for the then chairman of the company, C.J. Seelen, to remark in the presence of the Union Minister of State, V.N. Gadgil, on the occasion of the commissioning of a high-tech professional equipment factory at Pimpri, that Peico was actually not becoming a trading concern (*EPW*, 20.10.1984). The data in the annual reports of his company, however, indicate that the denial is not legitimate.

If we take for example the sales volume in 1984, then as much as 37% consisted of goods which have been purchased by Peico in their finished form. Some of the products have been organised in Table 5.3 according to their lincensed capacity, in-house production, purchases and sales. The goods include radio sets (744,000 purchased on a total sale of 1,572,000), tape recorders (81,000/186,000), and lamps (26 million/ 80 million). Whereas the excess sales oves in-house production as well as over lincensed capacity is considerable, with regard to a number of other products, particularly televisions, dry battery cells and domestic appliances, the sales appear to consists solely of third party products.

As it stands, low-tech products remain the mainstay of the output of the company. Table 5.4 shows that the lighting sector may be losing some of its relative importance. In 1981, it still represented 44% of the turnover. Its decrease afterwards can only partially be explained by the faster growth of the lamp output in the subsidiary ELMI. The audio products also have lost in relative importance, but still account for roughly one-third of the sales. The most significant growth has been reported in the sales of domestic appliances and dry batteries. These sectors, together with the income from installations (mainly lighting and communication installations) and from (marine product) trading, account for 84.5% of the turnover. The non-consumer products during the last ten years have continued to represent around 15% of the output. Professional equipment appears to have grown significantly. Almost half of the production under this heading is, however, made up of welding electrodes, a production branch which Peico sneaked into by taking over a sick company after it had managed to acquire 25% of the shares as well as the control over the technology. Specialised tools, electronic measuring instruments and medical equipment account for hardly five per cent of the activities. A comparison with Table 5.1 earlier, which gives the worldwide production structure of Philips N.V. is instructive since it establishes that at the world level professional and industrial equipment represents more than 45% of the output. Lighting and audio-visual home electronics which in India account for approximately 70% to 80% of turnover, in the worldwide production do not reach much beyond 35%. India appears very much as a mass maket for relatively low-tech consumption goods.

**Table 5.3 : Peico : Production and Trading Component of its Products, 1984**

| Product | Licensed Capacity | Production | Purchase | Sales | Excess Sales |
|---|---|---|---|---|---|
| Radio Sets | 1000 | 880 | 744 | 1572 | 78.6% |
| Tape Recorders | 20 | 115 | 81 | 186 | 61.7% |
| Television | 0 | 0 | 11 | 11 | — |
| Electronic Components | 456 | 365 | 373 | 226 | 0 |
| Dry Battery Cells | 0 | 0 | 53 | 52 | — |
| Domestic Appliances | 0 | 0 | 25 | 23 | — |
| Lamps | 30 | 26 | 57 | 80 | 207.7% |
| Electronic Measuring Instruments | 30 | 12 | 11 | 14 | 16.6% |

*Notes* : 1. Excess sales is calculated in relation to the in-house production and not in relation to the licensed capacity.
2. The production is expressed in thousands, except for lamps (x million).

*Source* : Peico Electronics and Electricals Ltd., Annual Report 1984.

**Table 5.4 : Output Structure of Peico, 1974-1984**

| Product Line | 1974 | 1979 | 1984 |
|---|---|---|---|
| Industrial, Medical and Welding | 7.09 | 7.21 | 9.06 |
| Intercom Apparatus | 2.76 | 1.48 | 0.93 |
| Electronic Components | 5.47 | 7.03 | 5.55 |
| Lighting and Batteries | 43.45 | 42.18 | 38.70 |
| Audio | 37.53 | 34.69 | 30.26 |
| Domestic Appliances | 0 | 0 | 6.13 |
| Installations, Services, Trade | 1.75 | 4.85 | 7.55 |
| Others | 2.88 | 2.22 | 1.74 |
| Total | 100 | 100 | 100 |

*Notes* : 1. Industrial and Medical Apparatus include specialised tools, electronic measuring instruments and welding electrodes and equipment.
2. Audio in 1984 includes televisions.
3. The sales figures of lamps exlude the lamp sales made by the subsidiary company ELMI. In 1984, the newly started production of dry batteries (2.18%) has been added.
4. Due to rounding, the totals may not add up to 100.00.
5. Trade includes only one particular item, namely marine products, and thus excludes the trading activities which have become visible in Table 5.3.

*Source* : Annual Report of Peico.

## 5.2. Indigenisation and Performance

Most foreign companies at the time of Indianisation under the FERA guidelines, adopted a number of measures including the prerogative of appointing the managing director and the regulating of the use of trademarks and the corporate name. Peico also adopted these two specific measures. In what follows we will examine the management structure in detail. The strength of the Board of Directors of the Peico Electronics and Electricals Limited has been raised from five in 1967 to eight in 1981. Until 1968, the majority of the Directors had been foreigners. Subsequently, well before FERA, the company started inducting more and more Indian directors on the Board. Since 1972 the composition of the Board of Directors changed in favour of Indians. Three directorships of the company—Chairman-cum-Managing Director, Technical Director and Director of Finance and Administration—remained to be held by foreigners till 1974. Only in 1975, the technical directorship was temporarily transferred to an Indian, the then 45 year old Mr. S. Venkataraman, who held the technical directorship till 1983.

Apart from the technical director, there are three other full-time Indian directors on the Board. They are in charge of marketing, personnel-cum-administration and the liaison executive for government contacts at New Delhi. They all joined the company a quarter century ago and have served in various posts. One of them, Mr. S.G. Phaterphekar, who looks after the head office at Calcutta, is stated to hold 22 directorships (S.P. Varma 1983, p. 248). These three directors are holding 3692 equity shares out of 18,000,000 equity shares. This negligible number of shares in their hands shows that they are merely salaried managers of the company.*

The Chairman-cum-Managing Director of the company is invariably a foreigner. The last two directors of the company served in the office for a five years' period each and were also Chairman-cum-Managing Director of the Electric Lamp Manufacturers (India) Private Limited and up to recently, Chairman of Duphar-Interfran Ltd. In addition, the present expatriate managing director is also the director of Hind Lamps, of Webel Telecommunications and of Music India Limited.

Peico, as stated earlier, has chosen to promote its own employees to the Board of Directors. There is, however, a limit to their number. Under the Articles of Association of the company, it is stipulated that as long as Philips NV holds a minimum level of the equity of the Indian company,

*In 1981 the total remuneration to the six directors on the payroll amounted to Rs. 1.5 million. The other two Indian directors are not mentioned on the company's payroll. One of them who has been on the Board since 1969, is a partner in the firm of Crawford Bayley and Company, the legal advisers of the Company. The other one was appointed as a director on September 29, 1980 at the request of the financial institutions who subscribed to the issue of Rs. 80 million debentures.

it would have the right to appoint one-third of the Directors on the Board as well as the Chairman and Managing Director. The company's top management is thus still safely under control of the parent company, despite the FERA measures.

One of the aims of the FERA guidelines was the preservation of foreign exchange through the increase in exports and through a relative decrease in the outward flow of dividends for foreign equity. Our calculations show that the expected net positive result has not fructified in the case of Philips. We have estimated the balance of payments effects of Philips-Peico in Table 5.5. Information is available only for the years after 1973 as statements on the earnings and expenditures in foreign currency in the annexure to the profit and loss statements. Due to the enactment of FERA the companies having non-resident interest are expected to declare these accounts.

Over the period of 1973-1984 Peico, i.e. without taking into account the other Philips controlled companies (ELMI, Duphar, Hind Lamps, among others) caused a drain on the country's foreign exchange resources of Rs. 193 million, i.e. if only the direct imports are taken into consideration. The inclusion of the indirect imports, i.e. those procured through government channelising agencies, alters the picture drastically. The trading balance has been widening sharply from around Rs. 25 million in the mid- and late-seventies to more than Rs. 100 million in the mid-eighties. Exports totalling Rs. 599 million were very much inferior to the aggregate import figure of Rs. 929 million. The dismal export performance as compared to the imports is less dramatic when only the direct imports are taken into consideration, but also in this case the trading account is getting more and more out of balance. It went up to Rs. 163 million in 1985.

On the basis of our tabulations it also appears that the foreign currency involved in the trading activities is much higher than the actual drain of surplus, in which we have included the dividends, interest charges, commission fees, servicing fees as well as a rest category which may contain certain foreign exchange payments which are not strictly speaking a drain of surplus. Actual dividends absorbed only 8.7% of the foreign exchange cost. The net current effect over a

**Table 5.5 : Peico : Balance of Payments Effects, 1973-84**

(Rs. in Millions)

| Year | Exports at fob | Total Imports | Dividend | Commission and fees | Others | Drain of Surplus | Gross Out-flow (3+7) | Current Effect |
|---|---|---|---|---|---|---|---|---|
| 1973 | 11.9 | 25.6 | 7.3 | 3.8 | 0.4 | 11.4 | 37.0 | —25.1 |
| 1974 | 33.7 | 47.0 | 3.8 | 6.1 | 0.4 | 10.3 | 57.4 | —23.6 |
| 1975 | 31.6 | 31.4 | 0 | 5.9 | 0.6 | 6.4 | 37.8 | −6.1 |
| 1976 | 43.1 | 45.6 | 10.0 | 7.1 | 0.8 | 17.9 | 63.5 | —20.4 |
| 1977 | 45.2 | 66.3 | 4.7 | 2.5 | 1.1 | 8.3 | 66.3 | —21.1 |
| 1978 | 51.1 | 62.1 | 13.2 | 4.1 | 1.5 | 18.8 | 80.9 | —29.4 |
| 1979 | 51.0 | 62.7 | 10.6 | 5.2 | 1.9 | 17.7 | 80.4 | —29.4 |
| 1980 | 44.0 | 90.7 | 9.1 | 6.0 | 1.7 | 16.8 | 107.5 | —63.6 |
| 1981 | 64.5 | 101.0 | 9.6 | 3.4 | 3.8 | 16.8 | 117.8 | - 53.4 |
| 1982 | 73.2 | 157.7 | 9.6 | 1.0 | 5.3 | 15.9 | 173.6 | —100.5 |
| 1983 | 74.8 | 115.4 | 11.6 | 6.7 | 2.8 | 21.1 | 136.5 | −61.7 |
| 1984 | 75.4 | 162.7 | 10.3 | 6.0 | 5.6 | 21.9 | 184.6 | —109.2 |
| Total | 599.4 | 929.3 | 99.5 | 57.8 | 26.0 | 183.5 | 1142.5 | —543.3 |

*Notes* : 1. Imports includes all the raw materials, spare parts etc., which have been consumed in the production process and which have been imported either directly or indirectly through government trading companies, as well as the direct import of capital goods.

2. During the period no foreign capital has been brought into the country. The net effect in the last column is therefore the outcome of exports (and related income) minus exports minus drain of surplus.

3. The drain of surplus includes columns 4, 5 and 6. The latter column may include miscellaneous expenses which are not directly to be considered a drain of surplus. More details, however, are not available.

*Source* : Annual Reports of Philips India and Peico.

period of twelve year is, however, quite considerable, namely Rs 543 million. If the recent trends are any indications, the negative balance will take on dramatic proportions. Even presently the outflow of foreign exchange resources is as high as the total value of production in the high tech sector, i.e. specialised tools, measuring instruments and medical apparatuses.

The negative trade balance has persisted despite the fact that Peico has been awarded the status of an export house. Exports started in 1966 and in the early seventies increased to reach a record level valued at 5.9% of sales in 1976, i.e. at a time that the government made it clear that foreign controlled companies under the purview of the FERA act should honour their export obligations. In the following years, exports have again started declining. Table 5.6 clearly shows this development. It also brings out the fact that the company has been receiving substantial subsidies from the government. According to the claims of the company, most of its exports have been on a voluntary basis, with the exception of welding electrodes, in which case a condition had been put by the government that ten per cent of the annual output should be exported. A similar obligation has been imposed by the government while issuing a letter of intent in 1984 for the manufacture of an additional one million pieces of audio products. The export obligation, which usually is restricted to a number of years, indicates that the foreign company, if confronted with strict government regulations, takes its export endeavour serious but will return to production for the internal market after it has fulfilled the time restricted orders. The exports of Peico presently consists of radio receivers, loudspeakers; potentiometers, and marine products. The latter item in 1983 accounted for 61% of the export earnings. In 1984 it accounted for 39.5%. A rather simple arithmetic exercise leads us to the conclusion that, at least during the last couple of years, hardly two per cent of Peico's products were sold in other countries. Since the identity of the countries to which the exports took place is not known, a substantial part of its may have found its way to bilateral rupee trade countries from which no hard foreign currency was derived.

**Table 5.6 : Philips India : Export as a Percentage of Turnover, 1966-1985**

(Rs in millions)

| Year | Export | Export % of turnover | Exports subsidy and duty draw-backs |
|---|---|---|---|
| 1966 | 0.7 | 0.30 | — |
| 1967 | 0.2 | 0.01 | — |
| 1968 | 0.9 | 0.30 | — |
| 1969 | 7.5 | 2.40 | — |
| 1970 | 10.6 | 2.80 | — |
| 1971 | 6.0 | 1.20 | — |
| 1972 | 10.4 | 2.10 | — |
| 1973 | 11.9 | 2.30 | — |
| 1974 | 33.5 | 5 40 | — |
| 1975 | 31.6 | 5.30 | — |
| 1976 | 43.1 | 5.90 | 9.73 |
| 1977 | 45.1 | 5.60 | 10.15 |
| 1978 | 51.0 | 5.60 | 10.13 |
| 1979 | 50.8 | 4.90 | 12.14 |
| 1980 | 43.3 | 3.60 | 9.62 |
| 1981 | 61.3 | 4.12 | 8.20 |
| 1982 | 72.9 | 4.04 | 8.87 |
| 1983 | 74.8 | 4.22 | 8.16 |
| 1984 | 75.4 | 3.55 | 7.82 |
| 1985 | 61.6 | 2.35 | 9.98 |

*Source* : Annual Reports of the Company.

Philips started its activities in colonial India as a trading company, and subsequently has turned into a major producing and marketing company of various types of electrical and electronic goods. The data on turnover which has been collected from 1958 onwards (see Table 5.7) indicate a simple annual growth rate of more than fifty per cent. Since it can be argued that the simple rate of growth presents a distortion because of a likely low initial turnover volume, the

## Table 5.7 : Growth of Peico since 1957

| Year | Net Worth Rs. mill. | Share Capital Rs. million | Reserves | | No. of share-holders | No. of employees | Sales |
|---|---|---|---|---|---|---|---|
| | | | Rs. million | Per cent | | | |
| 1958 | 26.7 | 22.0 | 4.7 | 18 | 17,517 | 1,554 | 45 |
| 1959 | 27.3 | 22.0 | 5.3 | 19 | 16,023 | 1,667 | 49 |
| 1960 | 28.4 | 22.0 | 6.4 | 23 | 15,054 | 2,134 | 56 |
| 1961 | 29.5 | 22.0 | 7.5 | 25 | 14,596 | 2,469 | 68 |
| 1962 | 31.1 | 22.0 | 9.1 | 29 | 14,100 | 2,759 | 89 |
| 1963 | 33.4 | 22.0 | 11.4 | 34 | 13,786 | 3,064 | 106 |
| 1964 | 38.3 | 22.0 | 16.3 | 43 | 13,365 | 3,714 | 114 |
| 1965 | 49.7 | 26.0 | 23.7 | 48 | 14,135 | 4,215 | 135 |
| 1966 | 62.6 | 36.4 | 26.2 | 42 | 13,945 | 5,052 | 188 |
| 1967 | 67.2 | 36.4 | 30.8 | 46 | 13,972 | 5,087 | 234 |
| 1968 | 75.6 | 36.4 | 39.2 | 52 | 13,752 | 5,466 | 266 |
| 1969 | 90.3 | 36.4 | 53.9 | 60 | 13,492 | 6,017 | 302 |
| 1970 | 105.4 | 54.6 | 50.8 | 48 | 13,620 | 6,587 | 377 |
| 1971 | 134.2 | 54.6 | 79.6 | 59 | 13,675 | 6,929 | 466 |
| 1972 | 158.1 | 54.6 | 103.5 | 65 | 13,698 | 7,193 | 491 |
| 1973 | 212.8 | 67.9 | 144.9 | 68 | 32,748 | 7,495 | 504 |
| 1974 | 244.0 | 135.8 | 108.2 | 44 | 32,216 | 7,728 | 616 |
| 1975 | 235.5 | 135.8 | 99.7 | 42 | 32,432 | 7,406 | 592 |
| 1976 | 242.7 | 135.8 | 106.9 | 44 | 31,780 | 7,622 | 721 |
| 1977 | 260.2 | 135.8 | 124.4 | 48 | 31,617 | 7,989 | 798 |

| | | | | | | | |
|---|---|---|---|---|---|---|---|
| 1978 | 275.6 | 163.0 | 112.6 | 41 | 31,870 | 8,183 | 901 |
| 1979 | 307.5 | 173 8 | 134.5 | 44 | 64,642 | 8,451 | 1030 |
| 1980 | 342.4 | 180.0 | 162.4 | 47 | 62,092 | 8,409 | 1199 |
| 1981 | 377.3 | 180.0 | 197.3 | 52 | 59,252 | 8,655 | 1488 |
| 1982 | 575.1 | 216.0 | 359.1 | 62 | 58,848 | 8,850 | 1805 |
| 1983 | 591.2 | 226.0 | 375.2 | 63 | 58,895 | 8,867 | 1769 |
| 1984 | 595.6 | 216.0 | 379.6 | 64 | 58,836 | 8,975 | 2251 |
| 1985 | 701.3 | 216.0 | 485.3 | 69 | 60,924 | 9,028 | 2556 |

*Source* : Annual Reports of the Company.

index of growth after 1974, the crucial year in which the FERA act became operational, will be used as an additional comparative exercise. In ten years' time, the index of sales increased from 100 to 380 in 1984, representing a simple growth rate of 38%.

It is often mentioned that the Peico products, especially in view of the link with the Philips logo, are bound to have an advantage over products of less known and less reliable companies. One significant aspect which actually may lay at the basis of this position is often forgotten, namely the brisk advertising activities of the company. Expenditure on advertisements alone, according to our calculations, on an average amount to close to two per cent of sales. In addition, the company has developed an intricate network of dealers all over the country. The dealers have been organised into three different categories. The most important category, the class A dealers, used to be bound by strict agreements which are drawn up by the various dealers associations, e.g. the authorised radio dealers association. The clauses in the agreement between the company and the radio dealers stipulated that "the dealer shall carry out at his own expenses advertising campaigns to promote the sales of the company's products in accordance with the company's policy laid down for the purpose". Although the last stipulation was afterwards deleted on the authority of the MRTP Commission, the structure of dealers associations has remained intact and provides the company with a powerful sales promotion instrument (B. Rajender 1982, pp. 72-76).

At the time of the incorporation of the company in 1930, it started with a modest authorised capital of Rs. one lakh and a paid-up capital of Rs. 45,000. After independence, the amounts were increased to Rs. 5 million and Rs. 2.5 million respectively. New increases in equity were permitted by the government of India in 1957 (Rs. 5 million), in 1967 (Rs. 100 million), in 1974 (Rs. 200 million), and in 1983 (Rs 300 million). By 1985, the paid-up capital had increased to Rs. 216 million. The total net worth totalled more than Rs. 700 million which put the company among the thirty biggest private companies in India. The increased capital base of the company is to a great extent on account of the growing volume of retained profits, as emerges from column 4 of Table 5.7. The reserves in 1985 represented 69% of the net worth of the company.

The analysis of the shareholders' capital reveals only one aspect of the financing policy of a foreign controlled corporation. A more detailed view will result from the analysis of the sources of finance for gross investments. The financing policy has two implications. In the first place, if the MNC depends heavily on local funds, the indigenous firms may accordingly find it more difficult to get access to liquidities. In the second place, a decreasing inflow of new foreign capital in conjunction with the payment of dividends on increasing (bonus) share equity will cause a negative effect on the balance of payments.

In addition to the internally generated capital, loans from the local capital market and institutions have regularly made an important contribution to the total working capital of the company. In Table 5.8, the sources of funds have been calculated by B. Rajender (1982) since 1957, the year in which Philips India turned into a public limited company. During a period of a quarter a century, Philips-Peico derived most of its funds from local and internal sources. The remaining contribution, amounting to a mere Rs. 20.8 million over the total period came from foreign sources, which by any stretch of imagination cannot be considered a significant amount.

If the present trend continues—there is no indication to assume that it will not—, the total foreign contribution to gross investment before long will have declined to less than one per cent: whereas the internal sources in the total capital stock grew from 22% in 1957 to close to 78% in 1981, the foreign stock declined during the same period from 28% to less than 3%. In terms of new flows, the contribution was even much lower: foreign sources during the period 1970-1980 provided only 0.1%, with one peak of 10% in 1973, as a consequence of which its share in the stock position increased marginally to 6%. Loans from local banks, equity participation and debentures have also decreased in importance, but still remain at a significant level of 19.1%. During the last couple of years, borrowings from local banks and institutions appear to have been growing (Sridhar Krishna 1982, p. 25).

**Table 5.8 : Philips India: Relative Share of the Sources of the Funds**

| Year | Reserves including bonus issues | Depreciation | Total Internal | Local Banks & financial institutions | Borrowing from local capital market | Local contributions to equity net of bonus issues | Total local | Local & internal | Foreign contributions to equity net of bonus issues | Finance for gross investment (Rs. millions) |
|---|---|---|---|---|---|---|---|---|---|---|
| 1957 | 12.5 | 9.5 | 22.0 | 26.6 | — | 23.3 | 49.9 | 71.9 | 28.0 | 35 |
| 1958 | 15.2 | 12.0 | 27.2 | 16.1 | — | 25.8 | 41.9 | 69.1 | 30.9 | 32 |
| 1959 | 16.0 | 14.9 | 30.9 | 14 0 | — | 25.0 | 37.0 | 69.9 | 30.0 | 33 |
| 1960 | 21.8 | 15.0 | 36.8 | 22.7 | — | 18.4 | 41.1 | 77.9 | 22.0 | 44 |
| 1961 | 18.9 | 15.2 | 34.1 | 33.5 | — | 14.7 | 48.2 | 82.3 | 17.6 | 56 |
| 1962 | 22.1 | 17.7 | 39.8 | 29.8 | — | 13.8 | 43.6 | 83.4 | 16.6 | 59 |
| 1963 | 22.6 | 18.5 | 41.1 | 32.5 | — | 12.0 | 44.5 | 85.6 | 14.4 | 68 |
| 1964 | 26.6 | 20.4 | 47.0 | 29.3 | — | 5.4 | 34.7 | 81.7 | 18.3 | 76 |
| 1965 | 26.3 | 18.2 | 44.5 | 34.6 | — | 6.4 | 41.0 | 83.7 | 14.5 | 105 |
| 1966 | 26.0 | 16.7 | 42.7 | 43.2 | — | 4.3 | 47.5 | 90.2 | 9.7 | 156 |
| 1967 | 27.2 | 21.0 | 48.2 | 29.4 | 9.0 | 4.1 | 42.5 | 90.7 | 9.2 | 166 |
| 1968 | 27.5 | 22.3 | 49.8 | 31.2 | 7.7 | 3.5 | 42.4 | 92.2 | 7.8 | 195 |
| 1969 | 31.4 | 22.3 | 53.7 | 29.1 | 6.9 | 3.1 | 39.1 | 92.8 | 7.0 | 217 |
| 1970 | 31.4 | 21.7 | 53.1 | 33.0 | 5.6 | 2.5 | 41.1 | 94.2 | 5.7 | 266 |
| 1971 | 44.5 | 27.3 | 71.8 | 13.5 | 5.9 | 2.7 | 22.1 | 93.9 | 6.0 | 252 |
| 1972 | 47.3 | 28.3 | 75.6 | 11.5 | 5.2 | 2.3 | 19.0 | 94.6 | 5.3 | 288 |
| 1973 | 50.8 | 27.1 | 77.9 | 7.6 | 4.2 | 4.0 | 15.9 | 93.9 | 6.0 | 349 |

| | | | | | | | | | | |
|---|---|---|---|---|---|---|---|---|---|---|
| 1974 | 52.6 | 27.1 | 79.8 | 7.5 | 3.7 | 3.5 | 14.8 | 94.6 | 5.3 | 396 |
| 1975 | 50.0 | 30.7 | 80.8 | 6.5 | 3.7 | 3.5 | 13.8 | 94.6 | 5.3 | 400 |
| 1976 | 49.6 | 33.6 | 83.2 | 4.7 | 3.5 | 3.3 | 11.6 | 94.9 | 5.0 | 418 |
| 1977 | 49.8 | 34.9 | 84.8 | 4.0 | 3.3 | 3.1 | 10.4 | 95.3 | 4.7 | 451 |
| 1978 | 49.9 | 36.4 | 86.4 | 3.7 | 2.4 | 2.9 | 9.1 | 95.5 | 4.4 | 481 |
| 1979 | 47.5 | 35.3 | 82.9 | 7.2 | 1.6 | 4.8 | 13.6 | 96.6 | 3.4 | 551 |
| 1980 | 42.5 | 31.8 | 74.4 | 5.2 | 12.6 | 4.6 | 22.4 | 96.9 | 3.0 | 681 |
| 1981 | 44.9 | 32.8 | 77.7 | 3.4 | 11.4 | 4.3 | 19.3 | 97.1 | 2.8 | 723 |

*Source* : Annual Reports of the Company as Computated by Basuthkar Rajender (1982).

*Note* : The percentage may not always add to 100%, due to rounding.

During recent years, there has been a marked decline in the profitability ratios, as the last column in Table 5.9 indicates. Net profit as a percentage of net worth which had been consistenly between 15 and 20%, barring a few exception, after 1981 dropped to a one digit number, and in 1983 even reached as low a score as 2.9 per cent. The fast growth in shareholders' interests is only partially responsible for the decline, because even in absolute terms, net profits after a temporarily increase around 1980 have remained at the level reached during the 1970s. One major development has been the consistent rise in depreciation and interest charges. Both items together, which in 1975 totalled Rs. 40 million, by 1984 had risen to Rs. 132 million and accordingly caused a slow-down in the growth of gross profits and even a stagnation in taxes. Since on the other hand, the company continued to pay higher dividends, more recourse had to be taken to loans to finance the big expansion programmes. Once the investments start throwing off results, the profitability ratios may again return to their normal levels.

Before leaving this section, it may be interesting to have a look at the comparative behaviour of Peico within the corporate structure of Philips. Earlier we have seen that the dividend remitted to the parent company during the last couple of years amounted to around ten million rupees as compared to around five million in the mid-seventies. The increase is not dramatic since much of the difference can be accounted for by inflation. Nevertheless, if we aggregate the drain of surplus on account of dividends, interest and commission fees, and compare it with the actual share of Philips in the paid-up of the capital (i.e. 40%), the ratio in 1983 for example, which was admittedly a bad year for the company, was as high as 20.5 per cent. The drain of surplus (columns 4+5 in Table 5.5) in absolute terms was actually higher than the net profit declared by Peico. Although we do not intend to stretch this argument too far, the relative low profit ratios of subsidiaries of multinational companies in particluar years do not necessarily or automatically cause a decline of income from profits for the parent company.

Before comparing the profitability of Peico with that of the parent company, a general idea will be presented on the

**Table 5.9 : Peico: Profits, Dividends and Taxes, 1958-1984**

(Percentages and Rs. Million)

| Year | Gross Profit to Sales | Taxes as % of Gross Profits | Net Profit | Dividends | Profit Retained as % of Net Profits | Net Profit to Net Worth |
|---|---|---|---|---|---|---|
| 1 | 2 | 3 | 4 | 5 | 6 | 7 |
| 1958 | 12.0 | 51.9 | 2.6 | 1.9 | 28.1 | n.a. |
| 1959 | 12.0 | 47.5 | 3.1 | 2.6 | 14.8 | n.a. |
| 1960 | 11.3 | 54.0 | 2.9 | 2.6 | 9.0 | n.a. |
| 1961 | 9.7 | 54.5 | 3.0 | 2.6 | 12.0 | n.a. |
| 1962 | 13.6 | 70.8 | 3.5 | 2.9 | 18.3 | n.a. |
| 1963 | 15.6 | 70.5 | 4.9 | 3.3 | 32.6 | n.a. |
| 1964 | 19.7 | 71.4 | 6.4 | 4.0 | 38.1 | n.a. |
| 1965 | 16.8 | 68.7 | 7.1 | 4.7 | 34.1 | 14.3 |
| 1966 | 17.1 | 62.3 | 12.1 | 6.5 | 45.9 | 19.3 |
| 1967 | 18.6 | 67.8 | 14.0 | 6.9 | 50.6 | 20.8 |
| 1968 | 17.3 | 66.6 | 15.3 | 7.3 | 52.4 | 20.2 |
| 1969 | 17.4 | 64.5 | 18.7 | 8.4 | 55.2 | 20.7 |
| 1970 | 17.8 | 63.2 | 24.7 | 10.9 | 55.8 | 23.4 |
| 1971 | 24.9 | 66.6 | 38.7 | 13.1 | 66.2 | 28.8 |
| 1972 | 20.5 | 65.5 | 34.0 | 13.1 | 61.5 | 21.6 |
| 1973 | 18.2 | 64.3 | 32.7 | 16.3 | 50.2 | 15.4 |
| 1974 | 18.7 | 67.0 | 38.0 | 12.9 | 66.1 | 15.6 |
| 1975 | 8.6 | 60.5 | 34.9 | 12.0 | 63.0 | 6.4 |
| 1976 | 9.5 | 63.5 | 25.0 | 16.3 | 34.8 | 10.3 |

(*Contd.*)

**Table 5.9** (*Contd.*)

| 1 | 2 | 3 | 4 | 5 | 6 | 7 |
|---|---|---|---|---|---|---|
| 1977 | 11.4 | 58.9 | 37.3 | 19.8 | 46.8 | 14.3 |
| 1978 | 11.8 | 64.0 | 38.2 | 26.0 | 31.9 | 13.9 |
| 1979 | 13.3 | 68.4 | 43.5 | 29.4 | 32.2 | 14.1 |
| 1980 | 13-0 | 63.0 | 75.5 | 32.4 | 43.6 | 16.8 |
| 1981 | 12.3 | 63.4 | 67.3 | 32.4 | 51.9 | 17.8 |
| 1982 | 6.3 | 54.3 | 51.8 | 38.9 | 24.9 | 9.0 |
| 1983 | 1.9 | 49.7 | 17.7 | 34.6 | 0 | 2.9 |
| 1984 | 4.5 | 53.8 | 46.6 | 43.2 | 6.9 | 7.8 |
| 1985 | 2.0 | 37.3 | 30.3 | 32.4 | 0 | 4.3 |

*Notes* : 1. Gross profit is calculated net of depreciation.

2. Net profit represents profits after tax but before deduction of investment allowances reserves.

3. Profit retained is the gross result of net profits minus dividends disregarding transfer of balances from previous years and from investment reserves.

*Source* : Annual Reports of the Company; B. Rajender 1982, p. 134.

performance of the Philips subsidiaries in the Third World in general. A similar exercise has been undertaken earlier in the case of Unilever, but unlike the practice in that concern, overall figures of Philips N.V. as contained in the annual reports, do not include the non-consolidated companies. The overall statistics in Table 5.10, do therefore not include the activities of Peico. The activities have been grouped under three areas, viz. Europe, North America and the Rest of the World. The last category can be taken to be broadly identical with the developing countries, although it also includes Japan, Australia, New Zealand. The latter countries represent approximately three per cent of the corporate structure.

The changes which have taken place in the corporate asset structure, profit generation and employment position indicate two basic shifts. On the one hand, we notice a dramatic growth in the importance of the North America operations. The share of assets located in the USA and Canada has more than doubled between 1976 and 1984, albeit on the basis of a more capital-intensive production structure than either in Europe or in the Third World. On the other hand stands the fast decline of the importance of the European operations. From an overwhelming 74.4 per cent of the corporate assets located in the European countries in 1976, the percentage has gradually declined to 60.4 per cent in 1984, despite an increase in absolute terms from 22.4 billion florins to 32.9 billion florins. In the rest of the world, assets have less than doubled and have, in proportion to the overall assets, remained more or less static at around sixteen per cent.

The second important observation to be derived from Table 5.10 is the respectively relatively low and relatively high contribution to the overall profits by the units operating in Europe on the one hand and in the developing countries on the other hand. In this respect, the year 1981, when the developing countries contributed almost twice as much to the overall profits than what either its share in assets or employment would warrant, stands out as exceptional.

Conclusions on differing rates of profitability in OECD countries and developing countries cannot be drawn without a caveat. The usefulness of aggregate calculations for this purpose

**Table 5.10 : Philips N.V. : Geographical Distribution of Assets, Profits and Employment (1976-1984)**

| | 1976 | | | 1984 | | |
|---|---|---|---|---|---|---|
| | Assets % | Profits | Employment | Assets % | Profits | Employment |
| Europe | 74.4 | 61.6 | 71.7 | 60.4 | 47.9 | 61.6 |
| North America | 10.3 | 14.7 | 9.9 | 23.3 | 26.7 | 17.7 |
| Rest of the World | 15.3 | 23.7 | 18.4 | 16.3 | 26.3 | 20.6 |
| Total Magnitude | 30.100 | 2226 | 392 | 54.535 | 3473 | 344 |

*Note* : The magnitude has been expressed in million florins for assets and profits, and in thousand numbers for employment.
*Source* : Annual Reports of Philips N.V.

are namely distorted by the fact that a substantial part of the output is not sold directly to third parties, but to subsidiary companies in other areas. For example, Philips in the EEG 1982 accounted for 59 per cent of the output, but for only 45 per cent of the sales. Developing countries on the other hand accounted for only 10.0 per cent of output, but for 18 per cent of sales and for for as much as 31.5 per cent of profits. Since a substantial part of the profit derives from the sale of products produced elsewhere in the world, the accounting of the profitability of the invested capital in the various regions is distorted, the more so since the possibilities for transfer pricing are manifold. This, however, does not mean that no general conclusions can be drawn. From the material, the picture emerges that the activities in the Third World *do have* an exceptional contribution to the profits of the corporate group.

Let us now again turn our attention to the profitability of Peico in comparison with its parent body. It is evident from Table 5.11., in which the ratio of profit to the net worth of both the companies is calculated over a period of ten years, that the Indian subsidiary is more profitable than the overall worldwide operations. In all the years, except probably in 1983, the profit rate of Peico has been substantially higher than that of its parent body. The higher profits in India stand in sharp contrast to the low remuneration for labour. Whereas in the EEC countries around half of the sales revenue accrues to the work-force, in India only around 15 per cent of sales revenue is spent on wages and salaries (B. Rajender 1982, p. 125).

## 5.3. Monopoly Position and Linkages: The Lamp Industry

The industrial licensing system is an instrument in the hands of the Government to regulate new investments in accordance with the plan objectives. The licensing system was adopted with a view to protect small-scale industries and to regulate foreign private investments and technical collaboration in such a manner that local entrepreneurship and indigenous technology and knowhow would be provided

**Table 5.11 : Gross Profit/Net Worth Ratio of Peico and Philips**

| Year | Peico | Philips N.V. |
|---|---|---|
| 1972 | 71 (64) | 26 |
| 1973 | 49 (43) | 32 |
| 1974 | 52 (47) | 24 |
| 1975 | 29 (22) | 12 |
| 1976 | 35 (28) | 21 |
| 1977 | 40 (35) | 21 |
| 1978 | 43 (39) | 20 |
| 1979 | 48 (45) | 19 |
| 1980 | 49 (45) | 16 |
| 1981 | 54 (49) | 17 |
| 1982 | 29 (20) | na |
| 1983 | 19 ( 6) | na |
| 1984 | 32 (17) | na |

*Notes*: 1. Trading profit has been calculated as the proceeds from deliveries, prior to interest charges.
2. Between brackets the gross profit ratio net of interest.

*Source*: Annual Reports of the respective companies; B. Rajender 1982, p. 108.

with a certain degree of protection. After the adoption of the licensing system, all large industrial houses would require government approval prior to expansion. Additionally, for certain industries the entry by industrial monopoly houses was strictly prohibited (e.g. in the production of one-band radio's, tapes, dry battery cells, refrigerators, etc.)

It would be interesting to analyse Peico's production behaviour in respect of the licensing policy. We have examined the excess capacity from the legal viewpoint, that is to what extent it is exceeding its licensed capacity by more than five per cent. In almost all the years between 1971-1980, almost half of the products were being produced excessively. The actual production was very much above the licensed capacity in items like lamps, filaments, fittings, etc. In the period 1978 to 1980, the company's lamp production was below the newly granted license, which in fact regularised the excess capacity, but if we look at the purchase of the company from third parties, the aggregate lamp sale by Philips turns out to be more than double its production. Instead of producing excessively in its own plants, which in the past had attracted the attention of political parties and committed economists and journalists, the company has shifted to a strategy of purchasing from other producers and selling the same under its brand name. The new strategy seems therefore geared at reducing the in-house excess production and to contractually purchase the output of smaller producers. This out-house production is also taken recourse to in the case of those products which the company is not allowed to produce itself, like dry battery cells, casette tapes, refrigerators, kitchen machines, etc. Information on some of these products has been given earlier in Table 5.3. Here we would like to concentrate on one of the two products which traditionally has been the mainstay of the companies' activities in India, namely incandescent lamps. Lighting products, together with audio products, represent close to seventy per cent of the turnover. In both ranges of products, Peico may be considered to have acquired an absolute monopoly position. Even if the aggregate statistics of the Directorate General of Technical Development, the principal technical advisory organisation to the Government of India on technical and industrial matters, may have left some production units from its purview and may not be fully accurate, the overall production figures in for example the radio industry are too obvious to be dismissed because of possible accounting errors. The DGTD in 1981 counted eight registered units with a total production in the organised sector of 1.56 million radio sets, valued at Rs. 4.0 million rupees (DGTD 1983, p. 29).* The annual report of Peico on the other hand reported the production of 911,000 sets and the sale of 1.29 million sets with a value of Rs. 3.9 million rupees. Radio sets, with the exception of one-band

*According to the area survey Electronics Industry in India (Electronics Information and Planning, December 1981, p. 161), total radio production, inclusive of unregistered units, totalled 5.5 million.

radio's, it appears, are almost exclusively marketed by Peico. Only a few indigenous producers of low-priced radios are left as independent producers. The rest have been either liquidated or have been integrated as suppliers to the Peico concern. On the basis of the same aggregate sources, Peico accounts for 51 per cent of the tape recorders and combination sets (90 per cent of the value) and for 75 per cent of the record players (92% of the value of sales).

The electric lamp industry offers a good example of the extent to which and the way in which a multinational corporation has succeeded in establishing itself in a monopoly position. The electric lamp industry in India originated in 1934 with the poineering efforts of Bengal Lamps Works Limited. Presently the industry is spread all over India, mainly in the organised sector. There are quite a few small scale units manufacturing GLS and FT lamps. It is to be noted that small scale units are producing mainly miniature and auto bulbs. In the early seventies, there were as many as 127 GLS lamp units in this sector. The number came down to 50 by 1977 due to the competition from the organised sector units and the lack of adequate resources with the small scale units. Further, for critical components, these units have to depend on the organised sector units. It is difficult to assess their production capacity. However, it can be estimated that it is around five per cent of total GLS lamp production. Aggregate licenced and installed capacity of the organised sector according to the DGTD is 256 million for the manufacture of GLS lamps and 32 million for FT lamps. The actual production of GLS and FT lamps in 1982 was 272 million and 32 million pieces respectively.

The organised sector had recently seventeen units manufacturing general lighting service (GLS) lamps and eleven units manufacturing fluorescent tube (FT) lamps. GEC and AEI recently merged and formed a company called Genelec Company which is getting bulbs from ELMI and Hind Lamps. Its brand name is Osram. Crompton Greaves is also getting products for its trade from the above companies. Apart from this Crompton took over the management of Toshiba Anand, its products being manufactured under the brand name of Crompton. With the exception of Beneal Lamp Works, the rest of the major electric lamp producing units in India either had or are having a foreign collaboration with internationally well-known companies. In the case of Philips (presently called Peico Electronics and Electrical Ltd.), technical assistance is even now generally available from its parent company (N.V. Philips). Hind Lamps Ltd. and Electric Lamp Manufacturers (India) Pvt. Ltd. (ELMI) had technical collaboration agreements with N.V. Philips, but the agreement has not been renewed after its expiry. Mysore Lamp Works Ltd. had a technical collaboration with General Electric but in this case also after the expiry of the agreement, it was not renewed. Sylvania and Laxman, Toshiba Anand Lamps, ECE, and HMT are the four existing large scale units in whose case foreign technical collaboration is still in vogue. The first one has a collaboration arrangement with Sylvania of U.S.A., the second one with Toshiba of Japan and last two with Tungsram of Hungary. The remaining units registered with DGTD are not dependent on foreign know-how. According to the DGTD, no financial collaboration is now permitted for the manufacture of GLS and FT lamps while technical collaboration with royalty payment may be allowed for FT lamps.

Yet, in 1982, a new agreement was approved in the case of Punjab Anand Batteries Ltd. with Philips N.V. for the production of 55 million GLS lamps. Philips has argued that new developments have taken place in the technology of lamp making and that the new agreement would allow for an upgrading of the technology. The perusal of the claims (Usha Menon 1984), however, shows that the changes to be brought about are of a minor nature and are mainly related to automation aimed at an increase in efficiency.

The lamp industry has been exempted from the licensing provision of the Industries (Development and Regulation) Act 1951. This facility is, however, available subject to the condition that the industrial undertaking does not require imported materials, imported capital goods or foreign collaboration. This facility is therefore not available to industrial undertakings, falling under the purview of MRTP Act and FERA, to which the MRTP Commission has to issue a license prior to the entry into the production line or the expansion of business. Philips India had a production capacity of 5 million GLS lamps after it purchased the bankrupt Osler company in 1962. In 1965, the company applied for an additional capacity of 3 million GLS lamps at a time that the Planning Commission directed the government, in view of the growing demand for electric bulbs, to allow all existing firms an expansion of 3 million GLS lamps. One year later it again secured a license for the production of 1.5 million FT lamps along with its components. Until 1975 its licensed capacity remained at 8 million GLS lamps and 1.5 million FT lamps. Philips formally applied in 1974 for further expansion of 9 million GLS lamps and 2.25 million FT lamps, and in the meantime started producing more than what it applied for without the approval of the concerned authority.

In 1975, after an investigation by the MRTP Commission, the approved capacity was marginally increased to 11.5 million pieces. Philips India accordingly raised its installed capacity, and, except for the exceptionally low output in 1975, continued to produce around thirty million lamps a year.* In 1978, the capacity, then expressed in terms of two shifts, was ultimately raised to thirty million pieces. Peico, as it appears from Table 5.12, in the following years kept its output within the regularised limits. If we, however, look at the total sales of the company, the picture undergoes a dramatic change. By 1983, sales were 2.5 times above the permitted productive capacity.

Peico's share in the organised sector's licensed capacity was 12 per cent of GLS lamps and 14 per cent of FT lamps in 1980. If we go by its market share, however, Philips accounted for 30 per cent of GLS lamps and more than half of FT lamps (Peico, Annual Report, 1980; Electric Lamp and Component Manufacturers Association, Directory 1980, Bombay). During the last couple of years the sales of lamps by

*The degree of excess production was surrounded by the prevailing confusion over the definition of installed capacity. The licensing committee recommended that after 1969, the capacity sbould be expressed in terms of two shifts (MRTPC 1975, p. 95). The licensed capacity prior to that year could therefore be treated as a one shift capacity, and could be interpreted as allowing for a corresponding higher actual production. From 1970 onwards, however, it was clear that the permitted production was fixed at 11.5 million pieces.

**Table 5.12 : Lamp Production Capacity and Sales of Philips-Peico**

(Million Pieces)

| Year | Licensed Capacity | Production | Sales |
|---|---|---|---|
| 1962 | 5.00 | 3.3 | n.a. |
| 1964 | 5.00 | 5.9 | n.a. |
| 1966 | 9.50 | 9.7 | n.a. |
| 1968 | 9.50 | 18.6 | n.a. |
| 1970 | 9.50 | 23.4 | n.a. |
| 1972 | 9.50 | 23.5 | n.a. |
| 1973 | 9.50 | 24.1 | 44.2 |
| 1974 | 9.50 | 27.6 | 42.5 |
| 1975 | 11.50 | 18.5 | 41.2 |
| 1976 | 11.50 | 28.4 | 54.0 |
| 1977 | 11.50 | 28.6 | 63.2 |
| 1978 | 30.00 | 28.9 | 63.0 |
| 1979 | 30.00 | 27.1 | 57.7 |
| 1980 | 30.00 | 28.6 | 57.9 |
| 1981 | 30.00 | 29.9 | 63.5 |
| 1982 | 30.00 | 29.1 | 64.6 |
| 1983 | 30.00 | 28.9 | 76.2 |
| 1984 | 30.00 | 26.4 | 79.9 |
| 1985 | 30.00 | 21.1 | 70.4 |

*Source* : MRTP Commission 1975, p. 26, and the annual reports of Philips India and Peico.

the company has increased considerably and, although we don't have the exact figures on the total production of bulbs by the other companies, the share of Peico is not likely to have decreased. The sales record of lamps sharply increased from 58 million pieces in 1980 to 80 million pieces in 1984. The in-house production in the latter year amounted to only 26 million pieces. Most of the sales thus originated from other companies.

The developments appear to suggest that, in the government effort to gain control over monopoly practices, the ceiling on the productive capacity of the big firms can work as a useful mechanism, but, even if rigorously implemented, leaves the possibility of the formation of a monopoly position through the indirect control over the production and market structures unaffected. As a matter of fact, government has not only refrained from introducing a restrictive legislation, but in a number of cases has stimulated the big companies to act as trading companies. The recognition as an Export House, for example, requires the aspiring firms, among others, to include in their exports ten per cent of products originating in the small scale sector.

If the official production figures of Peico can be treated at their face value, the explanation for the excessively high sales should be looked for in the intra-firm supplies by two affiliate companies (Hind Lamps and Elmi), and in the dominant position in the production of components which allows for a putting-out system with smaller companies. We shall first have a look at the control over the market of the final product. In the first place, Philips N.V. has entered into a technological agreement with the Anand Lamps which in 1987 was expected to reach an output of 25 million lamps. In the second place, although Peico till 1982 had only 35 per cent share participation in the Electric Lamp Manufacturers Company, its management and technical staff come under the direct control of Peico. ELMI operated as a manufacturing enterprise for the benefit of its promoters until it was taken over by Peico. Prior to the takeover, the RBI had directed ELMI to dilute its 100 per cent foreign equity to a level not exceeding 40 per cent. The company, instead of diluting the shares through a public issue, sold its non-Philips shares to Peico, an operation which was not strictly illegal in view of the fact that Peico by then had become a non-FERA company. Many objections to the take-over by a multinational MRTP company were, however, raised since it increased the monopoly hold over the industry, and could not be considered as being conducive to the stimulation of indigenous private or public enterprises. Indrajit Gupta, the communist member of parliament and a widely respected trade union leader of long standing, wrote a letter to R. Venkataraman, the Minister of Finance, with the appeal to conduct a probe into what he called a shady deal (*Business Standard*, 12.08.1980, and 20.09.1980). The minister answered in the negative to a number of questions which were also raised in parliament, stating in clear terms that "No permission has been given to Peico Electronics and Electricals Ltd. to acquire controlling interest in the holding of any multinational in India" (Statements 4671 and 2701 in December 1980). The issue was considered quite sensitive, particularly in view of the fact that ELMI had the largest lincensed capacity in the organised sector. The deal nevertheless went through, and as such illustrates the way in which the Indian cabinet, despite sound arguments of a political as well as of a techno-economical nature, chose to bend its policy in favour of a multinational corporation.

The multinational lamp manufacturer, who incidentally has never received a license to start the production of bulbs, thus succeeded in building up a monopoly position. The combined production of Peico, Elmi and Hind Lamps in 1982 amounted to 41 per cent of the lamp market. Since Peico, in addition to its procurements from the two related companies, has also entered into purchase agreements with small companies, total sales may be close to fifty per cent of the market.

We shall now illustrate that the monopoly hold is even more secure over the lamp component than over the final product. An important feature of the lamp industry is the vertical growth of large units who produce not only the finished end products but the various components as well. It will appear that Peico has established itself as the largest supplier of electric lamp components on which most other units, including the major ones, are dependent.

Tungsten filament or coil, the most important component required in the manufacture of lamps, is produced on the basis of imported rods. The effort by Mishra Dhatu Nigam Ltd. (Midhani), a public sector unit, to produce the rods in India itself, appears to have reached only the experimental stage. The tungsten metal is extracted in India by a public sector undertaking and is then exported for further processing into wires. Peico receives the rods from its parent company under an automatic import license for further processing into coils. At present there are ten units manufacturing filaments. While five of them produce filaments for their own consumption, the other five units supply filaments to other units as well. Among these units the position of Peico is predominant (see Table 5.13).

**Table 5.13 : Licensed Capacity and Production of Filament Coils 1979**

(Million Pieces)

| Name of the Firm | Licensed Capacity | Production | Capacity Utilisation % |
|---|---|---|---|
| Peico Electronics & Electricals Ltd. | 100 | 103.0 | 103 |
| Sylvania & Laxman Ltd. | 29 | 12.0 | 41 |
| Toshiba Anand Lamp Works Ltd. (captive unit) | 20 | 5.0 | 25 |
| Bengal Electric Lamp Works Ltd. (captive unit) | 15 | 8.0 | 53 |
| Pradip Lamp Works Ltd. (captive unit) | 10 | — | 0 |
| Bharat Electrical India Ltd. (captive unit) | 15 | — | 0 |
| Mysore Lamp Works (captive unit) | 10 | 1.3 | 13 |
| Jay Electric Wire Corporation | 30 | 1.5 | 5 |
| Hindustan Machine Tools Ltd. | 110 | — | 0 |
| Kalpana Industries Ltd. | 26 | 25.0 | 96 |

*Source* : Electric Lamp & Components Manufacturers Association Directory, 1980.

As in the case of tungsten filament, molybdenum thick wire also is still not available in India. In incandescent lamps, molybdenum wire is used as the mandrel around which the tungsten filament is wound as well as support hooks and pins. In total six units have received a license to produce molybdenum wire, but except for Peico, no other unit has reached the stage of production as yet.

Glass shells and tubings are equally important components in the production of incandescent and fluorescent lamps. Most of the units, both small and medium scale, are dependent on large scale units like Peico. The combined production of Peico, Hind Lamps and ELMI, who are all under direct or indirect Philips management, represent two-thirds of the total output of glass tubings and glass shells (see Table 5.14).

**Table 5.14 : Production of Glass Shells (Million Pieces) and Tubings (Tonnes) in 1979**

| Name of the Firm | Glass Shells | Glass Tubings |
|---|---|---|
| Peico | 28.8 | 36.00 |
| Hind Lamps | 126.4 | 8.99 |
| ELMI | 34.5 | 8.66 |
| Pengal Electric Lamp Works | 31.5 | 8.23 |
| Toshiba Anand Lamps | 11.5 | 5.60 |
| Sylvania & Laxman | 29.4 | 7.17 |
| Electric Construction Company | 18.0 | 4,00 |
| Hindustan Machine Tools | n.a. | n.a. |

**Source** : Electric Lamp and Components Manufacturers Association Directory 1980; Annual Report of Peico, ELMI and Hind Lamps, 1979.

If the quality of these products is not up to the mark, the dependent units would face a high rejection rate during the production process of electric lamps, and thereby would suffer losses. During the MRTPC enquiry on Philips' proposal on the expansion of light bulb production, an objector stated that: "there have been some problems in the dimension of the lead glass tubings, which have resulted into very high rejection rate in our manufacturing, but since we have no alternative, we have to accept whatever quantity we get from them" (MRTPC 1975, p. 74). Secondly, if the supplies are not made in time, the dependent units lose their market share also. For example, high wattage lamps have a particular market season. Since, according to our information, the supplies of high wattage shells often do not reach in time, the dependent units lose their market. If the glass shells reach them too late, the small and medium scale industries are hence afterwards saddled with stocks, payments for which have to be made in advance.

There are three units which produce fluorescent powder, namely Peico, Sylvania and Toshiba Anand. All three of them are also manufacturing FT lamps. Peico has the largest production unit. Its production in 1980 actually amounted to four times the combined output of the other two units. The company nevertheless asked for a new license which in 1981 was rejected by the government (which later was followed by a positive decision on the application for a fifty per cent expansion of the glass shells capacity). Whereas both other units practically exclusively produce for their own captive consumption and as a rule attain less than half capacity utilisation, Peico maintains almost full capacity utilisation, and sells close to 80 per cent of its output. As in the case of molybdenum wire, in fluorescent powder also Peico enjoys an absolute monopoly. In respect of two other components, namely lamp caps and lead-in wire, Hind Lamps and ELMI are the only lamp manufacturing units who supply to other units.

The MRTPC in its report of 1975, which approved of the further expansion of the Philips lamp production in India, stated that the company had witnessed the fastest growth in the industrial sector since its establishment in 1962, "partly because it is the largest producer of raw materials and components in the country. . . . This (virtual monopoly) could not but effect the working and growth of other units" (MRTPC 1975, pp.106-107). The apparent plan of the government in the early sixties to work for a kind of cooperative organisation for the production of components in which Philips and other Indian producers would participate, was abandoned becauce of the unwillingness of Philips to join such a venture (MRTPC 1975, p. 107). The government seal on further expansion enabled the company not only to continue its dominant position in the industry, but also to acquire an absolute monopoly in some of the electric lamp components. Collaboration agreements have been allowed for the manufacturing of the end product (bulbs) without insisting on the transfer of the technology needed for the production of the major component, tungsten filament, the raw material of which is exported from India.

As a final note it should be mentioned that the success of Peico in the lamp industry has to a certain extent been due to government patronage. The diversification from general sales of light bulbs to large scale lighting projects has led to the successful cornering of many government sponsored contracts. The lighting arrangement as well as the sound and communication system for the Asian Games in 1982, the lighting arrangements at the Khajuraho temples, the lighting and sonorisation of the Brindavan Gardens at Mysore, the public address and lighting system in the Calcutta metro, and a number of street lighting and airport lighting installations are some examples of government contracts, even bypassing the public sector undertaking HMT which has reached a stage of closing down its lamp division. It is an irony that in the home basis of HMT, Hyderabad, Peico is planning to undertake a huge expansion of its tube lamp and glass shells capacity.

The story of the operations of Philips Gloeilampenfabrieken in India confirms the correctness of the slogan "A Household Name for Fifty Years" which recently used to be advertised with great vigour. The company has expanded very rapidly, especially during the last fifteen years, and in general has maintained a high profit ratio. The company, on the basis of its sound financial position and its unmistakably huge reservoir of sophisticated technology, could have contributed to a strengthening of the infrastructural basis of the Indian industy. Most of its production, however, remains in the consumer sector, and particularly in consumer products like radios and lamps which can be, and actually have been produced on the basis of indigenous technological know-how, and which, moreover, have in many cases been assigned by the government for production in the small-scale sector.

The present trend, in spite of the occasional contribution in the field of sophisticated instruments, seems to be even more in the direction of expanding into a wide range of consumer products. The expansion, diversification and product modernisation are not so much induced by the desire to contribute to the development of the country, but, as the then chairman and managing director, C.J. Seelen, remarked in his address to the 1982 annual meeting of shareholders, "to maintain leadership position". The audio range of products has accordingly received what he called "a complete revamp—a step highly appreciated by dealers and consumers alike". Whether the step should also be appreciated from a developmental point of view is less apparent. It caters to a pattern of consumption which is associated with the emergence of a prosperous upper middle class. The better-off strata of society have now been given an outlet for their wealth which is in any case not being tapped by the government for social redistribution or investment. Peico allows them to eat away their own future in the form of audio-visual gadgets. The steep increase in resource mobilisation, sales and profits on the basis of the production of sophisticated luxury items may not be exactly the contribution from a multinational corporation with its vast technological resources which an underdeveloped country should be waiting for.

Left on its own, Peico is likely to continue concentrating on the product sectors in which it has established a dominant position, in some cases even an absolute monopoly position. The control over a whole range of audio and lighting products may be considerably more than is visible through direct market sales. The monopoly over strategic components augments its sway over the particular industrial sector, as been demonstrated in the case study on the lamp industry. The impunity with which the company is allowed to exceed its officially licensed capacity and to extend into new areas where its entry is legally questionable (*e.g.* battery cells, refrigerators and casette tapes), socially irrelevant (*e.g.* audio racks) or a multiplication of already existing production capacities (*e.g.* minicomputers which are already produced by public sector enterprises in Kerala and Uttar Pradesh), seem to indicate that the bargaining power of Peico is based on extra-economic factors.

It is hardly conceivable that the expansion of Philips N.V. into the Indian lamp industry has been allowed by the government on the basis of sound techno-economic arguments. In a relatively simple technology area, for which in addition to indigenous capabilities collaborators can be found all over the world, Philips, without originally getting a license, has been allowed to successively establish its control over Osler Lamps, ELMI, Hind Lamps and Punjab Anand Lamps. If the term monopoly has any meaning, either in the learned economic treatises or in the relevant government departments, it should be applied to the position of Philips N.V. in India: if for whatever reason, including political pressure, the headquarters in Eindhoven would decide to do so, they could throw the Indian subcontinent into darkness. After all, Peico (and ELMI) remains a foreign controlled company. Unlike Hindustan Lever, it has a strong expatriate management. It has now got a Dutch chairman and managing director (M.C. Guepin), a director (R. van Graafeiland), as well as technical director (J. Huart), and has also brought the ELMI factory under close managerial control by the induction of P. van Strijp as the manager. With them, the Indian chapter of Philips is in safe hands, the more so since, as Guepin confided (de Volkskrant, 11.11.1985), with the new economic policy of Rajiv Gandhi, "Philips has hit the jackpot".

# 6

# *Research and Development*

A well balanced and appropriate scientific and technological infrastructure is an essential component of economic development. Hence multinational corporations have been welcomed by the underdeveloped countries as the suppliers of modern technology. Yet also criticisms have been raised against them for not transplanting the technology they import into the countries of the third world. One of the apparent lacunae in the process of transferring and developing the technology which has been brought in, is the disinclination to start in-house Research and Development in the host country. Studies on R&D by MNCs in the developing countries (Germides 1977, OECD 1981, United Nations 1973) have generally pointed out that the multinational corporations locate their research work in their home countries, less in other developed capitalist world, and almost nothing in the underdeveloped countries. Yet is has been noticed that recently many foreign firms have been setting up sizeable R&D departments in India. Out of the eighteen companies in the private sector which spent more than Rs. ten million on R&D in 1980-81, at least twelve had foreign equity participation. Hence it becomes all the more necessary to study the possible determinants of their research work, so as to ascertain the nature of the trend. The present survey, apart from mapping out the contours of the in-house R&D by Dutch companies in India, will also attempt to explore the character and determinants of this R&D. It should help us to assess the contribution the corporations are presently making and are likely to make in the future to the development and upgrading of the scientific and technological infrastructure of underdeveloped countries like India.

Research and Development is the means by which the process of innovation is brought about. While an innovation can rise directly from the process of production itself, it usually arises as the result of systematic experimentation carried out outside the sphere of production. R&D activity leading to innovation can be conceptualised as a series of steps as follows: a. basic research; b. applied research; and c. experimental development research. Such a differentiation is necessary on the one hand to differentiate R&D activities from normal production activities and on the other hand to differentiate between the various activities involved in the innovation chain. These activities have different implications for costs, risks and organisational structures involved.

Applied research and development research can further be classified according to their organic connection with production. A differentiation can be made between the R&D which is product-oriented, process-oriented or raw material-oriented. There is a more concrete and aggregate level of characterising R&D, namely the level of typologies. The typologies take, apart from the purely technical aspects, the social dimensions of the research activities into consideration. Most of the studies on R&D have been done in the developed capitalist countries. They have developed a typology that characterises R&D as offensive, defensive, imitative, dependent, traditional, etc. (Freeman 1974, pp. 55-250; Nystrom 1979). Since the applicability of this type of typology even to developed capitalist countries is questionable (Uhlmann 1979), its applicability to underdeveloped countries becomes even more so. As a matter of fact, the study of thc R&D activities of MNCs outside their home countries and even more so in underdeveloped countries has been a neglected area of research. One of the pioneering works in this area (Kaplinsky and Chisthi 1977) studied the MNCs in India and Kenia, but did not use any typology for analysing the character of the R&D.

The developmental implications of the different types of R&D need to be kept in mind while developing typologies appropriate to the third world, since their contribution in upgrading the local scientific and technological gap has been considered as the main expected function of MNCs. With this perspective in mind, the following typologies are suggested: local R&D, global R&D, adaptive R&D and transfer R&D. Central to this typology is the conception of different levels of capabilities in the home and host countries of the multinationals. We characterise as local R&D, the R&D conducted by a multinational which is at the same level as the scientific and technological capabilities existing in the host country, and which is oriented towards the solution of problems arising in the local production structure. When a multinational undertakes such an R&D, it cannot be considered to bridge any technological gap. Indeed, such a firm can be considered to be behaving like any comparable local company.

Local R&D can be further subdivided into three subdivisions: a. local adaptive; b. local dependent, and c. local independent. In *local adaptive R&D* the work involves essentially modifications, to suit the local conditions and is conducted either on an imported technology or on a technology in local use. In *local dependent R&D*, applied research is also undertaken in addition to experimental development, but it is not done on the core problem. Thus for example, applied research can be done on the methods of separation of by-products from fermentation, but as long as research on the upgradation of the bacteria are not conducted, the R&D remains dependent on crucial inputs from abroad. *Local independent R&D* can be considered the ideal type of local R&D. It consists of both applied research and experimental development and is oriented towards the solution of the crucial aspects of the problem faced. The second type of R&D, classified as *global R&D* is that performed in the underdeveloped host country for problems arising out of the production process outside the host country. The scientific level of this research is the same as that existing in the host country. The location of this type of R&D away from the production can take place as a result of the introduction of the division of labour into a single innovation chain. Such a geographical dispersal of the innovation chain is facilitated by the modern developments in communications and R&D management. Global R&D can be again subdivided into two sub-groups, global independent and global dependent. Whereas in *global independent R&D* the applied research deals with the crucial aspects as well, in *global dependent R&D* only the peripheral components of applied research are conducted in the host country. While both types of global R&D would not lead to the local productive utilisation of the scientific capabilities, the impact of the global dependent R&D would be particularly pernicious.

*In adaptive R&D*, the firm undertakes modifications to suit local conditions, but the level of expertise is superior to that existing in the host country. This type of R&D is closely related to the import of technology. Import of technology, whether or not embodied in machinery, requires modifications. In carrying out these modifications often problems arise that can only be resolved by experimental work, whereby the MNC makes use of basic and applied research conducted in the home country. This work can be either product-oriented, process-oriented or raw material-oriented. Since the market conditions are different in the underdeveloped countries, often product-oriented development becomes necessary. The same is true for process-orientation, since abundance of cheap unskilled labour and comparative scarcity of skilled labour are specific to the situation in the underdeveloped country. Along the same lines, differences in the availability and prices of raw materials also induce raw material-oriented modification.

The fourth type of R&D can be termed as *tranfer R&D*. In this case, applied research and experimental development research are undertaken to solve local problems and the level of scientific and technological capabilities employed are higher than those existing in the host country. In this case, the multinational sets up a production process at a higher level that that existing in the country and progressively undertakes modification, experimental development and applied research. We can also refer to this type of R&D as real R&D as opposed to a mere import of technology.

The characteristics of the different types of R&D are given in Table 6.1.

## 6.1. R&D Policy

After Independence, when India launched a programme of industrialisation, the need to upgrade the existing technologies

**Table 6.1 : Typology of R & D by MNCs in an Underdeveloped Country**

| Year | Relation to the local level of science and technology | Production orientation | Nature of dominant activity |
|---|---|---|---|
| Local R&D | Comparable | Local | Applied research and experimental development |
| Global R&D | Comparable | Foreign | Applied research |
| Adaptive R&D | Higher | Local | Modification |
| Transfer R&D | Higher | Local | Applied research and experimental development |

*Source* : Usha Menon 1982, p. 21.

was recognised. With this objective, a chain of national laboratories was established in the fifties. Yet, in course of time, it was found that there was very little link-up between the laboratories and the industry, and that R&D continued to be highly concentrated in the government sector.

Measures to promote indigenous R&D, especially in the private sector, were introduced in the late sixties, mainly in the form of income tax rebates. Discussions on the measures to promote R&D were held during this period, and in April 1972 a working group on "Policy in Regard to Execution and Commercialisation of R&D in the Private Sector Industry" was constituted under the Chairmanship of Dr. Y. Nayudamma. The Nayudamma Committee submitted its report in October 1974, but in the meanwhile measures had already been taken regarding the promotion of indigenous technology. A scheme for granting recognition to in-house R&D units came in operation in 1973. The recognition, granted by the Department of Science and Technology, is initially for a period of three years and is to be renewed after approval by an expert team. Accordingly, there was a sharp growth in the number of R&D units. As the end of 1983 there were 668 units recognised by the Department of Science and Technology, up from around 200 in 1970, prior to the inauguration of a number of incentive policies (DST 1984b, pp. 3-5).

The most important of the schemes introduced by the Government of India for the promotion of in-house R&D deals with (a) import facilities, (b) preferential treatment in licensing of production capacities, (c) concessional finance, and (d) fiscal incentives. Under the various schemes, the recognised R&D units in 1981 were allowed to import Rs. 65 million worth of equipment, machinery, raw materials, etc. The expenditure on R&D is deductible from income tax up to 133 per cent. Also an investment allowance of up to 35 per cent is deductible by users of the know-how developed indigenously.

Expenditure on research and development has increased significantly, both in absolute terms and as a percentage of the GNP, although it is still far behind the developed capitalist and socialist countries. Expenditure as a share in the GNP has risen from 0.18 per cent in 1958-59 to 0.61 per cent in 1978-79 and to 0.85 per cent in 1982-83, which compares rather unfavourably with, for example, the Netherlands (1.9%), Japan (2.4%), the USA (2.6%), and the USSR (4.9%). In comparison with the developing countries, e.g. with Pakistan (0.2%), Philippines (0.2%) and even South Korea (0.7%), India performs fairly well (DST 1984a, p. 30). The comparison in terms of expenditure per capita, however, brings out in stark contrast the vast gap between India and the developed countries. Whereas in 1977, the Netherlands spent US $ 136 per capita and the USA $ 1204, the Indian figure was as low as $ 0.98 (Usha Menon 1982, p. 34). Another indicator of the research activity is the number of patents filed in the country. Out of a total number of 18620 patents in force in 1982-83, only 3329 were Indian and the rest (82.3%) were foreign. Out of the 1950 new application filed by foreign countries in 1983, 714 came from the USA and more than 200 each from the FRG and the United Kingdom. The Netherlands filed 59 and 42 applications in 1982 and 1983 respectively (DST 1984a, pp. 51-54).

In general, the government does not distinguish between Indian and foreign firms, although the intention underlying the Industrial Licensing Policy Statement of February 1973 was aimed at excluding FERA and MRTP companies from undertaking research in a considerable number of industries unrelated to their business. The proposals in 1974 of the official Nayudamma Committee put a special check on the big private research centres. In the report, a neat distinction was made between in-house R&D and autonomous R&D centres. Research was expected to be engaged in without any government restriction as long as it was related to the business for which the companies had received a license. As such, R&D should enable them "to adopt technologies imported from the principals, utilise local materials and equipment and develop new technologies. R&D should help them to avoid seeking extensions of collaboration/consultancy/ R&D agreements with their principals. The companies should also ... negotiate the sale of technology to firms within the country or for re-sale to their principals and other companies abroad on suitable terms".

The R&D centres set up by foreign companies as autonomous organisations should be subject to a different set of conditions. Periodically they should report their results to the competent authority:

> It should be ensured that the work programme is related to the overall interests of the country and the results patented or otherwise are available for exploitation in India on negotiable terms. The government may consider having nominee(s) on the Boards of Management of such R&D Centres (quote in Usha Menon 1982, pp. 32-33).

The Nayudamma Committee recommendations, which could have gone a long way in making the know-how of the foreign companies available to the Indian industry at large, were not made into official policy. On the contrary, the government has started relying on the independent and untransferable research contributions of the foreign ccmpanies as the main element in the technological upgrading of the country. Whereas earlier, public sector research was considered an essential counterweight to the restrictive control of MNCs on the reservoir of technology, in the 1980s, government has extended a warm hand to the MNCs who now actually are expected to counsel the authorities instead of the other way round. This is symbolised at the highest level by the fact that in the main technology advisory body to the Prime Minister, two of the six members are representatives of foreign firms.

One feature which distinguishes R&D in India from that in the developed capitalist countries is its concentration in the government sector. If we look at the sources of the funds used in all R&D efforts in the country, the situation hardly compares with the industrialised countries where private sector funding is more or less equal to government funding. In India, government sources account for 87 per cent (DST 1984a, p. v). The decreasing share of this sector, which includes both the research institutions linked to the various central and state departments and the public enterprises, may indicate that the private sector has recently started picking up. If one excludes the research efforts in government research institutions and compares the in-house research and development in the government public sector undertakings and the private sector, the latter turns out to have a slightly higher outlay (Rs. 1614 million as compared to Rs. 1242 million in 1982-83).

In both sectors there was, in constant prices, practically a doubling of research efforts between 1976 and 1982. The respective performances in terms of R&D intensity during the last couple of years have been of similar magnitude, as Table 6.2 shows. The aggregate figures obviously do not represent a reliable figure on the R&D intensity in the various industrial sectors. With regard to the public sector, for example, the intensity is quite high in telecommunications (6.96% of sales), defense (3.48%), electricals and electronics (2.08%), and rubber goods (2.05%). The industrial groups in the private sector with a more than two per cent research intensity are scientific instruments, telecommunications, machine tools and drugs.

The aggregate figures indicate that the public sector undertakings perform below the average of the private industry. The inference is that the public sector is bound to lose in

**Table 6.2 : R&D Intensity and Advertising by Public and Private Companies (1982-83)**

(Rs. in Millions)

| | Public Sector | Private Sector |
|---|---|---|
| R&D Expenditure | 1242 | 1614 |
| Advertising Expenditure | 71 | 662 |
| Sales | 21543 | 23672 |
| R&D to Sales (%) | 0.58 | 0.68 |
| Ads to Sales (%) | 0.03 | 0.28 |
| Ads to R&D (%) | 4.99 | 41.02 |

*Source* : DST, R&D in Industry, 1982-83. p. 58.

competition with the private sector undertakings. In some important industrial groups, the relative and absolute differences are so big that it can be safely concluded that the public sector has been made to give up any pretension about playing a domineering role. The amount spent on R&D by the public sector enterprises as a percentage of the total in some of the important industries in 1983 was as follows: 8.13 per cent in chemicals, 10.25% in pharmaceuticals, 5.71 per cent in industrial machinery, 0.32 per cent in transportation (DST 1984a, p. 22).

In the next section, we shall have a closer look at the position of the Dutch multinational corporations in India who operate in some of these sectors and some of whom are regarded as having an excellent R&D record.

## 6.2. R&D by Indo-Dutch Companies

In the 1970s, seven of the companies with Dutch equity participation conducted in-house R&D. They are Hindustan Lever, Peico, Organon, Duphar-Interfran, Nocil, Century Enka and Vicon. The recognition of the R&D unit by the Department of Science and Technology has been taken as the criterion in determining which unit conducts R&D. The recognition by the Department is necessary to obtain the various concessions offered by the government. Hence, it is likely for the figures supplied by the companies to the government to be on the high side. All the same, in this survey, they have been taken at face value. The fact that the Department of Science and Technology independently tries to verify this information is a deterrent on the companies for claiming wildly exaggerated efforts.

The Dutch or Indo-Dutch companies conducting in-house R&D, include such giants as Hindustan Lever and Philips as well as such pigmies as Vicon. As is to be expected, the bulk of the research expenditurec omes from Hindustan Lever and Philips. In 1977 they accounted for 39% and 42% of the total expenditure on R&D by the companies (see Table 6.3). Also in terms of employment in R&D, Peico and Hindustan Lever are far ahead of the others. Each of them employs more people in R&D than all the other companies put together. Whereas Peico employed considerably more staff (456 in 1976 as compared to 214 by HL), it had less highly qualified personnel (38 post-graduates as compared to 45 at the HL research centres).

Further details of the R&D work conducted by these companies, especially regarding their nature and orientation is dealt with separately. Although the data on which our description and analysis take place may be slightly dated, and may not reflect the state of affairs in the 1980s, they present a comprehensive picture for the period under study. There are no indications that the general trend has undergone a drastic change in the later period.

Century Enka produces nylon yarn under a collaboration agreement with Algemene Kunstzijde Unie N.V. of Arnhem in Holland and Glanzstoff A.G. of Wuppertal in the BRD, who have merged as AKZO N.V. The technical collaborations were entered into in 1967 for a period of five years. The technical collaboration agreement with AKZO specified that additional know-how would be available from AKZO without extra payment for a period of ten years. At the same time Century Enka contracted to put their full know-how in the field of nylon yarn at the disposal of AKU and Glanzstoff. In return for the delivery of know-how for the nylon plant, AKZO was given a

**Table 6.3 : Total R&D Expenditure in Indo-Dutch Companies, 1973-79**

(Rs. Lakh)

| Name of the Company | 1973 | 1974 | 1975 | 1976 | 1977 | 1978 | 1979 |
|---|---|---|---|---|---|---|---|
| NOCIL | 57 | 65 | 75 | 35 | 41 | 46 | 58* |
| Century Enka | 5.4† | 5.4† | 15.5* | — | 17.8 | — | — |
| Organon | 2.5 | 3.9 | 6.9 | 9.1 | 11.9 | 15.00** | 6* |
| Vicon | — | — | — | — | 0.79 | 1.65 | 1.47 |
| Duphar Interfran (Chemical) | — | — | — | 5.5† | 5.5† | 5.5† | 1.5* |
| Duphar Interfran (Pharmaceutical) | — | — | — | 3.2 | 1.97 | 2.6 | 2.5* |
| Peico | — | 100 | 138 | 126 | 167.2 | 189.3 | 242.6 |
| Hindustan Lever | 102 | 125 | 112 | 132 | 157 | 188* | 185** |

*Source* : Usha Menon 1982, p. 42.
*Notes* : †average over three years.
*budgeted figure.
**estimated figure.

total of 47,250 shares in the company amounting to 27 per cent of the equity.

Although research work, according to the company, was started in 1970, it applied for recognition by the Department of Science and Technology only in 1976 and did not maintain separate accounts of R&D work. The R&D activities were not separate from quality control on production. There was only a part-time R&D manager and no separate R&D laboratory, except for a small room. One spinning grid was isolated from the main spinning assembly and some experiments were conducted on this. The situation had not improved till 1979, but it was reported in April 1980, that from the end of that financial year separate accounts would be maintained for R&D. They were planning to set up an R&D Centre for work on engineering of polymers and fibres.

The R&D figures available for Century Enka are not very reliable, since expenditure on trouble-shooting, etc., is included. The R&D intensity, as calculated on the basis of recurring R&D expenditure, works out to be 0.66 for 1979-80. In 1979 Century Enka employed 11 people full-time and 10 people part-time on R&D. The R&D intensity as calculated on the basis of the total number of people employed works out to be 9.7 full-time equivalent to per thousand employees.

Some of the R&D work reported seems to be of a purely trouble-shooting nature. For example, one of the yarns produced by Century Enka used to create serious problems of deposit formation during processes of warping and knitting. White powder used to be deposited on guides, combes, etc. R&D work concentrated on this problem and changed the process of spinning of this denier. Work has also been directed towards creating product differentiation/modification. Thus a sparkling effect, "even better than that produced by the competitor", were produced. Some process improvements were also undertaken. Higher speeds were achieved in the twistron process for nylon-6 yarn. Some amount of work is also directed towards import substitution. Thus new spin finishes were introduced in place of the imported ones. Some imported parts of the machinery used, like the bars which provide pre-tension to yarn during draw-twisting, were substituted with those manufactured by local parties.

Century Enka has not taken out any patents. The R&D work appears to involve only minor modifications, although it cannot be ascertained whether this was at a level higher than the level existing in India.

*NOCIL* (National Organic Chemicals India Ltd.), in which the Royal Dutch Shell has an equity participation, entered into a technical collaboration with Shell in 1964. With the start of the production of petrochemicals (PVC products) in 1968, a Technical Service Centre was started at Worli in Bombay. According to the company, R&D work was started at this centre, but till 1976, no separate accounts were maintained and no full-time person was made in charge. In 1979, a Dutch national was appointed as the R&D director and a separate centre was constructed adjoining the factory in Thane. The recurring R&D expenditure as a percentage of the total turnover in 1978-79 had reached only 0.36 per cent, well below the national average in the chemical sector of 0.99 per cent.

R&D work at Nocil appears to fall into two broad groups. One area of research is the scaling up of the know-how obtained from the regional research centre of the National Research Development Corporation at Hyderabad and Jorhat, particularly pertaining to pesticides. The other one is related to the modification of the existing production process to suit local condition.

The utilisation of local know-how for the production of insecticides seems to have taken place under special circumstances. Given the advanced stage of the development of the know-how in the national laboratories, Nocil was, according to confidential sources, not allowed to import the know-how, and as a compromise had to use the local know-how. This scaling up of the local technology can be characterised as local R&D.

The modification work was directed towards the creation of new PVC products (heat resistant cables, building profiles, foam PVC, etc.). Some of the process development arose out of modifications to suit Indian conditions. The company for example successfully developed fibre grade ethylene glycol from the aqueous waste, which in Europe goes into the production of anti-freeze. The modifications seem to be carried out under the technical guidance of the principals and would thus fall under adaptive R&D.

Incidentally under the 1978 agreement entered into between Nocil and Shell, the latter company was granted "the right to use a royalty-free, non-exclusive irrevocable license" under the patent right acquired by Nocil.

*Organon,* a pharmaceutical subsidiary of AKZO, started a chemical laboratory in 1972 and a pharmaceutical laboratory in 1975. Both establishments are attached to the respective factories in Calcutta. The R&D intensity of the company as a percentage of the net sales in 1981 was hardly 1.04 per cent (0.65 per cent in 1979 and 1.35 per cent in 1980). The sharp fluctuations can be attributed to the clubbing together of recurrent and capital expenditure in the annual accounts. The expenditure compares unfavourably with the industry average of 1.58 per cent and 1.95 per cent for the private sector in 1978-79 and 1980-81 respectively. The higher percentages which were quoted earlier in the reports of the Department of Science and Technology (2.3 per cent in 1978), were up to eighty per cent on account of expenses on raw materials etc., which seems to be rather on the right side.

The utilisation of indigenous raw materials for the products of the company seems to have been the most important objective behind the setting up of the R&D programme. Thus, when in 1972 the first laboratory was set up, work was undertaken on pilot plant production of diosgenin from dioscorea roots. Diosgenin forms the main raw material for all the hormones which are produced by the company. In 1975, progress was reported in the field of production of human gonadotrophin from the urine of pregnant women. The company has also undertaken the screening of medicinal plants of indigenous origin for the extraction of the active principle.

The construction of a new research centre, involving Rs. 30 million, started in 1982. One of the main activities envisaged in the new laboratory appears to be the setting up of an animal house, complete with toxicology and pathology laboratories, for experiments with animals. Work will also be undertaken on the development of better drugs for tropical diseases and on the pharmacological use of herbs and plants.

The research on tropical diseases can be considered local R&D since it is meant for the local market, and since the scientific level is comparable to the one at IICB in Calcutta and the Central Drug Research Institute at Lucknow where, according to Organon, similar work is conducted. The company as a matter of fact in the past has signed quite a number of collaboration agreements with the various national laboratories at Calcutta, Lucknow, Jammu, Bangalore, Jadavpur, etc. It is quite likely that the setting up of a major animal house might not be directly related to the research programme Organon undertakes for its production in India, but that it may be used to test drugs developed elsewhere also, in which case the research would fall under the type global dependent. Drug research of the global dependent type has been warned against by Iyengar, a technical consultant: "Since R&D expenses in India are relatively low, the facilities of some of these laboratories are utilised to carry out the basic research as required by their parent companies who themselves carry out the intermediate and penultimate stages, keeping the Indian subsidiary completely in the dark" (Iyengar, p. 9).

*Duphar Interfran*, another pharmaceutical company, which till 1981 was a subsidiary of Philips and was then sold to Solvay of Belgium, employed seven people in the R&D department, in 1979. The total expenditure as a percentage of the sales amounted to 0.48% in 1978-79, well below the national average. In the pharmaceutical laboratory, which absorbed almost twice as much funding as the chemical laboratory, the work seems to be oriented towards the production of new formulations. It essentially involves minor modifications of products for which the technology was received from Indian research institutes or from its principle. Paracetamol, obtained from the Central Drug Research Institute at Lucknow, was scaled up in this laboratory.

*Vicon* at Bangalore, one of the smallest Dutch companies in India, produces combine harvesters and threshers. The company claims to have started R&D activities in 1969, but as late as 1980 the work was done either in the production area itself or through the services of outside consultants. According to the accounts, 0.86% of total sales was spent on R&D, which compares unfavourably with the annual average in the agricultural machinery sector of 1.51% in 1978-79 (DST 1981b, p. 28), but which is more than one would expect from a company without a separate R&D area. Vicon claims to have taken up the production of new products like a stationary multicrop thresher and a multipurpose tool carrier which was developed on the basis of a design supplied by the research institute ICRISAT. Vicon has been importing prototypes for further development in India and is interested in setting up a tropical agricultural machinery research laboratory in Bangalore. By and large the work at Vicon at present appears to involve only minor modifications, routine design work and trouble-shooting.

*PEICO Electronics and Electricals India Ltd.* operates in a field which is largely science-based. R&D can therfore be expected to play an important part in the activities of the company. Information on its activities is, however, difficult to come by since it is even more reticent than other companies in publishing detailed information. The annual reports, for example, do not give any information regarding R&D expenditure.

At present Peico has ten laboratories recognised by the government. They are attached to the production units in Loni, Pimpri, Kalwa and Calcutta. According to Peico, R&D work in these laboratories started right from the inception of production, thus for example at the radio factory in 1948, but it appears that these were mere quality control and component-testing laboratories. In 1979-80, the Indian laboratories of Philips employed 456 people, which, for a fruitful insight could be compared to the 19000 persons employed by the parent company in 1964. Philips N.V. in 1969 spent 6.92 per cent of its income on R&D (Van der Geest, 1978, p. 47). In 1982, the percentage stood at 7.3 per cent (Annual Report, 1982).

For the Indian concern as a whole the research intensity was 2.4 per cent in 1979 and 1.9 per cent in 1980 (calculated on the basis of budgeted and estimated figures of total expenditure). In 1979-80 the factories to which laboratories are attached had an intensity of 61.1 per thousand employees.

The research intensity as measured by the recurring R&D expenditure, which is a better measure of assessing the intensity, shows that it has been increasing gradually from 1972 onwards from 1.12 per cent of total turnover to 1.83 per cent of turnover in 1978 (see Table 6.4.). After that it shows a tendency to decline. Peico, unlike Hindustan Lever, has been spending more on R&D than on advertisement. This is to be expected since in the electronic industry R&D is more important than in

**Table 6.4 : Peico Advertising and R&D Expenditure 1970-1981**

(Rs. Lakh)

| Year | Turnover | Total R&D | Recurring R&D Expenditure as % of 2 | Advertising | R&D as % of 5 |
|---|---|---|---|---|---|
| 1 | 2 | 3 | 4 | 5 | 6 |
| 1970 | 3768 | 42.5 | 1.1 | 74.8 | 57 |
| 1971 | 4656 | 67.4 | 1.1 | 65.8 | 102 |
| 1972 | 4911 | 63.0 | 1.1 | 80.3 | 79 |
| 1973 | 5043 | n.a. | n.a. | 74.7 | n.a. |
| 1974 | 6156 | 100.0 | 1.3 | 86.3 | 116 |
| 1975 | 5920 | 138.0 | 1.7 | 112.0 | 123 |
| 1976 | 7208 | 126.3 | 1.6 | 90.1 | 140 |
| 1977 | 7981 | 167.2 | 1.8 | 112.2 | 149 |
| 1978 | 9011 | 189.3 | 1.8 | 119.8 | 158 |
| 1979 | 10298 | 242.6 | 1.8 | 122.2 | 198 |
| 1980 | 11980 | 227.3 | 1.7 | 185.9 | 122 |
| 1981 | 14883 | n.a. | n.a. | 227.0 | n.a |

*Sources* : Internal Reports and Annual Reports of Philips India. Some of the component figures are estimates on budgeted expenditure (See Menon 1982, pp. 65-66).

the soap industry. Both in terms of personnel and in terms of financial outlay, Peico as a matter of fact compares quite well with the other companies in the private sector (0.7 per cent on sales and 23 staff per 1000) and in the public sector (2.1 per cent on sales and 25 staff per 1000). Small scale units in the electrics and electronics industries on the other hand appear to be incurring a higher outlay, namely 2.7 per cent on sales (DST 1984b, p. 17).

It can be noted that although the radio and tape laboratories employ the maximum number (256 in 1980), the level of skill of those employed is comparatively low, since it employs no one with a doctorate degree and only 14 with a masters degree. On the other hand, the laboratory attached to the factory at Loni Kalbhor, producing electronic components, employed 144 people of which 4 had a Ph.D. and 12 a masters' degree. All the laboratories of Philips have been headed by Indians except for the electronic instruments laboratory at Pimpri, which in the early seventies was headed by Mr. N. H.W. Vrijenhoek. In 1984, Venkataraman, the Indian technical director of Peico Ltd. was shifted to the headquarters in Eindhoven and was replaced by the expatriate Director Huart.

The important research centres in terms of total expenditure are attached to the radio factories in Calcutta and Pimpri, and particularly to the electronic instruments unit at Pimpri and the electronic components unit at Loni Kalbhor. The Kalwa welding electrodes factory on the other hand has a relatively low research intensity (less than one per cent of the turnover). The instruments factory at Pimpri is the most R&D intensive, both in terms of recurring expenditure (11.4%) of sales in 1979 and in terms of R&D staff (161 per 1000 employees).

An analysis of the R&D work undertaken by Peico is best dealt with product-wise. Radios which form the most important electronic product of Peico, fall essentially into two categories, the cheap standardised radios and the more expensive radios. Not only the R&D, but also the production techniques employed in the two cases are different. Cheaper radios costing up to Rs. 500 are produced in Pune, while the more expensive radios are produced in Calcutta. Production outside the factory, in small scale units, is resorted to on a large scale for cheap radios. Approximately 60 per cent of the production is carried out within the factory premises and 40 per cent outside the factory. Such a system is also resorted to in the case of tape recorders in Calcutta.

The Central Development Laboratory in Pimpri designs new models of radios based on the information supplied by the industrial design department. Whereas the designs for the mechanical parts are got from Holland, the rather simple circuitry is developed in Pimpri. In the case of the more expensive radios as well as in professional microphones and scientific industrial instruments, no new circuit designs are introduced in India. The developmental work in India consists mainly of substituting local components in the designs developed in Holland.* Changes in the circuitry are only made when the substitution becomes too tedious. When changes are made, then the advice/permission of the parent company is taken before production is started. It is significant in this respect that Peico has not introduced any product on the basis of designs developed in India.

The dependence on the parent company is almost total in the case of items that are exported. Thus for example, whereas for multimeters all the technology comes from Holland, for the locally sold oscilloscopes some efforts are made to adapt to the local requirements. Also in the case of the more sophisticated equipments like exclusive microphones and some two-in-ones, imported kits are merely assembled here, and that too sometimes in the small scale sector. The professional electronic equipment factory which uses very sophiscated imported equipment for production does so at assembly lines guided by imported computerised machines.

The dependence of Peico on technical support from Holland is exemplified by a few instances. In spite of having, apart from the equity participation, a separate technical agreement operative for a period of ten years from 1967 onwards for the production of fluorescent lamps, fluorescent powder and glass products, Peico requested the Government of India in 1977 for a further renewal of the technical collaboration agreement. When analogue multimeters were to be produced by Peico in 1980, the necessary drawings and designs had to be imported from Eindhoven. The drawings were made in Holland specially for Peico, since the manufacture of such multimeters were not being undertaken elsewhere.** When the halogen lamps which

*Peico mentions the development of an electronic system for the different functions of a record player like 'start', 'stop' and automatic tripping. Since these circuits are already developed in Europe, the maximum Peico can do is merely to substitute for example a voltage dependent resistor with local diodes. What needs to be mentioned is that this work is at the border line between experimental developmental work and routine application. The work has a very low level of uncertainty.

**The multimeters produced by Peico were made essentially for export, and there seems to be a possible case of transfer pricing since the ex-factory value of one multimeter was Rs. 675.70 while f.o.b. value was only Rs. 439.70 in 1978.

were being produced under technical collaboration, developed problems, the development laboratory in India was apparently not capable of handling it. The faults were rectified under simulated conditions in Holland and later in field studies conducted in India by technical experts from Holland. The dependence in this field appears to continue because the collaboration agreement was asked to be extended in 1980.

The only field in which Philips India has undertaken any applied research is in the area of materials. The Central Chemicals and Materials Laboratory in Loni, which employs 20 to 25 people, is its only laboratory where research projects not related to day-to-day problems are undertaken. The materials testing laboratory was converted into a materials development laboratory in 1963. In the mid-sixties, in view of the foreign exchange difficulties, it was decided to undertake substitution work with local materials. At first, locally available materials such as Litanium oxide were processed to be used as electronic materials. Later, alternative materials were developed to be used instead of materials not locally available like Bismuth. All this resulted in the setting up of a unit with a very competent team which is supposed to be the second strongest unit outside Holland in ceramic and piezo-electric materials. In 1975-76 it was decided that this laboratory should function as one of the know-how centres of Philips International. As a know-how centre, it appears to play a subordinate and supportive role to the work conducted in the Netherlands. It actually keeps track of developments in the Far East. Apparently the local availability of cheap infrastructural facilities like the electron microscope in the government-owned National Chemical Laboratory have added an impetus to the development of the laboratory.*

Thus it seems that Peico in the past has undertaken mainly local adaptive research, in spite of the large number of people employed in the R&D department. This work became necessary under conditions of import substitution, when imported components were substituted by the local components. The only

*The NCL microscope is available at the rate of Rs. 300 per hour (in 1981), which according to a high level employee of Philips would not even cover the interest on the capital employed.

applied research, undertaken in the area of materials, was also formulated under the stimulus of import substitution.

## 6.3 The Case of Hindustan Lever

Traditionally, Unilever has been a company that paid scant attention to research and development. This flows frow the nature of the main products manufactured by the corporation, namely margarine and soaps. For Unilever, marketing skills have been traditionally the most important asset (Wilson 1976, pp. 64-68). The situation changed in the late fifties and sixties. In course of time a number of research laboratories were established. By 1982, the research division consisted of nine central laboratories in England, the Netherlands, the United States, France, Germany, Turkey and India (Van der Geest 1978, p. 62). The central research laboratories undertake work of a more fundamental nature. The share of expenditure on basic research has been increasing from 10 per cent (1959) to 25-30 per cent of the total R&D expenditure in 1979 (De Haan, 1981, p. 132). Applied research is being undertaken in more than hundred laboratories all over the world.

The employment at the Andheri Research Centre in Bombay has not expanded significantly (from 207 in 1972 to 250 in 1981), although the qualifications of the staff have improved considerably. Both Doctorate and Master Degree holders form each one-fifth of the total employment.

In order to assess the research intensity of Hindustan Lever in terms of sales, we have calculated an average of current R&D expenditure and the capital expenditure over the previous five years. The latter has been done in view of the high fluctuations in capital expenditure and in view of the fact that the equipment is expected to be used over a number of years. The result of the calculations can be seen in Table 6.5. Research intensity, it appears, has rather decreased than increased. In the early eighties it was on an average 0.10 points below the intensity reached in the early seventies. In comparison with the rest of the private companies and the public sector companies operating in the same industrial fields (an intensity of around 0.15 per cent), the performance of HL is relatively better. A comparison between the outlay on research and advertisements, however,

### Table 6.5 : R&D Intensity of Hindustan Lever, 1964-1984

(Expenditure in Lakhs)

| Year | Capital R&D Expenditure | Av. Cap. R&D Expenditure[1] | Recurring R &D Exp. | Sales | R&D Intensity[2] | R&D Intensity of Unilever Ltd. |
|---|---|---|---|---|---|---|
| 1 | 2 | 3 | 4 | 5 | 6 | 7 |
| 1965 | 2.21 | | 11.85 | 7148 | | n.a. |
| 1966 | 4.07 | | 16.84 | 8467 | | n.a. |
| 1967 | 58.58 | | 22.93 | 9328 | | n.a. |
| 1968 | 64.39 | 25.85 | 44.02 | 9259 | .75 | n.a. |
| 1969 | 9.93 | 27.84 | 54.61 | 10879 | .76 | n.a. |
| 1970 | 11.02 | 29.60 | 64.33 | 11921 | .79 | n.a. |
| 1971 | 13.04 | 31.39 | 72.40 | 13410 | .77 | n.a. |
| 1972 | 34.00 | 26.48 | 79.00 | 14044 | .75 | n.a. |
| 1973 | 15.00 | 16.60 | 87.00 | 13268 | .78 | n.a. |
| 1974 | 25.00 | 19,61 | 100.00 | 14865 | .80 | 0.8 |
| 1975 | 11.00 | 19.61 | 101.00 | 20597 | .59 | 1.1 |
| 1976 | 16.00 | 20.20 | 116.00 | 21299 | .64 | 1.1 |
| 1977 | 25.00 | 18.40 | 132.00 | 26168 | .57 | 1.2 |
| 1978 | 34.88 | 22.38 | 145.73 | 30100 | .56 | 1.2 |

(Contd.)

**Table 6.5** (*Contd.*)

| 1 | 2 | 3 | 4 | 5 | 6 | 7 |
|---|---|---|---|---|---|---|
| 1979 | 73.92 | 32.16 | 166.00 | 35574 | .56 | 1.3 |
| 1980 | 134.02 | 56.76 | 201.03 | 44632 | .58 | 1.3 |
| 1981 | 69.31 | 67.43 | 241.39 | 53365 | .58 | 1.4 |
| 1982 | 92.43 | 80.91 | 262.42 | 54940 | .62 | 1.5 |
| 1983 | 67.83 | 87.50 | 288.11 | 56515 | .66 | 1.6 |
| 1984 | 94.00 | 91.52 | 341.00 | 61692 | .70 | 1.5 |

*Notes*; 1. Average of current year and four preceding years.
2. Calculated on the basis of the five year average of capital expenditure and current R&D expenditure as % of current sales.

*Source* : Internal company records, as calculated by Usha Menon; Annual Report Unilever.

reveals that research takes the second place. In none of the years for which information is available, did recurring R&D expenditure exceed that on sales promotion. On an average it was less than half, e.g. Rs. 43 million compared to Rs. 99 million on advertising in 1984. We have seen earlier, in Table 6.2, that for the private sector in general the relationship between R&D and Advertising is just the other way round, namely twice as much money being spent on the former.

The average research intensity of the world-wide research activity of Unilever, which has been computed in the last column of Table 6.5 presents a distorted picture in the sense that it is calculated on the basis of the overall turnover. It may be assumed that in some of the geographical areas, e.g. the two home countries of the corporate group, the intensity will be much higher. Even then, the aggregate average reveals not only a substantially higher average but also, unlike the trend in Hindustan Lever, an increase in intensity, up from 0.8 per cent in 1974 to 1.6 in 1983.

The R&D activities of Hindustan Lever can be divided into three broad periods. Roughly, they are period I (1969-63), period II (1963-75) and period III (1975 onwards). Such a division is at variance with the one proposed by HL itself, namely the period of import substitution (1960-1970), the period of progression into areas hitherto unexplored (1970-75), and the period of exploration into areas outside the traditional business interests from 1975 onwards (HL 1982). According to our division the first period was dominated by adaptive R&D and the second one by local R&D. While local R&D continues to play an important role in period III, there is a growing importance of global R&D (Usha Menon 1982, pp. 79 ff). Whereas period II fell essentially under a regime of import substitution, period III coincides with the regime of growing import liberalisation.

In 1959-60 an R&D division, employing only a few research workers, was started in the Bombay factory of HL. The research was directed at the production of dehydrated peas, instant foods, etc. According to HL, the research unit was started "with the principle object of meeting needs for growth and diversification. Specific requirements of consumer preference, costs and climatic conditions in India are of importance in this work" (Information supplied by HL to Government of India in 1972). This research was obviously adaptive research aimed at adapting the basic know-how which the parent company had to the local conditions.

The work related to the substitution of tallow and edible oils by minor oils in soap-making dominated the R&D during the sixties. The ut.lisation of minor oils, apart from throwing up a number of technical problems, necessitated the development of special catalysts. In July 1967, the research centre at Andheri which had been sanctioned in 1962, started functioning and continued to concentrate on the extraction and upgrading of minor oils from lemon grass, eucalyptus, cinnamon leaf, etc. Since the parent company did not possess any know-how in this field and since research laboratories like RRL Hyderabad and the Indian Institute of Petroleum at Dehra Dun did, the R&D was essentially of a local character (see section 6.4 later).

After around 1974, when the R&D intensity started declining, the focus shifts away from oils and fats into new areas (Table 6.6).

**Table 6.6 : Distribution of R&D Expenditure in Hindustan Lever 1975-1981**

| Division | 1975 | 1978 | 1981 |
|---|---|---|---|
| Soaps & Detergents | 45 | 35 | 21 |
| Chemicals | 14 | 21 | 23 |
| Corporate Interests | 12 | 16 | 31 |
| Personal Products | 8 | 11 | 10 |
| Animal Feeding Stuffs | 10 | 8 | 5 |
| Foods | 3 | 7 | 6 |
| Exploratory | 8 | 2 | — |
| Total | 100 | 100 | 100 |

*Source* : Information supplied by Hindustan Lever to GOI in 1976, 1979 and 1982.

A scrutiny of the R&D undertaken during this period shows that while developmental work on oils and fats continues, it is no more the focus of attention. Although research on 'older' areas, as well as energy saving exercises continues, agriculture and chemicals constitute the new foci of attention. The importance of these areas for Hindustan Lever is reflected in the fact that in 1978 it set up a Research Foundation "to support research in other R&D centres in the country in the fields of Agriculture, Animal Husbandry and Industrial Chemicals" (Annual Report, 1978). The shift in R&D emphasis by Hindustan Lever took place against the background of a progressive liberalisation in the import policy of the Government of India, in addition to various incentive schemes, among which the increasing facilities for imports of equipment.

Research in the area of chemicals can be divided into three broad areas—fine chemicals, inorganic chemicals and agricultural inputs. Research on all these areas can be considered local R&D.

Research on fine chemical is a continuation of the research conducted earlier on extraction and upgradation of perfumary chemicals from Indian raw materials. The chemicals produced have included linalol from Beta pinene, citral, phenyl ethyl alcohol and linalyl acetate. This is an area in which the corporate Unilever company does not possess much know-how, and it is our distinct impression it has greatly gained from this R&D by its Indian subsidiary.

It has recently been reported that Hindustan Lever has taken up research on 'Single Cell oil production by protoplastic fusion'. This is done by trying to introduce the genes for the production of oil into the yeast. One major advantage of single cell systems of production is that products from any geographical region in the world can be obtained in vitro. This has obvious advantages for the western countries, which have to depend on imports. This research could thus be characterised as global, although we are not in a position to characterise it as either dependent or independent. For the time being its suitability in countries like India as a means of of augmenting the scarce supplies, as well as its commercial validity his doubtful.

Production of oil by means of cell suspension cultures is not a realistic proposition for solving the oil shortage in India. Even according to Unilever,

> Because of the high capital cost of the equipment necessary to extract the end products from the cells and media, we are limited at present to research on high value products such as perfumary components and valuable compounds derived from oils and fats. We believe that production of large tonnages of protein fats and carbohydrates is still best done by agriculture (Economic Times, 30.04.82).

In response to the policy of the Government of India to allow foreign companies having more than 40% of foreign equity share to operate only in Appendix I industries, Hindustan Lever entered a new area of business after 1974. They started the production of sodium tripoly phosphate, even though the parent company Unilever did not possess any know-how in this field. This entry into heavy chemicals took place after a considerable amount of controversy. The know-how for the production of STPP was obtained from Albright & Wilson (U.K.), and in 1974 Hindustan Lever started undertaking supportive R&D. Their research work succeeded in developing a process for the recovery of orthophosphate from spent filter-cake, and involved general support activity for the phosphate business of the company. This R&D can be characterised as local adaptive R&D.

Hindustan Lever has been working on the microbial synthesis of dipicolinic acid and propionic acid. Dipicolinic acid is a substitute for phosphates used in detergents. Production of dipicolinic acid cannot be considered to be a high priority item for Hindustan Lever in India, since the eutrophication of inland waters due to phosphates has not yet emerged as a problem. On the contrary, it is a problem of a very urgent nature for Unilever. Unilever has spent more than 100 million guilders between 1967-1976, in trying to create a substitute for phosphates (Van der Geest 1978, p. 65). It was reported in 1981 that the work on dipicolinic acid was shelved after having completed the laboratory work.

It is not known whether this was due to lack of success in the project, or because the pilot plant is being put up elsewhere in the world. This work can be considered to be of global independent R&D type. Agricultural chemicals and other agricultural inputs are another area in which Hindustan Lever is undertaking research. The aim is to enter into the the new business opportunity given by the short duration varieties of pulses developed by the Indian Agricultural Research Institute. Hindustan Lever is undertaking research on packaging and delivery systems for rizobial cultures.

Another agrochemical which Hindustan Lever has already started producing is the plant growth nutrient. In August 1980 Hindustan Lever announced the discovery of a growth stimulator for plants. HL received a letter of intent on September 26, 1980 for the production of the same. The production of this growth stimulation was shown to be one of the R&D breakthroughs in a high technology area where no local expertise was available. This was one of the reasons for justifying the continuation of more than 40% foreign equity in HL. Hindustan Lever is said to have begun the work on triacontanol in January 1979. The production of traicontanol and its miraculous properties in plant growth are already well known phenomenon, but Hindustan Lever claims that they are the first to have discovered a process for the cheap and plentiful production of the chemical.*

*The claim was contested by Dr. P.J. Thomas of Kay Laboratories Pvt. Ltd., a small scale unit. He brought out the fact that the same nutrient with the active ingredient triacontanol was being manufactured by Kay Laboratories. This product sold as 'miraculan', was being marketed by NOCIL. HL has argued that Thomas is using the same technology as developed by HL, which he is said to have obtained while being an employee of Hindustan Lever. On the contrary Thomas maintains that there is nothing very sophisticated about the technology and that he has merely scaled up the process available in textbooks using standard techniques.

After the Kay Laboratories representation to the government, the cost per hectare of the HL product was reduced from Rs. 60 to Rs. 40. But Kay Laboratories is selling its product at Rs. 27. (*India Today*, Sept. 16-20, 1981, pp. 136-139). HL has argued that its product 'mixtalol' contains ingredients other than Triacontanol to neutralise any possible side effects.

The increasing importance of agricultural research in Hindustan Lever is indicated by the fact that during 1970-80 a new Agricultural Division was added to the research organisation. The importance of agricultural research is also reflected in the external projects financed by Hindustan Lever through the newly formed Hindustan Lever Research Foundation. Agriculture is the focus of this research foundation. Indeed, according to Hindustan Lever, the Research Foundation was established "in 1976 to support research work in areas of relevance in Indian agriculture and industry utilising products of agriculture" (HL Research Foundation, no date).

The interest of Hindustan Lever in agriculture can be seen in two ways. One is related to the general interest Hindustan Lever is bound to take in agriculture, due to its product diversification into agrochemicals such as fungicides and phosphatic fertilizers, etc. The other possible factor, which we want to explore, is the relationship of Hindustan Lever's research to the interest of Unilever in biotechnolgy. For lack of definite evidence, it is not possible to conclude definitively that Hindustan Lever's research in agricultural area is a global R&D, satisfying essentially the needs of Unilever. Yet it is important to investigate this further, especially in the light of recent evidence in the case of other multinationals (Menon 1982, pp. 122-126).

At the stage of research, tissue culture uses extensive scientific labour. Tissue cultures have to be recultured to fresh nutrient medium at regular intervals to replenish exhausted nutrients and to allow further morphogenesis. A recent American review on palm tissue culture puts forward the view that "The subculturing of callus and the separation and culturing of plantlets is a time-consuming labor-extensive process. Refinement of this procedure will determine the efficiency of the vitro propagation method for palms" (Tisserat 1981, p. 18). After transplanting to free living conditions also the plantlets require extensive care. The reduction of labour required is identified as one of the research directions in the rapid propagation of palms (Tisserat 1981, p. 25). While the reduction of labour involved can be achieved at the stage of commercial propagation by using microprocessors and continuous systems, such an option is not open at the stage of applied research. Given the cheapness of scientific labour with comparable skills in India, it is safe to assume that it should have influenced the decision of Unilever to conduct the research in India.

Our characterisation of the new phase, as one in which the global needs of Unilever begin to play an increasingly important role, seems to be justified by the remark of of Unilver that "our research centre in Bombay is also playing a valuable role in building our technological base ... It makes an important contribution to the local business and is also working on various developments in collaboration with our European Laboratories" (Unilever, Annual Report, 1981, p. 26).*

In 1982, it was reported that "the Research Centre has extensive facilities for biological clearance work as an extension of the Environment Safety Division of Unilever. Every new ingredient and product formulation is extensively tested for safety in use before it is marketed. In fact Hindustan Lever is the only manufacturer with such extensive safety testing facilities in the entire Indian consumer industry" (Hindustan Lever 1982). According to Hindustan Lever, the work includes toxicological tests on guinea pigs, mice, rats and rabbits. The moot question is that since the testing is an extension of the work at the Unilever Division, the products tested are likely to be not only those marketed by Hindustan Lever, but as well or even exclusively by Unilever. The labour intensive nature of the work involved seems to indicate such a possibility.

*Given the existing policy of the government of India to discourage foreign ownership of plantations, Hindustan Lever cannot be sure of being allowed to own plantations in the future. On the other hand, the possibility of Hindustan Lever being allowed to enter the seed market is also not real. According to the present regulation FERA and companies coming under MRTPA are allowed to invest only in Appendix I industries. Seeds are not included in the list of products in which a MNC is allowed to enter. Given the fact that the Government of India does not recognise patents or breeder's rights in agriculture, Hindustan Lever cannot also hope to licence this process to others and enjoy technology rents. Given these factors, Hindustan Lever cannot realistically plan for commercialisation of the know-how developed.

Hindustan Lever has undertaken a host of other research activities as for example in the case of toilet preparations. In this area, Hindustan Lever has developed a new skin lightening cream, after years of research. It was subsequently marketed under the brand name 'Fair and Lovely'.

### 6.4. HL and Oils

Rather than getting bogged down in a debate on social relevance, which research efforts to achieve a skin lightener are bound to generate, we shall presently deal in some more detail with the research area in which Hindustan Lever has claimed major successes, and on the basis of which it has actually been allowed to retain a foreign equity.

Traditionally, groundnut (47% of domestic production) as well as rape/mustard seeds (18 %) have provided for the bulk of edible oil production (*ET*, 13.02.1985). Since the increase in production has been far short of requirements, the utilisation of non-edible oils as a substitute in soap production, was advanced as one way of saving on the foreign exchange account. The structural shortage of indigenous oil bearing resources has led to a volume of edible oil imports which is by and large of the same magnitude as the internal production. Against this background, HL claims that its sophisticated technology has contributed to utilisation of non-edible oils as a substitute in soap making and that it thereby has contributed to the relative decrease of edible oil imports.

In a note submitted to the government in 1975, it was claimed that HL provided science and technology inputs for the use of "unknown or scarce indigenous materials, e.g. minor oils". As Usha Menon (1982, pp. 102 ff) has illustrated, the credit for both the propagation of the use of minor oils as a substitute and the extraction of the oils, however, does not go to Hindustan Lever. The credit for the propagation of the idea that India's shortage of oil could be partially met by the utilisation of non-edible oils in soap-making goes essentially to two government agencies, namely the KVIC (Khadi and Village Industries Commission) and the ICOC (Indian Central Oilseeds Committee). As early as 1954, a separate section for the utilisation of non-edible oils for soap-making was set up by the KVIC (Kane 1959, p. 171). The experimental survey and collection work through village cooperatives received a major filip with the formation of the technical sub-committee on non-edible oils by the ICOC in 1957. A series of surveys on the minor oils seeds potential in the different states of the country was published in its Indian Oilseeds Journal.

The ICOC distributed the research to be undertaken among four major research laboratories. The Regional Research Laboratory (RRL) at Hyderabad concentrated on cotton seed, castor, fatty acids and bleaching materials; the Department of Chemical Technology at the University of Bombay on non-edible oils, fatty acids and solvent extraction; the Oil Technological Research Institute at Anantpur on groundnut, cotton seed and certain lesser oilseeds; and the Harcourt Butler Technological Institute at Kanpur on rapeseed, mustard and linseed. Till then the non-edible oils used by the cottage industries for the production of washing soap were crushed in village *ghanis*, which managed to recover only around one-fourth of the fatty content. Work was therefore undertaken for better methods of oil extraction. Some interesting improvement on decorticators and solvent extraction units was made in the research laboratories as well as in the central research institute of the KVIC at Wardha (Patil and Bhushan 1964; Srivastava 1969, p.100). Hindustan Lever's contribution in the survey and recovery efforts at this stage was practically non-existent.

In the annual report of HL in 1959, the then chairman S.H. Turner mentioned that "great efforts are being made to collect minor oilseeds". The company refers to that statement as the point of reference on HL's early concern for the utilisation of minor oils (T. Thomas 1981, p. 108). The validity of its claim can be best assessed if the various minor oils are dealt with separately, which, for reasons of space, we shall do as briefly as possible. The study conducted by Menon (1982, p. 107 ff.) clearly establishes that with regard to castor oil, kusum oil, neem oil, karanja oil, and others the following situation prevailed : 1. The national research laboratories, among others. RRL at Hyderabad, have made breakthroughs in solvent extraction, hydrogenation and bleaching of the oils, and in most cases have taken patents for the same prior to HL; 2. The actual use of minor oil in soap production of HL has remained at a low level, which in any case was much below the consumption pattern in the traditional soap-making industry, e.g., whereas in 1966 only 4 per cent of the oil used in soap production by HL consisted of non-edible oils, in the KVIC soap units the share went up to almost 100 per cent (KVIC, *Annual Report* 1966); 3. The research efforts of HL were repeatedly in collaboration with the local scientific institutes, e.g., with the RRL at Hyderabad.

Some of these aspects will be further illustrated with reference to the case of sal fat. The utilisation of sal fat by HL has been the focus of a vigorous propaganda effort by the company. The fat had been traditionally extracted and consumed by the tribals and to a lesser extent by the non-tribal population in Orissa and Madhya Pradesh. Nowadays it is being used as a substitute for traditional oils in soap making as well as for cocoa-butter. The interest in the commercial utilisation of sal oil began only in 1966-67 when the Directorate of Non-Edible Oils and Soap Industry of the KVIC undertook the collection of seeds on an experimental basis in the Koraput district in Orissa (Laksmikantan and Gujarati 1969, p. 66; Jena 1969, p. 33). Similarly, interest in the collection and utilisation of the sal seeds was shown by J.P. Lath, who was a forest contractor in Sambalpur in the same state. According to J.P. Lath,

> The idea of utilising the oil on an industrial basis was propagated and I was introduced to this subject in 1958 by Shri B. Das and his efforts in convincing me of the vast potential of the forest produce, made me to take up the maiden venture in the field. It, however, took an appreciable time to compile all the data and secure a lease for sal seeds on an industrial basis after meeting the objections of the forest department. In 1966, we contacted the Regional Office, Oilseeds Development Hyderabad, Regional Research Laboratory and Dr. J.G. Kane of Bombay University whose interest and research works yielded most encouraging results and with their help *we were able to make some big*

> *industrial houses interested* in our project (Lath 1969, p. 29, stress added).

The story is confirmed by T. Thomas, the then Chairman of Hindustan Lever :

> When a forest contractor from Orissa approached us several years ago with a small quantity of sal seed, it was known that it had sal fat which had a very greenish colour but could be used in the manufacture of certain grades of soap. So we encouraged him to collect and supply the seed for extraction (Thomas 1981, p. 82).

At this stage Hindustan Lever was involved in the collection, as a very important, if not the most important buyer.

It is reported that the collection in Koraput district went up from 50 quintals in 1967 to 428 quintals in 1968 due to the interest shown by Hindustan Lever in buying the seeds (Lakshmikantan and Gujarati 1969, p. 37). But the leading and coordinating role in the whole operation was played by the Regional Office, Oilseeds Development, Government of India. Apart from M/s. Utkal Contractors and Joinery Pvt. Ltd., Sambalpur, belonging to J.P. Lath, and Hindustan Lever, other Companies such as Tata Oil Mills Co. Ltd. and M/s. Dulichand Omraolal & Co. were also involved in seed collection (OTAI 1969, p. 23).

As in the case of collection, Hindustan Lever has not played a pioneering role in the case of extraction technology either. Mechanical decorticators were developed at the research institutes at Anantpur and Kanpur. The oil, unlike other oil seeds, cannot be extracted in ordinary expeller units, and a new process technology for solvent extraction by means of a flaking machine was developed at the RRL in Hyderabad. The work was sponsored by the Utkal Contractors and Joinery Pvt. Ltd. at Sambalpur which in 1970 received the feasability report on a solvent extraction plant. The company was owned by J.P. Lath and supplied the extracted oil to HL. His company had earlier received a license to collect the sal seeds in Orissa on condition that he would set up a solvent extraction plant in the leased area. Accordingly, after receiving the technological data from the RRL at Hyderabad, his Orissa Oil Industries Pvt. Ltd. set up two plants at Rairangpur and Sambalpur (NPC 1980, pp. 29-30). With regard to the bleaching of the fat, i.e. the removal of the chlorophyl in order to make the colour attractive for application in cocoa butter and soaps, HL does claim to have developed a process. A patent (nr 137097) was applied for in July 1972. At earlier dates, national research institutes had reported success in bleaching the sal oil. In June 1970, the OIRI at Anantpur applied for a patent (nr 127314) on the basis of a technology which appears to be less energy intensive than the process for which HL applied for a patent two years later.

The upgradation of sal fat to obtain a cocoa butter extender has been the main aim of the utilisation of sal fat. Its potential use became known with the analysis of sal made in 1942 by Hilditch and Zaky, and later at the University of Bombay by the team of J.G. Kane. In 1970, HL filed an application for the fractionation of sal fat so as to remove the lower melting faction (Patent nr 129348). The exports which were done on this basis from 1974 onwards were not really cocoa butter substitutes, but more probably the sal stearin fraction which could then be mixed abroad with the palmitic fraction of palm oil. A breakthrough seems to have been achieved only in 1979 when a patent for the production of purified sal was made and when a pilot plant was set up for the upgradation of sal fat to chocolate butter standards. In the meantime Cadbury India Ltd. had also patented a process for the upgradation of sal fat to cocoa butter levels (Patent nr 147101) of September 1976). Tata Oil Mills Ltd. claimed in 1977 that they also had developed a substitute on the basis of mango kernel fat and sal fat. The R&D excellence of Hindustan Lever thus does not appear to be very exceptional, and certainly does not operate at a higher level than what the local scientists have achieved.

The picture that emerges from the involvement of Hindustan Lever in sal fat, as well as in the other minor oils, is that intensive linkages exist between the MNC and the local scientific and industrial organisations, and that HL occupies such a position in this structure that the maximum benefits accrue to it, particularly since at the level of publicity also, the company has managed to attract all the credits.

The general impression that MNCs do not conduct R&D in the underdeveloped countries and that when they do, it is a disguised form of quality control needs to be amended, as our study indicates. Out of the 14 companies in our sample, seven have recognised R&D units, and at present at least four of them undertake research in India.

An analysis of the R&D by the two major companies with a long history of R&D, Hindustan Lever and Peico, indicates that the import substitution policy had a positive impact on R&D intensity. But the most significant conclusion from our study is that R&D activities of multinaticnals need to be studied after disaggregation according to the different types. Thus, for example, two companies can have the same R&D intensity but one might be engaging in purely adaptive R&D, while the other might undertake local R&D of an independent kind. Our study also indicate the usefulness of studying in-house R&D according to the prevailing government policy, as, for example, in the import-substitution and in the export-promotion phase.

It seems that during the import substitution phase, multinationals undertake local R&D and adaptive R&D with a pre-dominance of the former. In other words, under pressure from government policy the MNC will undertake research to utilise local raw materials, provided that there exist suitable skills and facilities in the host country. We can also hypothesise from our data that a raw material oriented firm is more likely to undertake applied research.

During the phase of export promotion, global R&D enters as a significant component. The location of this type of R&D is facilitated by the liberal import of equipments, since this allows a combination of the sophisticated equipments from the advanced countries with the cheap scientific labour of the underdeveloped countries.

An export promotion policy can have a negative influence on the adaptive and local R&D of MNCs. One influence is exerted directly through the liberal imports which accompany export promotion schemes. Since raw materials of international standards are available it is no more necessary to undertake research to find local substitutes. Since raw material oriented research has been the most significant part of the local R & D by MNCs, this should have a depressing impact on the local R & D intensity.

An Export Promotion Policy affects negatively the propensity of MNCs to undertake local R&D in yet another way. The MNCs are given an opportunity to undertake exports rather than diversify into core sector activities which lie outside their area of operation. Since exports can be in sectors where the MNC already has expertise, the need to undertake local R&D will be reduced.

Our study indicates that the MNCs have a low propensity to undertake transfer R&D, which actually is the type of R&D that upgrades the local level of technology. In the next chapter we shall deal with another aspect of technology for which the multinational are generally invited in the developing countries, namely the so-called transfer of technology through the sale of embodied and/or disembodied know-how by foreign companies to their Indian counterparts.

# 7

# *Technical Collaborations*

Some general observations should be made about the significance of technical collaborations for the Indian industry, before dealing with specific instances of technical cooperation with Dutch multinational corporations.

Indian enterprises, both in the private and the public sector, after independence, were driven into a technological dependence upon foreign sources. Given the need for a rapid industrialisation and given the relative absence of the necessary equipment, know-how and know-why, the foreign source of technology worked as a short-cut in industrial development.

The buying of foreign technical know-how and operational skill helped the country in a short period of time to establish new industries at a relatively low cost.

Till the late fifties, when import license regulations became more stringent, the foreign companies operating from abroad preferred to sell finished products rather than patents and licenses. The cooperation with the socialist countries, which India resorted to in such important industrial fields like steel, petro-chemicals and pharmaceuticals, in conjunction with a policy of import restrictions, induced many foreign firms to start selling their know-how. Whereas there were only 248 technical collaboration agreements in 1951-1955, there were 1572 in the period 1961-1965 (Subrmaniam 1972). At that time they promoted the production of Rs. 23,300 milion worth of commodities, more than one-fifth of the country's overall industrial output. A survey of the big enterprises carried out by the Reserve Bank of India in the late sixties reveals that 82 per cent of them were set up with either financial or technical aid from foreign firms (Shirokov 1973, p. 227-299).

Thereafter, the number of agreements remained more or less at the same level. In the period 1973-1979 the foreign collaboration approvals even showed a marginal decrease to 1389 cases, or an average of 178 cases per year, but a new period of increasing reliance on foreign technology has recently started. The annual average number of agreements over the two years 1981 and 1982 went up to 490, and thereafter increased to an average of 918 agreements in 1984 and 1985. The steep increase in the number of approvals has occurred despite the fact that collaborations not exceeding one million rupees per year are permitted without formal approval and despite the fact that the government has given many incentives for in-house R&D, of which particularly the MNCs avail, as we have observed earlier.

The country-wise origin of the agreements can be judged from Table 7.1. The geographical concentration, which in the mid-fifties was for 40 per cent with England (A. Rahman 1970; Subramaniam 1972, p. 111), has undergone a fundamental reorientation. The United States and the Federal Republic of Germany have become equally important. The socialist countries who have been credited with helping India in building up a sophisticated capital goods industry in the 1950s-1960s were contracted to provide only four per cent of the total number of technical collaborations in the period 1977-1982.

## 7.1. Apprehensions on the Benefits Involved

Apart from the advantages at a relatively low social cost which the import of technology may have, depending on the type of technology which is contracted, a number of short term as well as long term inhibiting effects have emerged. Recently, a number of European researchers were funded by the EEC to do a survey of the technology suppliers (*EPW*, November 1985, pp. 1973-2094). In their contribution, Bell and Scott-Kemmis argue that a number of key features of technnological collaborations have changed. The most significant feautures which could be isolated in the past were : the predominace of large MNCs with an oligopolistic position in the particular technology and with a much superior knowledge of technology as well as an accumulated experience in bargaining over

**Table 7.1 : Country-wise List of Foreign Collaborations, 1957-1983**

| Country | 1957-76 | 1977 | 1978 | 1979 | 1980 | 1981 | 1982 | 1983 | 1977-83 |
|---|---|---|---|---|---|---|---|---|---|
| UK | 1165 | 59(9) | 61(5) | 63(9) | 110(17) | 79(9) | 106(14) | 119 | 597 |
| USA | 955 | 54(6) | 58(17) | 48(8) | 125(19) | 85(15) | 110(20) | 135 | 615 |
| FRG | 827 | 55(5) | 58(8) | 55(5) | 100(9) | 71(14) | 110(19) | 125 | 581 |
| Japan | 429 | 20(0) | 28(2) | 12(0) | 33(4) | 27(4) | 51(5) | 58 | 129 |
| Switzerland | 273 | 23(4) | 18(5) | 14(1) | 38(3) | 26(4) | 41(8) | 47 | 207 |
| France | 219 | 14(1) | 21(0) | 17(1) | 24(5) | 23(3) | 28(6) | 40 | 157 |
| Italy | 141 | 10(1) | 13(2) | 16(3) | 25(3) | 18(1) | 37(5) | 30 | 149 |
| GDR | 96 | 3(0) | 8(0) | 6(0) | 4(0) | 4(0) | 2(0) | 10 | 37 |
| Sweden | 87 | 4(0) | 8(2) | 5(2) | 10(4) | 11(0) | 15(4) | 15 | 68 |
| Netherland | 65 | 4(1) | 10(0) | 6(0) | 8(1) | 9(2) | 14(0) | 13 | 64 |
| CSSR | 63 | 2(0) | 1(0) | 2(0) | 4(0) | 0(0) | 5(0) | 2 | 16 |
| Denmark | 50 | 2(0) | 2(0) | 3(0) | 6(0) | 1(0) | 4(0) | 3 | 21 |
| Belgium | 44 | 2(0) | 0(0) | 3(0) | 2(0) | 1(0) | 4(0) | 8 | 20 |
| USSR | na | 3(0) | 3(0) | 2(0) | 6(0) | 2(0) | 2(0) | 4 | 22 |
| All Countries | 4845 | 267(27) | 307(44) | 267(31) | 525(71) | 389(56) | 591(126) | 673 | 3018 |

*Notes* : The number of technical agreements including financial participation as well is given between brackets.

*Sources* : India Investment Centre, *Quarterly Reports*; *Economic Times*, 19-11-1986 and 2-4-1984.

technology; the transfer of technology as one element within the broader strategy directed at global expansion, particularly the protection of markets and the sale of intermediate and capital goods; a complex of contractual conditions limiting exports and leaking of technology by the buyers and a prevalence of importers who were already subordinate agents of the MNCs, either as subsidiaries or as sales agents. The authors argue that on the basis of their survey of British companies some of the conditions and features have become significantly different (op. cit., p. 1976). Their evidence is, however, only convincing in respect of the assumed multinationality of the firms : in "only" 59 per cent of the cases the suppliers had widespread activities all over the world. It however, merely gives an indication of the number of firms and not of the relative weight of the operations involved or of the status of collaboration agreement.*

The most important objective for the foreign firms, in case of the British firms, are the circumvention of the trade restrictions (63%) and the return payment for technology (54%), followed by the protection of the export market, partially as a response to the emergence of competitiors in the Indian market (45%), and the opening of a new export market (43%). The motives of securing an export base from India is considered important by only 10 per cent of the technology suppliers, particularly in the cases of labour intensive exports directed at third country markets and of a phasing out of production in the U.K. Restrictive clauses, either on exports by the Indian firms or on the further development or sale of the acquired technology are not generally considered necessary since they on the one hand (did) not have the technological or managerial capacity to compete in the export market, and on the other hand *did not* have the engineering capacity to improve upon the technology : "Among firms whose agreements had

*Not all agreements are actually implemented. Fourteen per cent of the agreements covered in the RBI survey (RBI 1984, pp. 3-4) turned out to be infructuous for different reasons, such as the failure of collaborator to fulfill the commitments, non-feasibility on technical grounds, non-availability of foreign exchange, etc. It may be assumed that smaller companies rather than large multinationals will be confronted with some of these.

run long enough to allow comment on actual experience, almost all indicated that their expectations had been correct . . . ; but our impression from a few cases was that suppliers' concerns about these kinds of potential opportunity costs had commonly led to non-transfer of technology" (Bell and Scott-Kemmis 1985, p. 1979).

In another survey, in which the focus was not the official view of the exporters but the empirical evidence available from the Indian side, Nagesh Kumar (1985) has not noticed any changes for the better. He concludes, on the basis of a rather limited number of studies which have been undertaken thus far, that technical collaboration in combination with equity participation leads to a high import/value added ratio and to a poor export performance. The transfer of technology,* even in the case of public sector enterprises, has generally hindered the diffusion through sub-licensing or otherwise and has made only a limited contribution to the building up of a local technological capability. The statements on the dismal export performance are confirmed by the data in the Fourth Survey Report on Foreign Collaborations in Indian Industry, carried out by the Reserve Bank of India. The import content of firms with collaboration agreements, it appears, has risen quite sharply in recent years. Exports on the other hand have not picked up, and the RBI (1985, p. 41) notices that the tendency for the technology supplier "to impose export restrictions has increased over the period". The worsening balance of trade position and the inefficient resource mobilisation (in terms of a declining proportion of the value-added to total production) confirm many of the random critical assessments which have been made in the past.

A distinct disadvantage connected with the import of technology has been the growing bondage of the Indian firms, including some of the major ones, as we have already noticed in the case of Shell and Mafatlal, due to the practice of the foreign partner to attempt to participate in the equity of the

*Strictly speaking it is wrong, to talk about 'transfer of technology' when embodied or disembodied know-how is transferred to a contracting partner in an underdeveloped country. Transfer take place only if the knowledge applied in the creation of that product is transferred as well and gets absorbed at the level of not only the particular sector but of the economy as a whole.

company. The sale of technology therefore has opened a novel way for the penetration of foreign capital in the equity structure and actual management of Indian firms. In general, this has reinforced the dominance of the monopoly sector within the Indian economy, as Subhendu Das Gupta (1978) has rightly argued. The share of the Indian monopoly house as defined by the official enquiry committees, account for 25 to 30 per cent of all collaboration agreements. The two top houses, Tata and Birla, occupy the first positions in the number of collaborations, by far outstretching their immediate competitors Kirloskar, Bajaj, Walchand, Sarabhai, Shriram and Thapar. These firms taken together account for one-fifth of the collaboration agreements entered into by the Indian industry.

A second distinctly negative feature of an indiscriminate policy of technical collaborations are the repetitive imports of similar technology which prevent the building up of uniform standards and types of equipments, spare parts and raw materials, and thereby pre-empt the advantages which such a vast country as India would derive from the economics of scale. Subramaniam and Mohan Pillai (1972) have brought together a wide list of such repetitive imports.

A final aspect which may have negative consequences for the economy of the host country is related to the appropriateness of the technology. By appropriateness we do neither refer to aspects of scale nor to capital-labour ratio since these aspects of technology are no means in itself. We are rather concerned with the end-product. The regulatory government policy in the past to some extent had succeeded to tip the scales in favour of collaborations in the capital goods industry and had induced companies from capitalist countries to follow the lead given by the socialist countries, even in respect of collaborations with the public sector. The present trend, however, may reverse that practice. The government has removed a number of restrictions which have as a consequence that the public sector has lost the exclusive responsibility for particular industrial fields, that industries where only technical collaborations were allowed will now also have financial collaborations, and that in general the technology import policy has become more liberal. The change in policy has opened up many new avenues for technological collaborations for rather unwarranted product lines.

What is the position of the Dutch companies in this context. A detailed list of all the Indian companies who got the government approval for either technical or technical-cum-financial collaborations can be provided off the shelf by the Directorate General of Technical Development (DGTD 1980) and by the Indian Investment Centre (1982). Only a limited number of the agreements have not materialised, due to different reasons.* The agreements which have materialised have generally led to successful operations, at least from the point of view of the suppliers.

Charles Cooper (1985) in his study on the agreements between Belgian and Dutch companies and Indian firms has provided some very interesting data. In his assumption, an agreement can be deemed a failure if the supplier does not receive a lumpsum payment for the supply of the know-how and/or royalties to cover at least the management time and the technical assistance involved. One-fourth of the cases turned out to be failures. This appears to be on the high side, but a further disaggregation shows that whereas 82 per cent of agreements of the small non-MNC firms ended in failure, this was only the case with 2 per cent of the contracts of the Benelux MNCs. The disadvantage of the smaller companies seems to be structural (lack of resources to acquire the information and the relatively higher costs involved in managing the contract), and can only partially be related to the complexity of the Indian control system : "To clarify this it is helpful to recall how comparatively well supplied the MNC groups of firms are with relevant information. Benelux MNCs have joint ventures in the Indian market which generally speaking have some of the most skilled industrial managers in India in charge of them" (Cooper 195, p. 2020).

*On three such cases, information was supplied by the contracting firms : Voltamp Transformers and Smith Transformatoren (lapsed within the time limit set by the government), United Ink and Varnish Company and Wagemakers of Breda (the latter withdrew its offer for the production of spraying powder), and Transmissions Pvt. Ltd. and Altap for the production of conical cutters (not sanctioned by the government within a reasonable time). The latter was the only case in which the approval lag, which is so often focused upon the public complaints by the private sector, is known to have played a deterrent role.

It is interesting to note the difference in initiation of the agreements : whereas of the sample firms virtually all collaborations involving non-MNC Dutch firms were initiated by the Indian enterprises, this was the case with only 8 per cent of the agreements of the MNC group. For all practical purposes this means that the MNCs have and keep the initiative in their hands. They consider the risks of loss of control over technological knowledge in the case of inter-firm transfer of technology without equity participation too big. The MNCs accordingly "enter collaborations mainly because the Indian market for the products in question might be lost to them if they did not. Some MNC managers considered this to be a minimal reason for transferring technology; they argue that it encourages a defensive strategy whereby supplying firms 'stay out of India' for as long as possible—i.e., until they perceive that a competitor might enter ahead of them and exclude them from the market' (Cooper 1985, p. 2017).

## 7.2 Some Case Studies

If one goes by the official figures till 1982, Stami Carbon tops the list of technical link-ups with nine Indian companies, closely followed by Philips with eight companies and both Stork and Akzo-Organon with five. The importance of the companies as suppliers of technology to India should, however, not be determined on the basis of the number of collaboration agreements involved. Collaboration agreements as such are not necessarily a reflection of the technical link-up involved as is shown by the difference between the modus operandus of Unilever and Philips who have adhered to a diametrically opposite pattern, with the latter probably signing as many agreements as possible. The most important difference, in our view, however relates to the presence or absence of structural dependence which has accompanied the supply of technology.

The involvement of Stami Carbon, on the one hand, relates to the sale of technological know-how in the fertiliser industry without either managerial or financial involvement in the running of the receiving company. It has enabled the Indian companies and their Indian or foreign project contractors to design, construct and put the particular fertilizer plant into operation. The know-how and services provided include the transfer of erection and process data, the technical supervision up to the starting-up period and the training of employees. The agreements on designs and drawings, for example the coal handling technology transferred by IHC to Tata-Robins Fraser, are not to be treated as cases of 'technical collaboration', but rather as the sale of technologies on a lumpsum basis. In a technological sense the 'collaboration' is self-terminating and does not necessarily entail a structural, self-perpetuating link-up. Since this type of technology import, moreover, have taken place in the core sector of the industry, its overall impact on the development of productive forces may be considerable.

The opposite tendency, namely of one Dutch firm signing a multiple number of agreements with one Indian subsidiary, is very much prominent in two cases. Hazemeyer and Co. got the approval for four separate technical collaboration agreements with Electric Control Gear P. Ltd., for the production of fuses, switch gear and air circuit breakers. The other case is Philips India (Peico). Unlike Hindustan Lever, it has followed a policy of signing many collaboration agreements with its parent company Philps N.V., which in its turn has signed similar collaboration agreements with companies under the direct influence of Philips India, particularly with ELMI and Hind Lamps. The rationale behind such repetitive collaboration agreements of a peacemeal nature is not readily apparent. The suspicion that a company like Peico might use the technological contracts as an added means for transferring profits out of the country is not confirmed by the rough data on the drain of surplus of the various Dutch companies (Table 7.2).

Among the smaller companies on which some information could be collected, it appears that collaboration agreements quite often go hand in hand with either a financial participation or an agreement on the buy-back of the production. Marshall Engineering in Bombay, for example, has an agreement with Technodiamont of Amsterdam for the know-how of industrial diamond tools. After the cutting of rough diamonds, imported from the Netherlands, the polished product is returned to the parent company. The company claims to be "extremely happy" with this agreement. A similar agreement has been entered into by Gaitonde in Madras. Gaitonde, exporters of finished leather,

**Table 7.2 : Royalty Payments by Dutch Subsidiaries 1978 (Rs million)**

| Company | Total Foreign Exchange Utilisation | Drain of Surplus | Royalty and Technical Service Charges | 4 as % of 3 |
|---|---|---|---|---|
| Hindustan Lever | 117.3 | 28.6 | 2.8 | 10 |
| Peico | 57.7 | 18.8 | 2.5* | 13* |
| Nocil | 42.0 | 14.6 | 5.8 | 40 |
| Century Enka | 22.0 | 3.5 | 0.4** | 11** |
| Duphar Interfran | 6.3 | 0.7 | 0.3 | 41 |
| Wavin | 7.5 | 0.2 | 0.2 | 100 |
| Organon | 4.2 | 0.5 | 0.1 | 20 |
| ELMI | 5.0 | 0.1 | — | — |
| Hind Lamps | 4.5 | 0.01 | 0.01** | 100** |
| Maschmeyer | 5.5 | 0.1 | 0 | |
| Others | 0.8 | | | |
| Total | 272.3 | 67.2 | 12.0 | 19 |

*Source* : The Annual Reports of the respective companies.

*Notes* : *The Annual Report of Peico does not mention royalty payments separately. Our figure of Rs 2.5 million is composed of Technical Service Charges (calculated at Rs 1.04 million) and the rest category 'others' (Rs 1.46 million) which probably contains royalty payments in addition to expenditure under other headings.

**Century Enka and Hind Lamps have clubbed their royalty payments, if any, under the rest category 'others'.

bought the redundant machinery of a Dutch company for which it was a buying agent. In exchange for the imported machinery, Gaitonde agreed to supply its principals' requirements of finished leather. The transfer of technology in both cases appears to have accompanied a process of international redivision of labour. The more labour-intensive raw materials processing has been shifted to India and has increased the value-added of the exported product.

In the case of the smaller companies the tie-up between the

import of technology and the import of components and raw materials is clearly discernible. For example, Hazemeyer, which operates in the Kandla Free Trade Zone, imports on an average 97 per cent of its raw materials.* Such a tie-up does not readily appear from technical collaboration agreements which have been entered into with bigger Indian firms, which generally have multiple collaboration agreements with different foreign partners. Such examples are the link-up of Kirloskar (with Grasso) for the production of air cooling systems, Amar Dye Chemicals Ltd. (with Akzo for the production of PVC stabilizers), Gammon (with Stork) for the production of fibre glass propellors, and Larsen and Toubro (with Stork) for the manufacture of aerators used in thermal power plants. Usually a royalty of five per cent as well as lumpsum engineering fees are agreed on for a period of five to ten years. It appears that most of these collaboration agreements relate to the engineering sector and to products which generally can be classified as capital goods. As such, the transfer of technology could very well fit in with the strategy of industrial development and of widening and upgrading the technological infrastructure of the country.

Specific information on technical collaborations is difficult to obtain. From internal company sources we, however, have been able to construct the technical relationship between National Organic Chemicals and Shell and between Peico and Philips. In the next section, we shall deal with both these groups in some more detail.

On July 1964, the Mafatlal company NOCIL entered into a technical collaboration with SIRM (Shell Internationale Research Maatschappij) for the production of twelve different petrochemicals of which polyvinyl chloride with a 20000 tonnes design capacity was the most important one. The royalty of one to two and a half per cent on net sales value was to be effective for a period of ten years. The agreement provided for the supply of technical information relating to the modification of the licensed process for a period of five years after the start-up of the plant. A number of restrictive clauses were added to

*One of the conditions for operating in the KFTZ stipulates that the import content of the end product should not exceed 70 per cent (Agrawal 1982, p. 86).

the agreement. NOCIL was granted the non-transferable right to use the patent and the technical information on condition that "both during and after the expiry of the agreement the technical information shall not be disclosed to any third party".

Shell reserved for itself the right not only to utilise any modifications in the licensed process produced by NOCIL, but also the right to sub-license the process. The rights and obligations of the contracting parties were to be determined according to the laws of the Netherlands, and not to the Indian law.

At the same time as the technical collaboration agreement with SIRM, NOCIL also entered into an operating service agreement (OSA) with another Shell company, the Bataafse Internationale Chemie Maatschappij. The agreement was to be operative for a period of ten years from the starting up of the olefines plant. The operations for which Shell was to provide advice, assistance and services were all encompassing. It included the quality of the products, plant performance, operating techniques, laboratory methods, existing and future processes and equipment, safety measures, development reports, etc. The services under the agreement, which was to be exclusively governed by the laws of the Netherlands, ware supplied by Shell for the payment of a royalty of five per cent of the net sales value of the products.

Later developments indicate that neither the collaboration agreement with SIRM, nor the OSA provided technological competence to NOCIL either to introduce modifications or even to operate the plant at the licensed capacity. The OSA expired in January 1978. Shortly thereafter, the company applied for an extension of the OSA, at a payment of Rs. 5 million a year, with the argument that it was the only way to tap the know-how pool of Shell and thus to keep abreast of current international developments. The new OSA included even such non-specific operations as transport, safety, fire fighting, industrial hygiene, etc., which indicates that no independent know-how had been generated during the ten years the previous OSA was in operation.

Even minor modifications were only undertaken after the 'consent' or 'advice' by Shell. When, for example, the naptha cracker was to be replaced in 1977, the design work was undertaken at the Shell office. The same type of dependence came to the surface in the case of the catalyst change in the ethylene unit and the improvements in the vinyl chloride monomer and in the pvc units. In spite of the OSA, NOCIL has had to purchase know-how from outside the Shell company, namely from Goodrich (USA), Stauffer Chemicals (USA) and Vinatex Ltd. (UK). The particular technology was necessitated by the introduction of stricter pollution control under the Maharashtra Prevention of Water Pollution Act (1969).

The information on engineering and design work at NOCIL reveals the level of dependence and integration into the Shell group. We shall quote at length from NOCIL documents in order to show the extent of this integration :

> Shell has developed the design and engineering specifications which are derived largely from the Group know-how... So, a large measure of uniformity throughout group engineering work is thus achieved with all its attendent economic advantages... To keep uniformity in the design, Shell also sends sets of standard drawings advising typical arrangements.

In other words, the designs and engineering of NOCIL are fully integrated into Shell's system, with the corollary that it is less integrated into the national system : "Occasionally, the local suppliers or contractors are unable to meet the engineering and material requirements". A more detailed study of NOCIL as well as of the other foreign companies operating in India could possibly indicate that because of the lack of integration with the rest of the industry, the transfer of technology is often inadequate. Since the so-called transferred technology is, as a rule, restricted to the production circuit of the subsidiary, and is further developed and modified in the parent concern, the industrial sector as a whole is excluded from the benefits of the newly acquired know-how. One single private company, which initially has been given the exclusive access to the imported technology and thereby has acquired a by far advantageous position, will be determined to keep that position and may even go to the extent of gradually transferring more equity and managerial power to the foreign partner. Indeed, in exchange for the supply of new technology, the Mafatlal group recently has retreated into a junior position, reducing its equity in Nocil to 20 per cent and leaving Shell with 40 per cent of equity as the dominant partner.

The operations of Philips N.V. reveal a different aspect of MNC attitude towards the sale of technology. It has followed a policy of signing many agreements, both with its directly controlled companies and with companies with a substantial equity participation in addition to important managerial functions.

Usha Menon (1974) has collected data on as many as sixteen agreements which were signed with Peico, both at a time when, as Philips India Ltd., it was still a subsidiary of Philips N.V. and at the time when the foreign equity had been reduced to 40 per cent. In addition, Philips N.V. signed a number of agreements with ELMI, Hind Lamps, Webel and Punjab Anand Lamps.

According to Cooper (1985, p. 2016), companies who make heavy use of collaboration agreements do so "essentially because they perceive them as necessary to protect the 'high technology' they transfer". In the case of Philips-Peico, however, the technology which has been transferred has generally not been that exclusive that it needed special protection against competitors. We shall illustrate this with the example of the lamp industry, but first shall give a brief description of the agreements signed in relation to welding technology.

In the case of welding electrodes, the technical collaboration appears to have been used to gain control over the local company WELMA, with which an agreement for the production of welding rods was signed in 1964. The agreement specifically stipulated that the disclosure of the know-how was not allowed and that exports would only be allowed to some neighbouring countries. The agreement further specified that the services would include "written instructions and documentation which are drawn by Philips from time to time on the basis of developing techniques in respect of the electrodes". Five years after the commencement of the production line, the company had become a sick unit and was taken over by Philips India Ltd. which in 1976 applied for an extension of the agreement for five more years. It was argued that such an extension was necessary in order to get the following services from the parent company: product development, trouble-shooting, application know-how, process control, quality control, development of raw materials for import substitution. After more than ten years of operation, the dependence of Philips India on Philips N.V. had prevented them from becoming self-reliant in welding technology, even in respect of trouble-shooting and quality control. The Government of India rejected the proposal, but two years later approved another proposal for the purchase of ten different electrode formulations. Again in 1981, a technical agreement was entered into for the production of six types of welding equipment, at 5 per cent royalty. Both agreements still include such services as quality control which, as the document of the latter agreement records, "shall be done in the Central Quality Control Laboratory of our collaborators and advising us on areas of improvements".

In the case of lamps, as in the case of welding electrodes, a number of agreemets were signed. Lamps can be broadly divided in two groups, namely incandescent lamps and discharge lamps. The incandescent lamps or GLS (General Lighting Service) lamps, were introduced one century ago on the basis of carbon filament and later on the basis of tungsten filament. After 1934, the technology did not change until 1959 when iodine and bromine halogens were introduced into the lamp. The tungsten halogen lamp achieves higher efficiency but, since it is restricted to high wattage lamps, has not been able to replace the ordinary GLS lamps. Discharge lamps are of two types. The low pressure mercury vapour lamps, introduced in 1938, have not seen big developments during the last decades, except for the development of new phosphors and the introduction of smaller diameter (26 mm) lamps, which gives a ten per cent increase in efficiency. The sodium and high pressure mercury lamps which were also introduced in the 1930s are used in floodlight systems and for professional applications. They, unlike the low pressure mercury lamps, have undergone big improvements in efficiency and durability during the last decades.

In 1934, the first GLS production unit was set up by Bengal Lamp works without foreign technical collaboration. Soon afterwards, Philips Gloeilampenfabrieken, which had started its bulb production in 1891 and had been exporting to India, together with other European companies set up the ELMI factory in Calcutta. After independence the ELMI cartel got involved in the Bajaj enterprise Hind Lamps. In 1960 Philips India took over a sick lamp unit and with the existing license secured the basis to start its independent lamp production. Afterwards, production targets were revised upwards repeatedly and new licenses for the production of lamps and components were received, often after the approval of technical collaboration agreements.

The first agreement, for the production of fluorescent lamps, powder, tubes and shells, was entered into in 1966. The collaboration would be valid for a period of ten years and provided for comprehensive services to be extended by Philips N.V. in exchange for 2 per cent to 3.5 per cent royalty. The agreement stipulated that information should not be disclosed to third parties and that Eindhoven should receive all information and inventions from the employees of the Indian subsidiary free of cost. Inventions applied not only to the manufacture of lamps, but to the use and sale as well (article 14 of the agreement). In 1977, Philips India applied for an extension of the agreement. The company's argument that it needed the assistance of the parent company in view of the continuously changing technology, was rejected. The government argued that the know-how was available in India and that any new developments could be incorporated in view of the equity participation by Eindhoven in the Indian subsidiary. In 1983, however, a fresh application, this time for a technical as well as financial collaboration between Philips N.V. and Punjab Anand Lamps, was approved. The agreement, which is mainly in respect of improvements in the efficiency of production, is based on the payment of 4 per cent to 5 per cent royalty, double the royalty which was earlier agreed with Philips India. This handsome return, as Menon (1984, p. 23) argues,

> is effected on the production of GLS lamps whose technology for production is standardised, the only changes

> brought about being modifications in production technology. . . . In case the same output labour ratio was maintained as Philips India envisaged in the mid-seventies for its own production process, there should have been employment for at least 1335 people, but the proposal of Punjab Anand Lamps involves only 800 persons. The new proposal also appears to have a very high import content. In 1974, the machinery of Philips India had an import content of 65.7 per cent, but the proposal of 1981 involving Punjab Anand has an import content of 87.8 per cent.

In December 1972, Philips India and Philips Gloeilampenfabrieken entered into an agreement for the production of high pressure mercury vapour (HPMV) lamps. The agreement provided for similar terms in regard of royalty payments, transfer flow of information and non-disclosure as the previous agreements. Although it also provided for a comprehensive flow of information regarding product engineering, in 1980 Philips Peico again applied for the permission to import the drawings and designs for the production of higher wattage HPMV lamps. At first the government department concerned rejected the application. It argued that the technology for the production of high wattage HPMV lamps was well established in the country and that, as a matter of fact, Philips N.V. had already supplied the know-how to ELMI, the sister concern of Philips Peico. Yet, for reasons which on technical grounds remain inexplicable, the government ultimately allowed the import of the drawings and designs for a sum of Rs. 320,000 and the payment of royalty. The import of technology again envisaged the transfer of assembly instructions for the modification of the existing machinery, quality control and testing procedures. Such a comprehensive transfer would not have been necessary had any expertise been built up during the six years in which production of HPMV lamps had taken place.

The technical collaboration agreements in the case of halogen lamps also reveal the abject dependence of Peico on Philips N.V. The technical collaboration agreement in 1972 provided for the production of six types of lamps, including cine lighting and photocopying. In 1980, Peico applied for the extension of the agreement on the grounds that they had faced technical problems and that they had been able to achieve only one-fifth of the installed capacity. The lack of facilities with Peico to adapt and improve the imported technology is clear from the fact that the new agreement, like many other agreements in the past, provided for the "evaluation of our products as well as components/materials used therein in the Central Quality Control Laboratory of our collaborators and advising us on areas of improvements". Although in the agreement pious intentions were made about absorbing the technology and developing it further, the dependence is clear from the fact that when technical problems developed with the production of halogen lamps, the work on the necessary modifications was couducted in the Netherlands. It is worth quoting the words of Philips India, as it shows that the purchase of technology does not ensure *the transfer of technology* :

> With the assistance of the collaborators, we conducted extensive field study through a team of our field engineers. A detailed independent investigation was also conducted by our collaborators at their end who have ultimately developed new materials and process modifications exclusively for our country. Lamps were also made in Holland based on these and tested under simulated application conditions. . . . The main problem was the corrosion of molybdenum lead and the failure of the lamp pinch. After elaborate trials, our collaborators also sent their technical experts to India to make 'on the spot' studies in the field and in the factory and to train local personnel in the new process.

A technical collaboration agreement was in effect between Philips N.V. and Philips India for five years between 1970 and 1975 for the production of tungsten and molybdenum wire and coils. The terms were similar to the ones noticed in the other agreements. In respect of the reverse flow of technology it stated :

> Philips India shall inform Philips Holland of any invention process, working method or improvement, whether patentable or not, made or applied by the company in relation to the manfacture of products and shall grant to

> Philips and their associated companies a royalty free non-exclusive licence with sub-licensing rights for the whole world under any patent rights in any invention made by the employees of the company and applicable to the manufacture, use or sale of the products. (Article 12 of the agreement as quoted in Menon 1984).

In 1975 the government approved an application for the extension of the agreement. The company claimed that it had succeeded in introducing a new range of products due to its R&D efforts in the coiling division but that they wanted to produce still thinner molybdenum and tungsten wire for application in high wattage lamps for which the know-how of Philips N.V. was essential.

The survey of technical collaborations between Philips N.V. and Philips India-Peico could be extended to other products, such as radios, condensors and multimeters. Multimeters present an interesting case of international division of labour. In 1975, Philips India was given a license for the production of multimeters with the condition that 100 per cent of the additional capacity thus granted would be exported. In 1979, the company again approached the government for the import of the drawings and designs for the manufacture of a new type of analogue multimeters. The new type to be imported was actually not manufactured by Philips N.V., but had been developed and tested by them at Eindhoven after a market research to establish the potential outlet of the new product. Peico would receive the technology and would supply the multimeters to the parent company which would look after the maintenance of quality and the actual marketing. In the process, Philips India made serious losses on the export of multimeters. From the calculations on the basis of the official figures (Usha Menon 1984), we learn that for example in 1978, the ex-factory value of Rs. 675.8 per unit was substantially higher than the f.o.b. export value (Rs. 439.7).

From the cases which have been dealt with in this chapter, a number of conclusions can be drawn. Although it is assumed that multinationals are bringing in modern technology, and for that reason are welcomed by the local governments, a survey of the operations of the well-established Dutch companies shows that their significance by and large lies in low technology products. There are some indications that the control over technology has been used as a means of obtaining property control over the local company. This happened among others with Welma which fell into the hands of Philips and with Nocil which for all practical purposes has gone over into the hands of Shell. Diffusion of technology does not seem to have taken place. Even in the case of companies controlled by the same multinational (Peico and ELMI), the technology was not available to the sister company, let alone to the industry at large. The equity participation in a company does not necessarily involve access to technical information. We have seen in the case of Philips that the Indian counterparts, in addition to the outflow of dividends, have to make a number of extra payments for a number of technological agreements. One last remark which could be made concerns the relationship between export and import of technology. From the limited number of cases which we have surveyed it appears that an export-oriented strategy requires that the internationally set standards of quality and specifications are met, and that with that aim the recurrent import of drawings, design and, in specific cases, components, will become a structural aspect of the transfer of technology.

# 8

# *Concluding Remarks*

In the present study, we have brought together empirical data on the operations of a limited number of multinationals in an underdeveloped country. We have first traced how the country concerned, caught in a position of confrontation with and reliance on foreign capital, has taken great care in enacting discriminatory measures. The government policy in the past does not, however, seem to have achieved its major objectives of technological and financial self-reliance, a devolution of the concentration of economic power and a planned and rapid industrial development. The most recent apparent changes in the policy framework of the Government of India indicate that a new page has been turned in the economic strategy, leading to the so-called liberalisation of the economy. The new government of Mr. Rajiv Gandhi, determined to push India, at least the industrial sector, into a 21st century of efficiency and frontier technology, appears to be set on a continuation of the new policy framework initiated by his mother during her last years of government.

More than two decades ago, the first major study on the Corporate Private Sector commissioned by the Planning Commission had pleaded for such a change in policy. The argument was then put forward by R.K. Hazari that the licensing regulations aimed at dispersing economic power were based upon a complete misunderstanding of the underlying factors: "The implementation of this policy has actually left a legacy of uneconomical, small-sized plants, to say nothing of the foreign exchange cost it has entailed". Hazari (1966, p. 361) therefore pleaded for a due recognition of monopoly firms "as the necessary price to be paid for modern technology, till such time as the size of the market for individual products expands sufficiently to permit the economic working of a large number of producers of each product".

The premium on efficiency, which Hazari pleaded for, in the context of an infant industry, has gradually made its way into government policy. The present policy, indeed, is based on the understanding that the Indian industrial sector has taken off beyond its nascent state, and that in the new complex industrial structure a new set of regulations is required for a further breakthrough. The new policy would therefore have to be based on efficiency and competitive ability with a less cumbersome access to foreign technology.

At such a juncture, it would be useful to reflect on some of the data which our study has thrown up, since they relate directly to the role western firms and western technology have played during the 1970s. Our basic attempt has been to make a detailed study of the factual behaviour of a few important multinational corporations, and to shore up this picture of specific companies with aggregate data on the combined Dutch companies operating in India.

The research results can be grouped under three major categories, namely the business results proper, the relation between the government regulations and expectations and the factual behaviour of the multinational corporations, and finally, the contribution to the four major problem areas which each developing country is confronted with, namely the foreign exchange constraint, the transfer of technology, the creation of employment and the acceleration effect on the rest of the economy.

A survey of company results offers interesting material for an analysis of the economic as well as political power of foreign enterprises. A consistent high profit rate will tend to reinforce the already lopsided and oligopolistic nature of the industrial structure, and will lead to an accumulation of financial means which can be put to use in thwarting the emergence of small competitors and in extra-economic and straight political pressure on the development process. It may result in a situation where the successful operation of industrial enterprises forestals the acceleration of growth in the rest of the economy, particularly in a situation where the market is not expanding rapidly.

The data on the Dutch multinational corporations in India suggests that such a process is in operation. A comparison of the companies in the sample with the average local corporate concerns shows them to have a significantly higher efficiency, internal capital accumulation ratio and growth rate.

The buoyant position of foreign companies indicate that they are better equipped with financial, technological and managerial resources than the average local company, and therefore are bound to play an eminent role in a developing country which, in policy or in practice, gives ample leeway to the manipulation of market forces.

The exceptionally good performance of most Dutch companies may have been regarded as a foregone conclusion. Without the expectation of a high rate of profit and the concomitant accumulation of internal resources for further expansion, parent companies would not normally locate their physical capital in a developing country where the political risks remain high. As a matter of fact, governments in developing countries who invite the multinational corporations, expect them to be better at the game than the local firms. When in practice the foreign firms turn out to perform exceptionally well, as the Dutch firms have proved to do, it is not in the logic of the argument to turn the successful performance against them. The argument should rather concentrate on the impact their operation have, either positively or negatively, on the developmental pattern of the host country.

The various enactments aimed at simultaneously controlling the monopoly formation and tapping the ample managerial, financial, technological and marketing resources of foreign big business houses, do not seem to have worked. The developments over the last quarter of a century have not brought the country any nearer to its goal as declared in the preamble to the constitution, namely the goal of a democratic socialist republic. The long-term intention to achieve a self-sufficient industrial sector free of monopoly formations also appears to have been infructuous.

At a general level, it appears that the actual functioning has not been in accordance with the government regulations. Before further elaborating, a necessary caveat should be introduced, however. It may indeed well be that the government policy has been violated on major counts, but that nevertheless the restraints have made themselves felt. In other words, one could argue that since the violations have been kept within bounds, the ill effects on, for example, the balance of payments situation or the competitive ability of the non-monopoly sector, have been kept in check. Our difficulty with such an apology, which indeed has a certain validity, relates to the fact that it isolates the practical behaviour of the oligopolies from other variables operating in the field. A fifty per cent excess production does establish that the legal provisions have been violated. It does not establish that without the legal provisions, the production would have risen even further. It could even be argued that, given the relatively protected market and given the bureaucratic constraints which new entrants have to face, the established major companies stand to gain from the controls. The fairly extensive lobbying and intelligence network, which they have generally established, enables them to profit from the positive provisions of the legal framework without being really bound by the negative provisions. Other variables, such as the saturation of the market and the marginal profitability of additional production, may be more important than the regulatory government policy, and should be taken into account while assessing the latter. Since such a detailed study has not been undertaken, except for company-intern feasibility studies, we shall overlook the argument of the alternative situation, and shall concentrate on the extent to which the MNCs have functioned according to the policy laid down by the government.

The government of India in its policy framework, more precisely the FERA of 1973 and the various Import and Export Policy regulations, has made a much debated attempt to channel the financial flow of the multinational corporations into the earmarked sectors of industry and to restrict the outflow of foreign exchange. The enforcement of an expatriate minority share in equity, except for export-oriented production and high technology areas, would ultimately lead to the dual objective of a balanced foreign exchange position and of a diversification in the product-mix of the foreign firms.

The indigenisation of management and equity has indeed been realised. This, incidentally, is the aspect which has received most attention in the public debates, and thereby has reinforced the image of multinational corporations as national enterprises. The evidence, however, establishes that the process, albeit in a cautious form, was already in progress before the legislation was introduced, and that it in no way has reduced the foreign control over the company. Whereas the indigenisation of management has led to the emergence of a category of 'corporate citizens', the indigenisation of equity has led to the emergence of a sizeable group of interested shareholders and to the widening of the financial reach of the company.

The FERA, despite the publicly stated aim of controlling foreign resources, was essentially aimed at opening the expatriate ownership structure for participation by Indian citizens. In order to effectively control the drain of foreign resources, it would have been necessary to insert a clause on the maximum permissible repatriation of profits. A percentage of equity slightly above the international bank lending rate would have restricted the outflow, and, on the other hand, would have provided the parent company with a sufficiently high return on capital. In our sample, the return on exported capital, net of bonus issues, in recent years by and large has been well beyond 30 per cent.

In respect of payments for royalties and technical service fees, a maximum permissible amount, as a percentage of sales, was fixed by the FERA, and the drain of surplus on this account indeed seems to have been restricted. After 1974, the value of royalty payments and service charges in the case of all Dutch companies, has been stabilised at around six million rupees, which in fact means a significant decline both in relation to the total turnover and to the repatriation of dividends. Whereas in the case of Philips, which together with Nocil scores relatively high, royalty payments during the years 1973 and 1974 represented 0.87 per cent of sales and were practically on par with the repatriation of dividends, during the years 1980 and 1981, they amounted to only 0.34 per cent of sales and to less than half of the dividend transfer. Since the major Dutch companies operate in production lines in the consumer sectors where the technologies are generally aged and simple, the decrease need not be typical of all MNCs in India. The decrease in payments for technology, which can be observed in our case, was a direct function of the selective approval policy of the Government of

India. The selective procedure has created a situation in which many of the patents, on which the earlier collaboration agreements were signed, have expired. The sharp increase in new technology agreements from 1980 onwards will probably lead to an increase in royalty payments to a considerably higher level.

The divergence between the government policy and the actual behaviour of the multinational corporations can be most properly tested in relation to the licensing policy. The system of licenses, aimed at the exclusion of foreign companies from a number of industrial sectors and at the prevention of the emergence of unhealthy concentration of production, has attracted sharp criticism from the major industrial houses. They have maintained that the stagnation in the Indian economy was reinforced by the excessive bureaucratic restriction on their own expansion. The ample managerial, financial and technological resources, if they had not been hampered by government regulations, could have induced a much faster growth and diversification of production.

The concrete examples which we have used in our study, however, indicate that multinational corporations may have experienced some nuisance from the administrative provisions, but were generally not seriously restricted in their operations. The data suggests that the major concerns have managed to disregard most of the restrictions imposed by, for example, the Monopoly Restrictive Trade Practices Act. In chapter two, we have even suggested that a regulatory framework may be more advantageous to monopoly houses than to small and medium companies, for whose benefit it was intended. The major companies, through their resident managers at New Delhi, were kept abreast of the new directions of government thinking and were able to get the officers concerned engaged in protracted negotiations, ultimately leading to government approval or inaction. The smaller companies, as a matter of fact including the smaller foreign companies, usually do not have access to a similar power of influence.

The failure of the MRTP provisions has emerged as a prominent feature of the monopoly sector of Indian industry. Hindustan Lever and Peico, the two major companies which we have studied, appear not to have encountered any major obstruction from the ceiling provisions "imposed" by the Government of India. An analysis of the composition of the output, moreover, leads to the conclusion that products, for which no foreign collaboration was permitted or considered necessary or which were earmarked for the small scale and medium scale industries, continue to be produced on a large scale. This is not only the case with traditional products like vegetable oil, laundry soaps, radios, loudspeakers, agricultural machinery and lamps, but also in the case of newly introduced products such as tape recorders, casette tapes, refrigerators, hearing aids, dry cell batteries, digital clocks, etc. The products, which cannot be considered to make a net contribution to the technological capacities available in India, constitute for most firms almost the bulk of the output. The policy of indigenisation of products and production techniques appears to be at loggerheads with the emergence of a rich stratum, mainly in the urban areas. The type and the quality of the consumer products, the wealthy sections of society are looking for, are highly influenced by the trends blowing over from the Western countries. The huge amounts of money in their hands, in any case huge in relation to Indian standards, has led to a continuing building up of pressure on the government to change its policy and either allow imports of those products as a better alternative to the widespread smuggling operation, or to condone the production by companies which would normally not be entitled to move into the particular sector.

No doubt, in respect of certain products and certain activities, the restrictive framework has refrained the companies from extending into a wider field of activities. Hindustan Lever has as yet not been allowed to move into the palm oil plantations and Peico for a long time had been devoid of its own television production line. Multinational corporations may have realised that entry into hitherto banned areas, is a matter of time. Peico rather than pulling out of the T.V. industry, has skilfully emerged as an important source of components for some of the major Indian companies. The liberal imports of colour television sets from the Asian Games in 1982 onwards, was an additional argument for allowing Peico to start its own assembly line.

A rate of expansion well above the national average and a diversification of production may represent a violation of the laws operating in the country, but are on that ground not necessarily inimical to the industrial development of the country. Let us therefore summarise our evidence on the three major problem areas to which the MNCs are expected to contribute their share : capital, technology and employment. As a catalyst of growth, MNCs should register a positive effect in at least one of these areas.

In respect of the foreign exchange gap, it has been argued in the first chapter that, even according to the protagonist view, the contribution by multinational corporations should not be expected to play a positive role in the short run. Many studies indeed have provided evidence that foreign firms take out more investible funds than they pump in. Such a state of affairs could still be condoned if indeed the inward flow continued to operate, and if the multiplier effect on the national economy was large. The data on our sample of firms, however, suggests that the importation of capital has been tapering off. Retained profits at present constitute the largest part of the sources of finance (86 per cent of the additional funds over the period 1973-1980). In the same period, the other finances were provided by local borrowings and equity participation. This share in recent years in the case of most companies appears to be growing. The continuation of the latter trend would mean that under present conditions, the scope for expansion is so vast that internal resources do not suffice any longer as they used to do in the 1970s, and that the attraction of more local funds has become necessary. The conclusion could therefore well be that the MNCs, after an initial investment a couple of decades ago, are resorting to the internal capital market and thereby preempt the possibilities of the Indian enterprises for external financing. The net foreign contribution to equity in the meantime has dropped to a meagre of 0.4 per cent.

The import substitution effect, which should have triggered off a chain of increasing productive activities in the country, appears to be on the wane. Tne aggregate statistics establish that the import dependence of production turns out to be fairly high and is increasing, both in relation to the total productive consumption and in relation to the output value, thereby gradually reducing the multiplier effect the imported raw materials and components could have on industrial activities.

The control of foreign resources through the FERA was expected to result in an increase in exports. The FERA provisions, however, did not elevate the export norm into a guiding principle. It was only stipulated that those foreign companies intending to maintain more than half of the equity were required to export 60 per cent of their sales. Since only one major company (Hindustan Lever) as well as the latter entrant in the Kandla Free Trade Zone (Hazemeyer Elcon) decided to maintain a majority foreign equity, generally exports have not shown a substantial increase after the FERA was introduced in 1973. Our figures indicate that the growth in exports started in the late sixties and reached the highest level in the late seventies, where after it gave way to a relative decline. Throughout, exports as a percentage of sales only rarely reached two digital numbers. Even Hindustan Lever, which as per the FERA provisions is required to excel in exports, has hardly managed to cross the 10 per cent mark. While the declining export performance of most of the companies may be associated with changes in the world economy, it appears from our separate firm studies that the occasional stress on exports was useful to the companies in propagating their advantages to the Indian economy on the eve of government decisions on applications for further expansion.

Manufacturing activities appear to be essentially oriented towards the internal market or at the best towards foreign captive markets of India. The exclusion of exports to the East European rupee trade market and of the mercantile exports of third party products from the aggregate export figures, would bring the overall performance of exports in terms of hard currency down to hardly a few per cent of the output. The export propensity of multinational corporations, as we have indicated in chapter one, is secondary to the production for the local market, and, if it prevails, is conditioned by specific local factor endowments. India by and large does not seem to possess the specific set of endownments which could stimulate the export orientation of MNCs. The introduction of infrastructural, financial, political and technical facilities which might make the export-orientation more feasible, will lead to serious, self-defeating changes in the economy and would ultimately, given the closing of the rest of the world, have only a marginal positive effect.

The transfer of technology in recent years, particularly after it appeared that the net massive transfer of capital was not in the scheme of things, has been set apart as the area in which multinational corporations could play a developmental role. The results of our study do not lead us to share the optimistic expectation. It may not be fully valid to draw conclusions on the basis of a small sample, namely around two per cent of the total number of collaboration agreements signed by India and basically restricted to consumer products. Nevertheless, the data which has been collected gives significant insights in both the impact of collaboration agreements and the further upgrading of technology by MNCs through their local research centres.

Government regulations in the past have had a beneficial effect in terms of the elimination of certain restrictive clauses such as a ban on exports, and the fixing of a maximum on royalty payments. A number of fundamental problems, however, remain. In the first place, government policy has been based on negative premises, in the sense that it ordained for which products technical collaboration was not necessary in view of the already developed capabilities in the country. A positive approach would have concentrated on the active search for production processes which the country for its economic development was in need of. With the exception of the state sector, largely drawing on the know-how from East-European countries, such a policy has not been followed. The private sector was accordingly excluded from certain imports, but was free to sign contracts for products the social relevance of which for the Indian development process was, to put it mildly, questionable. Particularly during the last couple of years, this freedom has led to a growing number of agreements for luxury consumption products. The more wealthy and the more sophisticated the top income class has grown, the greater the pressure that has been built up for the import of non-developmental know-how. The fact that most companies in our sample operate in the consumer sector would, in this light, not appear to be accidental. A related adverse feature of the collaboration agreements follows from the impossibility of the Indian government to direct the foreign company into a specific type of transfer of technology. It is ironical that India for example still exports tungsten metal for further processing abroad before the upgraded product is re-imported by Philips into India for the production of filaments. In this case, the transfer of technology for the production of lamps, refers only to the know-how to be used in the last stage of the production process, and keeps the country dependent on the basic technology which the parent MNC is not pressed to transfer.

Another main problem, namely the phenomenon of the dead-end transfer, still remains. Although the production technology has been upgraded as a result of the technical collaboration agreements, one can hardly speak of a transfer of technology but rather of a contractually restricted sale of production know-how. The technology imported under the agreements hardly gets adapted and absorbed, One would expect this process to take place, first within the production process of the contracting partner, and after a certain time in the other production units in the country. Our evidence suggests that the process is interrupted after the technology has been received. When a new generation technology is required, it still needs to be imported. The private character of the purchase of know-how and the accompanying purchases of capital goods, spares and raw materials, creates islands of capital intensive production which do not foster the diffusion of technology, and even limit the multiplier effect in the sense that prospective ancillary units are often not in a position to satisfy the specifications and measurements necessitated by the new technology.

The absence of an effective transfer of technology can also be traced to the rising import content of the production materials. The increasing import content, without being explainable by an appropriate exchange in the product-mix of the company, would normally be related to the absence of upgrading R&D facilities. Our evidence, however, suggests that the widespread belief that MNC's in developing countries do not engage in research activities, needs to be modified. Seven of the fourteen companies in our sample have recognised R&D units, and at present at least four of them undertake significant research in India.

An analysis of the R&D by the two major companies with a long history of R&D, Hindustan Lever and Peico, indicates that the import substitution policy had a positive impact on R&D intenslty. It seems that during the import substitution phase, multinationals undertake local R&D and adaptive R&D with a predominance of the former. In other words, under pressure of government policy the MNC will undertake research on local raw materials, provided there exist suitable skill and facilities in the host country. An export promotion policy can have a negative influence on the adaptive and local R&D of MNCs. The influence is exerted directly through the liberal imports which accompany export promotion schemes. Since it makes available raw materials of international standards, it is no more necessary to undertake research to find local substitutes. Since the exported goods are expected to conform to international standards, this normally requires the utilisation of components of international specifications and international processes, leaving no room for even modifications. This general observation does not rule out the existence of niches where exports on the basis of local technology might take place.

The disaggregation of the overall research efforts has provided fruitful insights into the different types of R&D undertaken. What seems to be of overriding importance, from the point of view of a policy framework, is the level of technology involved. The multinational corporations in their research activities in India make use of local skills and know-how, and produce results at a level of sophistication which is generally comparable to the local competence. The conclusion to be drawn is that the upgrading of technology in the country is not likely to be the result of the research effort of multinational corporations. During the last couple of years, a new trend has shown up, however, namely the use of Indian laboratories for the global research requirements of the corporation. Global R&D, i.e. the use of cheap personnel for the research requirements of the parent company without a direct financial or technological benefit to the host country, appears to be of growing importance in the Peico and HL laboratories as well.

The generation of employment is a direct function of the capital intensity of the production process. The modernisation and increasing productivity have proceeded on the basis of a more or less stagnant labour force. It is important to realise that the private sector in India in general suffers from this dilemma. The rising investment cost per unit of labour has on the one hand increased the production manifold but has, on the other hand, made the problem of employment generation in industry more intractable. The development can be best characterised as involution. Employment generation in the organised private sector between the mid-sixties and 1985, according to the annual Economic Survey of the Government of India, grew from 3.8 million to 4.4 million, which indeed is a simple average growth of no significance.

The Dutch multinational corporations are no exception to this trend. They, however, argue that they contribute substantially to indirect employment generation, particularly through subcontracting. In general, the subcontracting units are set up by close relatives of company managers (as in the case of Peico in Calcutta) or by trading partners who get the half-fabricates and the necessary technology for further upgrading into the MNC trade mark product (as in the case of the soap subcontractors of Hindustan Lever). The installment of new machinery in the parent unit, e.g. a computerised PVC extruder unit in the case of the Wavin, will be followed by installation of the old machinery in a seperate, small scale unit de facto controlled by the company. On the basis of a rough calculation, the aggregate employment generation by the Dutch companies would reach a maximum of 50,000 of which 25,000 work outside the factory gate. The aggregate figure, given the decennia-long presence and given the vast sales and profit performance, cannot be considered to be impressive.

The picture which has emerged so far brought in focus a number of features which will contribute to a useful debate on the performance of MNCs in developing countries and on the significance of developing countries in the global strategy of the corporations.

The still missing link, namely the direct and indirect linkages with the rest of the economy was vaguely indicated in a number of cases. Particularly the process of subcontracting as noted in the case of Philips, Hindustan Lever, Lipton, Wavin, etc., opened up a new perspective of looking at the phenomenon of direct backward linkages. The many advantages associated with this system (low wages, a docile labour force, evasion of MRTP licensing procedures, access to government raw materials supplies, absence of fixed capital, the re-installation of discarded machinery, etc.) make it into a likely vehicle for expansion by giant companies. A separate study in a limited number of industries would certainly deliver interesting results. So would a study of direct forward linkages, for which the role of Philips in the manufacturing of (colour) televisions and of Nocil in the production of PVC-based durables could serve as illustrative examples. They could then be contrasted with examples of the absence of direct forward linkages, as e.g. in the case of Sodium Tripoly Phosphate production by Hindustan Lever, and thus complete the picture of both forward and backward direct linkages in the strategy of multinational corporations.

Aspects of indirect linkages, i.e. the impact on the industrial sector in terms of prices, technology, market share, etc., have been studied in two separate cases, namely Hindustan Lever in the detergent industry and Philips in the lamp industry. The studies have revealed that in both sectors, the MNCs concerned occupy a more dominant position than is discernible from a superficial observation. A market share of over fifty per cent in combination with the control over essential raw materials and with a much better efficiency in production, make for a domination over market and production factors. The threat which seems to emerge occasionally from units in the small scale sector is by and large constrained to a different market segment.

The analysis of the business results, the contribution to scarcity sectors in the economy (capital, technology and employment) and the discrepancy between policy and practice has, probably insufficiently, extended into the developmental implications of the Dutch multinational companies in India. Although on the many extremely vital issues which are involved, care should be taken in locating both the positive as well as the negative aspects, we have been confronted with ample evidence to conclude that (a) government policy suffers from abundant loopholes, both in the regulatory framework and in the application, and that (b) the big multinational corporations move forward according to their own laws without having, after many years of activity, a substantial positive effect on employment, broadening of the industrial structure and acceleration of the economy.

The alternative approach by the Government of India has got stuck mid-way. In the absence of alternative economic reforms, particularly in agriculture, and in the absence of a gassroot based countervailing political power, a choice has been made for a short term realistic approach, namely an acceptance of the multinational corporations, increasingly on their terms. While the policy framework gets more and more adjusted to the requirements of the indigenous and foreign monopoly houses, most evidence shows that such an opening up of the economy will strengthen the dual process of immiserisation of the vast majority of the population on the one hand and the prosperous vertical growth of a small section on the other hand. Without a drastic change of policy, the widening of the abyss will continue.

The countervailing power of foreign firms will lead to a further economic, political and social polarisation. The present trend of the operations of the Dutch MNCs in India is the opposite of what the present Prime Minister of the Netherlands called for in the discussion on the Brandt Commission Report on the North-South Programme for Survival (Aspecten 1980, nr 6, p. 244) : "We are bound to make them subservient to the development of the nations, for which the nations themselves bear the first responsibility".

If words have any meaning, it should be reflected in economic and political practice. The urgency for such a new practice, in our opinion, has been amply demonstrated by the material which has been collected in this study.

# Bibliography


**ANNUAL REPORTS**

AKZO N.V.
Century Enka Ltd.
Das Reprographics Ltd.
Duphar Interfran
Hind Lamps Ltd.
Hindustan Lever Ltd.
Electric Lamps Manufacturers (India) Ltd.
Kinetics Technology India Ltd.
Lipton India Ltd.
National Organic Chemical Industries Ltd.
Peico Electronics and Electricals Ltd.
Organon (India) Ltd.
Philips N.V.
Royal Dutch Shell
Stormac India Ltd.
Stovec Screens India Ltd.
Vicon Ltd.
Unilever Ltd.
Wavin (India) Ltd.
Government of India, Economic Survey
Government of India, Ministry of Commerce
Government of India, Monopolies and Restrictive Trade Practices Commission
Government of India, Annual Survey of Industries, Ministry of Planning
Government of India, Department of Industrial Development
Government of India, Annual Report on the Working and Administration of the Companies Act, 1956
Government of India, Department of Science and Techology

Government of India, Import and Export Policy, Ministry of Commerce
Khadi and Village Industries Commission
Regional Research Laboratory (RRL), Hyderabad
Reserve Bank of India, Report on Currency and Finance
World Bank, World Development Report

## JOURNALS AND NEWSPAPERS

*Aspecten van Internationale Samenwerking* (Aspecten)
*Blend, Lipton House Journal*
*Business World*
*Business India*
*Economic and Political Weekly* (EPW)
*Economic Times* (ET)
*Economy and Trade*
*Export Magazine*
*Financial Express*
*Fortune*
*Hamara*
*India Today*
*New Age*
*Nieuwe Rotterdamse Courant* (NRC)
*People's Democracy*
*Reserve Bank of India Bulletin*
*Social Scientist*
*Times of India* (TI)
*Transnational Information Exchange* (TIE)
*Volkskrant*

## BOOKS AND ARTICLES

Adam, Gyorgy (1975), 'Multinational Corporations and World-wide Sourcing'. In : Hugo Radice, *International Firms and Modern Imperialism*, Harmondsworth.

Aggarwal, H.P. (1982), *Business Collaboration in India*, New Delhi.

Aggarwal, V.S. (1982), *Guide of Company Balance Sheet and Profit and Loss Account*, New Delhi.

Ahluwalia, Isher Judge (1985), *Industrial Growth in India : Stagnation since the mid-sixties*, New Delhi

Alam, Ghayur (1985), 'India's Technology Policy and its Influence on Technology Imports and Technology Development. In Ashok Desai, 1985.

Amin, Samir (1974), *Accumulation on a World Scale*, New York.

Arnolds, A.L.M. et al (1978), *Investeren in Landen met een Verwerpelijk Regime*, Scheveningen.

Astapovitch, A.A. (1983), *The Strategy of Transnational Corporations*, Moscow.

Bagchi, Amiya Kumar (1973), "Foreign Capital and Economic Development". In : Gough and Sharma, *Imperialism and Revolution in South Asia*, New York.

Bagchi, Amiya Kumar (1975), *Private Investment in India : 1900-1939*, Madras.

Bagchi, Amiya Kumar and Nirmala Banerjee, eds. (1981), *Change and Choice in Indian Industry*, Calcutta.

Balasubramanyam, V.N. (1973), *International Transfer by Multinationals to India*, New York.

Balasubramanyam, V.N. (1980), *Multinational Enterprises and the Third World*, London.

Ballance, R. et al. (1982), *The International Economy and International Development : The Impact of Trade and Development on the Third World*, Brighton.

Banerjee, B.N. (1977), *Foreign Aid to India*, New Delhi.

Baran Paul, (1962), *Political Economy of Growth*, New Delhi.

Bardhan, Pranab (1984), *The Political Economy of Development in India*, New Delhi.

Barnett, R.J. and R.E. Muller (1974), *The Power of Multinational Corporations*, New York.

Barrat Brown, Michael (1974), *The Economics of Imperialism*, Harmondsworth.

Baruch, Friedrich (1962), *Grote Macht in een Klein Land*, Amsterdam.

Bhagwati, J.N. and P. Desai (1970), *India : Planning for Industrialisation*, Paris.

Beerends, Hans (1980), *Tien Jaar Nederlandse Ontwikkelingshulp*, Utrecht.

Behari, Bepin (1983), *Unemployment, Technology and Rural Poverty*, New Delhi.

Biersteker, T.J. (1978), *Distortion or Development? Contending*

*Perspectives on the Multinational Corporations*, Cambridge—Massachusetts.

Bol, Dick (1982), *Ekonomen en Armoede. Moedwil en Misverstand in de Ontwikkelingshulp*, Amsterdam.

Bornschier, V. and C. Chase-Dunn (1985), *Multinational Corporations and World Development*, New York.

Bose, H.C. a.o. (1974), *Private Foreign Investments in Developing Countries*, Paris.

Brandt Commission (1980), *North-South, A Programme for Survival*, London.

Bruinsma, Sam (1986), *Hollanders, Hulp en Handel*, Mimeo, University of Amsterdam.

Bouwman, Theo, ed. (1982), *Philips : International Reorganisation and Workers' Resistance*, Eindhoven.

Bright Jr., A.A. (1948), *The Electric Lamp Industry : Technological and Economic Development from 1800 to 1847*, London.

Carlsen, John and Peter Neerso (1973), 'Transfer of Technology to India : A Case of Danish Private Business Activities', Mimeo, Copenhagen.

Castro, Fidel (1983), *The World Economic and Social Crisis*, Havanna.

Chandra, Bipin (1979), *Nationalism and Colonialism in Modern India*, New Delhi.

Chandra, N.K. (1973), 'Western Imperialism and India Today'. *Economic and Political Weekly*, annual number.

Chandra, N.K. (1977a), 'Role of Foreign Capital in India', *Social Scientist*, April.

Chandra, N.K. (1977b), 'Monopoly Legislation and Policy in India', *Economic and Political Weekly*, special number.

Chandra, N.K., (1981), 'Monopoly Capital, Private Corporate Sector and Indian Economy', In : Bagchi and Banerjee (1981).

Chandra, N.K. (1985), 'Modernisation for Export-Oriented Growth : A Critique of Recent Indian Policy,' *Economic and Political Weekly*, 19 July.

Chandrasekhar, C.P. (1983), 'Imperialism and Industrialisation in the Underdeveloped Countries', *Social Scientist*, January.

Chandrasekhar, C.P. and Prabir Purkaystha (1982), Transfer

Pricing in the Indian Drug Industry', *Social Scientist*, January.

Chaudhuri, Pramit (1978), *The Indian Economy : Poverty and Development*, New Delhi.

Chaudhuri, Sudip (1979a), 'FERA Appearance and Reality', *Economic and Political Weekly*, 21 April.

Chaudhury, Sudip (1979b), 'Financing of the Growth of Transnational Corporations in India', *Economic and Political Weekly*, 18 August.

Chaudhury, Saumitra (1979), 'Nationalisation of Foreign Oil Companies', *Economic and Political Weekly*,

Chaudhury, Saumitra (1984), 'Indian Bourgeoisie and Foreign Capital : A Study of Congress Policy Towards Foreign Capital, 1931-1961', *Social Scientist*, May.

Chenoy, Kamal Mitra (1985), 'Industrial Policy and Multinationals In India', *Social Scientist*, March.

Chenoy, K.M. and N. Kumar (1982), 'Multinationals and Self-Reliance : A Case Study of the Drugs Industry', *Social Scientist*, April.

Chishti, S. (1985), 'Foreign Trade and Economic Development of India : Issues in the Eighties', Mimeo, IOS Tilburg.

Chitale, V.P. (1973), *Foreign Technology in India*, New Delhi.

Clairmonte, F. and J.H. Cavanagh (1983), 'Transnational Corporations and the Struggle for the Global Market'. *Journal of Contemporary Asia*, pp. 446-480.

Cohen, R.B. et al. (1979), *The Multinational Corporation : A Radical Approach*, Cambridge.

Cooper, Charles (1972), 'Science, Technology and Production in Underdeveloped Countries', *Journal of Development Studies*, October.

Cooper, Charles (1985), 'Technical Collaboration Between Firms in the Benelux and in India', *Economic and Political Weekly*, Special Number, November.

Corporate Studies Group (1983), Functioning of the Industrial Licensing System, A Report', Mimeo, New Delhi.

Crone, Fred and Henk Overbeek, eds (1981), *Nederlands Kapitaal over de Grenzen*, Amsterdam.

Czaya, Eberhard (1975), 'Internationale Konzerne in Entwicklungslaendern', *IPW Hefte*, nr 4, Berlin.

Das Gupta, Subhendu (1980), 'Foreign Technical Collaboration in Indian Business Houses, 1957-76', Mimeo, Calcutta.

De Haan, Warner, a.o. (1981), 'Een Zwaargewicht Slankt Af: Unilever 1965-1980', In : Crone and Overbeek (1981).

Delhi Science Forum (1985), *Bhopal Gas Tragedy*, New Delhi.

Department General of Technical Development DGTD (1983), *DGTD Report 1979-1982*, New Delhi.

Department of Science and Technology DST (1981a), *Research and Development in Industry—1978-79*, New Delhi.

Department of Science and Technology DST (1981b), *Plant Tissue Culture Status Report*, New Delhi.

Department of Science and Technology DST (1983), *Status of Biotechnology in India*, New Delhi.

Department of Science and Technology DST (1984a), *Research and Development Statistics, 1982-83*, New Delhi.

Department of Science and Technology DST (1984b), *Research and Development in Industry*, New Delhi.

Department of Science and Technology DST (1984c), *Annual Report*, New Delhi.

Desai, Ashok V. (1982), 'Foreign Firms in Indian Industry', Paper Presented at the Indo-Dutch Symposium on MNCs, New Delhi.

Desai, Ashok V. (1984). 'New Forms of International Investments in India', *Social Scientist*, June.

Desai, Ashok, ed. (1985), 'Foreign Technology Suppliers' View of Indian Industry', *Economic and Political Weekly*, Special Number, November, pp. 1975-2094.

Directorate General of Technical Development (1980), *Handbook of Foreign Collaborations*, New Delhi.

Di Marco, L.E. (ed.) (1972), *International Economics and Development*, New York.

Dunning, John (1971), *The Multinational Enterprise*, London.

Dunning, John (1972), *International Investments*, Harmondsworth.

Dunning, John (1981), *International Production and the Multinational Enterprise*, London.

Dunning, John (1983), 'Changes in the Level and Production of International Production'. In : M.C. Casson, *The Growth of International Business*, London.

Dunning, John, ed. (1985), *Multinational Enterprise, Economic Structure and Economic Competitiveness*, New York.

Dunning, John and John Cantwell (1984), 'The Emergence of Multinationals in the Organisation of International Production'. In : A. Fonseca, *Multinationals in Third World Countries*, Rome.

Dutta, A. (1982), 'Interview by Patriot Correspondent with Management of Hindustan Lever', typescript.

Emmanuel. Arrighi (1970), 'Demystifier les Antagonismes entre les Nations', *Politique Aujourd'hui*, January.

Emmanuel, Arrighi (1978), 'The Multinational Corporation and Unequality of Development', *International Social Science Journal*, nr 4.

Emmanuel Arrighi (1982), *Appropriate or Underdeveloped Technology*, Chichester.

Ezekiel, Hannan (1984), *The Economic Times Statistical Survey of the Indian Economy*, New Delhi.

Fieldhouse, D.K. (1978), *Unilever Overseas. The Anatomy of a Multinational, 1885-1965*, London.

Fibbe, F. a.o. (1976), *Het Nederlandse Bedrijfsleven in de Derde Wereld*, Haarlem.

Frank, A.G. (1967), *Capitalism and Underdevelopment in Latin America*, New York.

Frank, A.G. (1980), *Crisis in the World Economy*, London.

Freeman, Christopher (1974), *The Economics of Industrial Innovation*, Harmondsworth.

Freeman, Christopher (1977), 'Economics of Research and Development'. In : Spiegel-Rosing and De Solla Price (eds), *Science, Technology and Society*, London.

Friedlaender, Thomas (1981), *Imperialistischer Kapitalexport in die Entwicklungslaender*, Berlin.

Frobel, Folker et al. (1980), *The New International Division of Labour*, Cambridge.

Fundulis, Christos, et al. (1978), *Internationale Monopole*, Berlin.

Gallez, Agnes and J.L. Troupin (1981), 'La Strategie des Nouveaux Pays Industriels d'Asie', *Revue Tiers Monde*, nr 87.

Ganguly, A.S. (1981), 'Foreign Business in India : Hindustan Lever Ltd.', SRI Conference Paper, New Delhi.

Geertsema, Gert Jan (1982), 'Vicon and India', Mimeo—University of Amsterdam.

Geest, W. van der (1978), 'De Overheid en Beheersing van Technologie'' Mimeo—Sociologisch Instituut Leiden.

Germidis, Dimitri (1977), *Transfer of Technology by Multinational Corporations*, Paris.

Ghosh, D.K. (1980), 'Multinational Corporations in India: Trends and Performance, 1973-74—1978-79', *Company News and Notes*, June.

Gold, Bela (1979), 'Inter-Industry Repercussions of Major Technological Innovations'. In : M.I. Baker (ed.), *Industrial Innovation*, London.

Golt, Sydney (1978), 'Developing Countries in the GATT System', *Thames Essay* nr 13, London.

Gooskens, Pit (1984), 'Tussen Ekonomisme en Klassenstrijd. Een Onderzoek naar het Bewustzijn van Arbeid (st) ers in een Nederlandse Multinational in India', Mimeo—Universiteit van Amsterdam.

Government of India (1980), *Sixth Five Year Plan, 1980 85*, New Delhi.

Government of India (1982), *Basic Statistics Relating to the Indian Economy, 1950-52—1980-81*, New Delhi.

Government of India (1978), *Report of the High-Powered Expert Committee on Companies and MTRP Acts*, Department of Company Affairs, Ministry of Law, New Delhi.

Government of India (1985), *Seventh Five Year Plan, 1985-90*, New Delhi.

Government of India (1986 and earlier), *Economic Survey*, New Delhi.

Government of West Bengal (1981), *The IMF Loan. Facts and Issues*, Calcutta.

Goyal, S.K. (1979a), 'The Impact of Foreign Subsidiaries on India's Balance of Payments', Mimeo—Escap, Bangkok.

Goyal, S.K. (1979b), *Monopoly Capital and Public Policy*, New Delhi.

Goyal, S.K. (1983), 'NIEO and Transnational Corporations', *Secular Democracy*, annual number.

Gromyko, Andrei (1985), *The Overseas Expansion of Capital, Past and Present*, Moscow.

Guth, Wilfred (1963), *Capital Exports to less Developed Countries.* Dordrecht.

Hamilton, Clive (1983), 'Capitalist Industrialisation and the Four Little Tigers of East Asia', *Journal of Contemnporary Asia*, nr 1.

Hamilton, Geoffrey (1984), 'The Control of Multinationals', *IRM Multinational Reports*, nr 2.

Hanson, James (1975), 'Transfer Pricing in the Multinational Corporation. A Critical Appraisal.' *World Development.*

Hazari, R.K. (1967), *The Structure of the Private Corporate Sector*, Bombay.

Heininger, Horst (1978), *Internationale Monopole*, Berlin.

Helleiner, G.K. (1973), 'Manufactured Exports from Less Developed Countries and Multinational Firms,' *Economic Journal*, March.

Helms, Wim, a.o. (1978), De Internationale Herstrukturering van de N.V. Phillips Gloeilampenfarbiek,' Mimeo—Technische Hogeschool, Eindhoven.

Hindustan Lever (1956), *Amendment of Memorandum of Association.*

Hindustan Lever (1973), *Amendment of Memorandum of Association.*

Hindustan Lever (1977), *Prospectus for Issue of Equity Shares.*

Hindustan Lever (1982), *Where Innovative Technology Meets Basic Needs*, Bombay.

Hindustan Lever Research Foundation (nd), brochure.

Hammes, Enno, ed. (1985), *Multinationale Ondernemingen in de Derde Wereld*, Baarn.

Huizer Gerrit, ed. (1978), *Nederland en de Derde Wereld. Basisvragen over Ontwikkelinsgsamenwerking*, Alphen aan de Rijn.

Hymer, Stephen (1970), The Efficiency Contradictions of Multinational Corporations,' *American Economic Review Papers and Proceedings.*

Hymer, Stephen (1975), 'The Multinational Corporation and the Law of Uneven Development.' In : *Hugo Radice, International Firms and Modern Imperialism.* Harmondsworth.

Hymer, Stephen (1976), *The International Operations of National Firms*, Cambridge, Massachusetts.

Hymer, Stephen (1981), *Intra-Firm Trade and the Developing Country*, London.

ILO (1973), *Multinational Enterprises and Social Policy*, Geneva.

ILO (1976), *Social and Labour Practices of Some European-Based Multinationals in the Metal Trade*, Geneva.

ILO (1981), *Employment Effects of Multinational Enterprises in Developing Countries*, Geneva.

ILPIC (1969), *Report of the Industrial Licensing Policy Inquiry Committee*, Ministry of Industrial Development, New Delhi.

Indian Institute of Foreign Trade (1981), 'Role of Transnational Corporations in India's Exports,' Mimeo, New Delhi.

India Investment Centre (1981), *Foreign Collaborations in India, Policy and Perspective*, New Delhi.

India Investment Centre (1982), *Directory of Foreign Collaborations in India. Volume V: India—Other Countries*, New Delhi.

Indu Emencee (1981), 'The Dutch Multinational Corporations in India,' Position paper, Mimeo.

Indu Emencee (1982), 'Papers Presented at the New Delhi Symposium on Multinational Corporations, Mimeo,' New Delhi.

Indu Emencee (1983), Procceedings of the Workshop on the Indu Emencee Project,' Mimeo, Nijmegen.

IPSO (1982), *Multinationale Ondernemingen*, Amsterdam.

Iyengar, M.S. (n.d.), 'The Status of Research and Development in the Private Sector,' Mimeo, New Delhi.

Jena, B.C. (1969), 'A Search for Sal (Shorea Robusta) in Koraput'. In : OTAI, 1969.

Kane, J.G. (1959), *Soaps, Their Chemistry and Technology, Indian Central Oilseeds Committee*, New Delhi.

Kannapin, Klaus et al. (1915), 'Imperialismus und Industrialisierung der Entwicklungslaender.' *IPW Forschungshefte*, nr 2.

Kaplinsky, R. and Sumitra Chisthi (1977). 'Technical Change and the Multinational Corporations.' In : Germidis (1977).

Keunig, Ir. R. (1982), *Tne Role of Science and Technology in Developing Countries*, (Unilever) Rotterdam.

Khanna, Sushil (1984), 'Transnational Corporations and Technology Transfer: Contours of Dependence in the Indian Petrochemical Industry,' *Economic and Political Weekly*, Annual Number, August.

Kidron, Michael (1965), *Foreign Investments in India*, London.
Kindleberger, Charles, ed., (1970), *The International Corporations*, Cambridge/Massachusetts.
Kindleberger, Charles (1972), 'Direct Investments in Less-Developed Countries.' In : L.E. Di Marco, *International Economics and Development. Essays in Honor of Raul Prebisch*, New York, 1972.
Kindleberger, Charles (1973), *International Economics*, Illinois.
Kirkpatrick, C.H., N. Lee and F.I. Nixson (1984), *Industrial Structure and Policy in Less Developed Countries*, London.
Kostyukhin, Dimitry (1979), *The World Market*, Moscow.
Krishna, Sridhar (1982), 'Balance of Payments Implications and Financing Policies of Dutch Companies in India', *Indu Emencee Report*, nr 5.
Krishna, Sridhar and Amitava Mitra (1982a), 'Balance of Payments Implications. Statistical Appendix', *Indu Emencee Report*, nr 6.
Krisha, Sridhar, Amitava Mitra and J.M. Reddy (1983), 'Profitability of Dutch Companies and Comparable Indian Firms,' *Indu Emencee Report*, nr 14.
Krishna, Sridhar (1984), 'A Note on Transfer Pricing. Some Theoretical Issues and Empirical Evidence,' *Social Scientist*, May.
Kumar, Nagesh (1982), 'Regulating Multinational Monopolies in India,' *Economic and Political Weekly*, 29 May.
Kumar, Nagesh (1985), 'Cost of Technology Imports. The Indian Experience,' *Economic and Political Weekly*, nr 35.
Kurian, Mathew (1966), '*Impact of Foreign Capital on Indian Economy*, New Delhi.
Laclau, Ernesto (1971), 'Feudalism and Capitalism in Latin America,' *Journal of Contemporary Asia*, nr 67.
Laksmikanthan, V. and P.V. Gujerati (1969), 'Sal (Shorea Robusty).' In : OTAI, 1969.
Lall, Sanjaya (1974), 'Less Developed Countries and Private Foreign Direct Investments : A Review Article,' *World Development*, April.
Lall, Sanjaya (1975), 'Dependence, a useful concept in analysing underdevelopment,' *World Development*, nrs 11 & 12.
Lall, Sanjaya (1978), 'Transnationals, Domestic Enterprises and

Industrial Structure in Host LDCs : A Survey,' *Oxford Economic Papers*, July.

Lall, Sanjaya (1979). 'Transfer Pricing and Developing Countries,' *World Development*, January.

Lall, Sanjaya (1980 a), 'Vertical Inter-Firm Linkages in the LDCs : An Empirical Study.' *Oxford Bulletin of Economics and Statistics*, January.

Lall, Sanjaya (1980b), *The Multinational Corporation : nine essays*, London.

Lall, Sanjaya and Paul Streeten (1980), *Foreign Investment, Transnationals and Developing Countries*, London.

Lall, Sanjay and Ajit Singh (n.d.), 'Transnationals and Linkages with Domestic Enterprises. A Survey,' Mimeo, UN Centre on Transnational Corporations.

Lall, Sanjaya and Shariff, Mohammed (1983), 'Multinationals in Indian Big Business,' *Journal of Development Economics*, pp. 143-157.

Landelijke India Werkgroep (1981), *Blauwe Revolutie in India*, Utrecht.

Landelijke India Werkgroep (1982), 'De Nederlandse Kunstmesthulp aan India,' *India Nieuwsbrief*, nr 19.

Landelijke India Werkgroep (1985), *India als Melkkoe van de EEG*, Utrecht.

Lath, P. (1969), 'Sal Seeds (Shorea Robusta).' In : OTAI, 1969.

Leipziger, D.M. (1976), 'Production Characteristics in Foreign Enclaves and Domestic Manufacturing : The Case of India,' *World Development*, pp. 321-325.

Levkovsky, A.I. (1966), *Capitalism in India. Basic Trends in its Development*, New Delhi.

Lieten, G.K. (1980), 'Janata as a Continuity of the System.' *Social Scientist*, December.

Lieten, G.K. (1982), 'Some Questions Concerning Multinational Corporations', *Link*, 10 September.

Lieten, G.K. (1984), *Colonialism, Class and Nation; the Confrontation in Bombay Presidency around 1930*, Calcutta.

Lieten, G.K. (1985), 'India : Foreign Investment and the Domestic Policy Framework', *Development and Peace*, autumn, pp. 66-82.

Lieten, G.K. (1987), Indian Workers in Multinational Companies', *Economic and Political Weekly*, 2 May.

Lieten, G.K. and Detlev Haude (1984), 'Findings on Dutch Multinational Corporations in India.' In : A. Fonseca (ed.), *Multinationals in Third World Countries, Towards a Code of Conduct*, Rome/Freiburg.

Limqueco, Peter, and Bruce McFarlane, eds., (1984), *Neo-Marxist Theories of Development*, London.

Louisse, Jim (1978), 'De Relatie Tussen het Nederlandse Bedrijfsleven en de Officiele Ontwikkelingssamenwerking,' Mimeo, Vrije Universiteit Amsterdam.

Luedeman, Ernes (1982), *Die Wirtschaft der Kapitalistischen Laendern in Zahlen*, Berlin.

Magdoff, Harry (1969), *The Age of Imperialism*, New York.

Malyarov, O.V. (1977), 'The Problem of Monopolies in the Concepts of India's Socio-Economic Development.' In : Indian Statistical Institute, *Theories of Economic Growth of Asian Countries*, Calcutta, pp. 150-210.

Malyarov, O.V. (1983), *The Role of the State in the Socio-Economic Strucrure of India*, New Delhi.

Mandel, Ernest (1975), *Late Capitalism*, London.

Manser, W.A. (1973), *The Financial Role of Multinational Enterprises*, London.

Mantel, I.M. (1975), 'Sources and Uses of Funds for a Sample of Majority-Owned Foreign Affiliates of US Companies,' *Survey of Current Business*, July.

Markensten, Klas (1972), *Foreign Investment and Development : Swedish Companies in India*, Lund.

Menon, Usha (1980), 'World Bank and the Transfer of Technology; Case of Indian Fertiliser Industry,' *Economic and Political Weekly*, nr 34.

Menon, Usha (1982), 'A Survey, of R&D by Dutch Multinational Corporations in India, *Indu Emencee Report*. nr 13 (with K. Kumar).

Menon, Usha (1984), 'Transfer of Technology Agreements; some cases relating to Dutch companies in India,' Mimeo.

Menon, Usha (1986), 'Hindustan Lever and the Indian Soap Industry', *Social Scientist*, to be published.

Menon, Usha (1987), 'Nocil, An Investigation into Industrial Pollution,' Somo, Amsterdam.

Michalet, Charles-Albert (1976), *Le Capitalisme Mondial*, Paris.

Michalet, Charles-Albert (1977), 'Multinational Corporations and Transfer of Technology'. In : Dimitri Germidis, 1977.

Michalet, Charles-Albert (1985), *Les Multinationales Face a la Crise*, Geneve.

Monopolies Inquiry Commission (1965), *Report of the Monopolies Inquiry Commission*, New Delhi.

Mosley, P. (1986), *The Political Economy of Foreign Aid*, Brighton.

Moslowski, R. (1978), *Deutsches Gelt und Dritte Welt*, Wuppertal.

MRTPC (1973), *Majotity and Dissenting Report on Hindustan Lever*.

MRTPC (1974), *Report on the Proposal of Philips India* (*Medical Electronics Equipment*, New Delhi.

MRTPC (1975), *Report on the Proposal of Philips India* (*General Lighting Service Lamps and Fluorescent Tube Lamps*), New Delhi.

Myrdal, Gunnar (1972), *The Asian Drama*, Harmondsworth.

Nabudere, Dan (1978), *The Political Economy of Imperialism*, London.

Nagaraj, R. (1985), 'Some Aspects of Small-scale Industries in India', *Economic and Political Weekly*, 19 October.

Narayanan, Rajan (1980), 'Changing Face of Hindustan Lever,' *Business India*, July 21.

Nayar, Baldev Raj (1983), *India's Quest for Technological Independence : Policy Foundation and Policy Change*, New Delhi.

Nayar, Deepak (1978), 'Transnational Corporations and Manufactured Exports from Poor Countries', *Economic Journal*, March.

Nayudamma Committee (1974), *Policy in Regard to Execution and Commercialisation of R&D in the Private Sector Industry*, New Delhi.

NCAER (1959), *Transfer of Technology to India*, New Delhi.

NCAER (1971), *Foreign Technology and Investment : A Study of Their Role in India's Industrialisation*, New Delhi.

Needleman, L. a.o. (1970), *Balance of Payment Effects of Private Foreign Investments*, Unctad, New York.

Nikolayew, A. (1975), *R&D in Social Reproduction*, Moscow.

NISTADS (1984), *Transfer of Technology from National*

*Laboratories to Industry*. National Institute of Science, Technology & Development Studies, New Delhi.

Nixson, F.I. (1984), *Transnational Corporations and Economic Development*, Brighton.

NPC (1980), *Report on Study for Development of Soap Industry in the Small Scale and Rural Sector*, National Productivity Council, New Delhi.

Nukhovich, E.S. (1981), *Economic Relations with the Developing World : An Analytical Study of Capitalist and Socialist Approaches*, New Delhi.

Nurskse, R. (1966), *Problems of Capital Formation in Underdeveloped Countries*, Oxford.

Nyilas, J. (1977), *Theory and Practice of Development in the Third World*, Leiden.

Nyilas, J., *The Changing Face of the Third World : Regional and National Studies*, Leiden.

Nystrom, Harry (1979), 'Company Strategies for R&D'. In : M.J. Baker (ed)., *Commercial Innovation*, London.

OECD (1979), *Transfer Pricing and Multinational Enterprises*, Paris.

OECD (1981), *International Investment and Multinational Enterprises : Recent International Direct Investment Trends*, Paris.

Olle, W. (1983), *Deutsche Direktinvestitionen in Entwicklungslaender*, Bonn.

OTAI (1969), *Proceedings of the Seminar on Sal Seed (Shorea Robusta) of the Oil Technologists Association*, Kanpur.

Paerl, Eric (1971), *Nederlandse Macht in de Derde Wereld*, Amsterdam.

Paranjape, H.K. (1973), *Dissenting Note; the MRTP Report on Hindustan Lever*, New Delhi.

Paranjape, H.K. (1982a), 'The Vanishing MRTP Act', *Economic and Political Weekly*, 5 June.

Paranjape, H.K. (1982b), 'Controlling Multinational Corporations; An Anti-case Study'. Paper to the Indu Emencee Symposium on MNCs, August 1982, New Delhi.

Paranjape, H.K. (1985), New Lamps for Old!—A critique of the 'new economic policy', *Economic and Political Weekly*, 7 September.

Patel, Meena (1984), 'Private Foreign Investment and Balance of Payments Effects in India During 1960-70', *Indian Economic Journal*, pp. 62-69.

Patel, Surendra (1985), 'India's Regression in the World Economy', *Economic and Political Weekly*, 28 September.

Patil, M.S. and D. Bhushan (1964), 'Technological Research on Vegetable Oilseeds and Oils during the Third Five Year Plan', *Indian Oilseeds Journal*, January.

Patnaik, Prabhat (1972), 'Imperialism and the Growth of Indian Capitalism', In : Owen and Sutcliffe, *Studies in the Theory of Imperialism*, London.

Patnaik, Prabhat (1979), 'Industrial Development in India since Independence', *Social Scientist*, June.

Patnaik, Prabhat, ed., (1986), *Lenin and the Theory of Imperialism*, New Delhi.

Paul, M.C. and G.K. Lieten (1982), Lipton Tea Ltd., a profile of the company and its workers', *Indu Emencee Report*, nr 11.

Paul, Samuel (1984), 'Regulation of Transnational Corporations, *Economic and Political Weekly*, 25 February.

Pavlov, V. and R. Ulyanovsky (1973), *Asian Dilemma : A Soviet View and Myrdal's Concept*, Moscow.

Philips, Frederik (1978), *Forty-Five Years With Philips : An Industrialists' Life*, Dorset.

Radice, Hugo (1975), *International Firms and Modern Imperialism*, Harmondsworth.

Rahman, A. (1970), *The Financing of Scientific and Technological Research in India*, Paris.

Rahman, A. (1984), *Science and Technology in India*, New Delhi.

Rajendra, P. (1981), *A Case Book of MRTP Cases*, New Delhi.

Rajender, Basuthkar (1982), 'Peico Electronics and Electricals Limited : A Profile', *Indu Emencee Report*, nr 7.

Rajender, Basuthkar (1982a), 'The Position of Philips in the Electric Lamp Industry in India', Paper to the Indu Emencee Symposium on MNCs, August 1982, New Delhi.

Rajender, Basuthkar and G.K. Lieten (1985), 'The Sovereign Power of Philips in India', *Social Scientist*, March.

Rath, Ajay Kumar (1982), 'Hindustan Lever Limited : A Profile', *Indu Emencee Report*, nr 9.

Rath, Ajay Kumar (1982a), 'Unilever in India', *Social Scientist*, October.

Rath, Ajay Kumar (1983), 'Structural Features of the Indian Detergent Industry and the MNC Dominance', *Indu Emencee Report*, nr 10.

Ray, Rajat K. (1979), *Industrialisation in India : Growth and Conflict in the Private Corporate Sector, 1914-1942*, New Delhi.

Reiffers, Jean-Louis a.o. (1982), *Transnational Corporations and Endogenous Development*, Paris.

Reserve Bank of India (1968), *Survey of Foreign Collaboration in Indian Industry*, Bombay.

Reserve Bank of India (1974), *Foreign Collaboration in Indian Industry, Second Survey Report*, Bombay.

Reserve Bank of India (1980), 'Finances of Medium and Large Scale Public Limited Corporations, 1977-78', *RBI Bulletin*, May.

Reserve Bank of India (1985), *Foreign Collaboration in Indian Industry : Fourth Survey Report*, Bombay.

Reuber, Grant L. (1973), *Private Foreign Invesments in Development*, Oxford.

Ruigrok, Michel (1983), *Buitenlandse Bedrijven in de Geneesmiddelenindustrie in India*, Utrecht.

Rungta, Radhe Shyam (1970), *Rise of Business Corporations in India, 1851-1900*, Cambridge.

Sachar Committee (1978), *Report of the High-Powered Expert Committee on Companies and MRTP Act*, New Delhi.

Sachar, Justice R. (1982), 'The MRTP Act', Paper to the Indu Emencee Symposium on MNCs, August 1982, New Delhi.

Saini, M.K, (1981), *Politics of Multinational Companies*, New Delhi.

Sangal, P.S. (1981), *National and Multinational Corporations : Some Legal Issues*, New Delhi.

Sarkar, Sumit (1983), *Modern India 1885-1947*, New Delhi.

Sau, Ranjit (1981), *India's Economic Development : Aspects of Class Relations*, New Delhi.

Sauvant, K.P. and G. Lavipour (1976), *Controlling Multinational Enterprises : Problems, Strategies, Counterstrategies*, Boulder-Colorado.

Schellekens, Leo (1980), *Nederlanders in Azie, Afrika en Latijns Amerika, 1600-1900*, Nijmegen.

Schoo, Eegje (1984), *Nota Herijking Bilateraal Beleid*, The Hague.

Shchetinin, V.D. (1982), *US Monopolies and Developing Countries*, Moscow.

Shetty, S.L. (1978), 'Structural Retrogression in the Indian Economy Since the Mid-Sixties', *Economic and Political Weekly*, annual number.

Shirokov, G.K. (1973), *Industrialisation in India*, Moscow.

Sidharthan, N.S. (1979), 'Industrial Houses, Multinationals and Industrial Policy', *Economic and Political Weekly*, 21 July.

Sidharthan, N.S. (1981), *Conglomerates and Multinationals in India*, New Delhi.

Simoniya, S. (1985), *The Prospects of Capitalism in the Orient*, Moscow.

Singh, Rana (1982), 'The Role of Transnational Corporations, Implications for Economic and Technical Cooperation', *Development and Peace*, Spring.

SOBE (1977), *Philips Wereldwijd; een overzicht van de internationale produktiestruktuur van Philips*, Eindhoven.

Srivastava, H.K. (1969), 'Progress of the Non-Edible Oil Industry Under the Khadi and Village Industries Commission'. In : OTAI, *25 Years of R & D in Oils, Fats and Allied Industries*, New Delhi.

Streeten, Paul (1972), 'New Approaches to Private Investment in Less Developed Countries'. In : Dunning (1972).

Streeten, Paul (1976), 'Bargaining With Multinationals', *World Development*, March.

Subramaniam, K.K. and Mohanan Pillai (1979), *Multinationals and Indian Exports*, New Delhi.

Sutcliffe, Bob (1972), 'Imperialism and Industrialisation in the Third World'-In : Owen and Sutcliffe, *Studies in the Theory of Imperialism*, London.

Swami, Dhalip (1980), *Multinational Corporations and the World Economy*, New Delhi.

Szentes, Tamas (1983), *The Political Economy of Underdevelopment*, Budapest.

Szentes, Tamas (1984), *Theories of World Capitalist Economy : A*

*Critical Survey of Conventional, Reformist and Radical Views*, Budapest.

Taminiau, Boudewijn (1982), 'Backgrounds of Philips Internationalisation'. In : Bouwman 1982.

Tandon, Prakash (1971), *Beyond the Punjab*, New Delhi.

TAS (1973), *Nederlandse Hulp in Dienst van Kapitaalbelangen*, Nijmegen.

Tavis, L.A. (ed) (1984), *Multinational Managers and Poverty in the Third World*, Notre Dame.

Teulings, A. (1975), *Philips, Geschiedenis en Praktijk van een Wereldconcern*, Amsterdam.

Thomas, T. (1981). *Managing a Business in India*, Bombay.

Tisserat, Brent (1981), Date Palm Tissue Culture', Agricultural Research Service, US Department of Agriculture, August.

Tugendhatt, Christopher (1973), *The Multinationals*, Harmondsworth.

Uhlmann, L. (1979), 'The Typology Approach in Innovative Research'. In : Baker, *Industrial Innovation*, London.

Unctad (1981), *Handbook of International Trade and Development Statistics*, Paris.

Unesco, (1982), *Transnational Corporations and Endogenous Development*, Paris.

UNIDO (n.d.), 'Technological Self-Reliance of the Developing Countries : Towards Operational Strategies', *Development and Transfer of Technology Series*, nr 15.

Unilever N.V. (1982a), *De Plaats van Unilever in de Wereldekonomie*, Rotterdam.

Unilever N.V. (1982b), *Unilever en Haar Verantwoordelijkheden*, Rotterdam.

Unilever N.V. (1984), *Unilever in Ontwikkelingslanden*, Rotterdam.

United Nations (1973), *Multinational Corporations in World Development*, New York.

United Nations (1978), *Transnational Corporations in World Development, a re-examination*, New York.

United Nations (1983), *Transnational Corporations in World Development, Third Survey*, New York.

United Nations (1985), *Trends and Issues in Foreign Direct Investment and Related Flows*, New York.

Vaitsos, Constantine (1974), *Intercountry Income Distribution and Transnational Enterprises*, Oxford.

Van der Velden, Fons (1980), *Ontwikkelingssamenwerking Vanuit West-Europa met India*, Nijmegen.

Van der Velden, Fons, Amitava Mitra and G.K. Lieten (1983), 'General Survey of the Position of Dutch Companies in the Indian Economy', *Indu Emencee Report*, nr 4.

Van Klaveren, Maarten (1982), 'A Profile of the Philip Concern'. In : Bouwman, 1982.

Verma, S.P. (1983), 'Political Dimensions of Multinational Corporations in India', Mimeo, New Delhi.

Vernon, R. (1973), *Sovereignty at Bay. The Multinational Spread of US Enterprises*, Harmondsworth.

Vernon, R. (1978), *Storm over Multinationals*, Harvard.

Warren, Bill (1973), 'Imperialism and Capitalist Industrialisation', *New Left Review*, nr 81.

Warren, Bill (1980), *Imperialism : Pioneer of Capitalism*, London.

Wattkins, Steven Lane (1980), 'Foreign Investment Law and Policy in India', Mimeo, University of California.

Wilson, Charles (1954), *The History of Unilever*, London.

Wilson, Charles (1968), *Unilever, 1945-1965*, London.

Wilson, Charles (1970), *Geschiedenis van Unilever*, The Hague.

Wolfers, Ivan (1983). *Druppels Tegen Armoede*, Baarn.

World Bank (1985), *World Development Report*, Oxford.

# Index